# The Education of Black Males in a 'Post-Racial' World

*The Education of Black Males in a 'Post-Racial' World* examines the varied structural and discursive contexts of race, masculinities and class that shape the educational and social lives of Black males. The contributing authors take direct aim at the current discourses that construct Black males as disengaged in schooling because of an autonomous Black male culture, and explore how media, social sciences, school curriculum, popular culture and sport can define and constrain the lives of Black males. The chapters also provide alternative methodologies, theories and analyses for making sense of and addressing the complex needs of Black males in schools and in society. By expanding our understanding of how unequal access to productive opportunities and quality resources converge to systemically create disparate experiences and outcomes for African-American males, this volume powerfully illustrates that race *still* matters in 'post-racial' America.

This book was originally published as a special issue of *Race Ethnicity and Education*.

**Anthony L. Brown** is Assistant Professor in the Department of Curriculum and Instruction in the area of social studies education at the University of Texas at Austin, USA. He is a former classroom teacher and school administrator, whose scholarly interests focus on the education and learning experiences of African Americans. His work has been published in *The Urban Review*, *Teachers College Record* and *Race Ethnicity and Education*.

**Jamel K. Donnor** is Assistant Professor in Curriculum and Instruction in the School of Education at The College of William and Mary, USA. His research focuses on race and inequality, which encompasses three key areas: theory, policy analysis and the education of African American males. Theoretically, his interests in race are aligned with critical race theory (CRT). His work has been published in the *Journal of Educational Foundations*, *Educational Technology* and *Race Ethnicity and Education*.

# The Education of Black Males in a 'Post-Racial' World

*Edited by*
Anthony L. Brown and Jamel K. Donnor

LONDON AND NEW YORK

First published 2012 by Routledge

2 Park Square, Milton Park, Abingdon, Oxfordshire OX14 4RN
711 Third Avenue, New York, NY 10017

*Routledge is an imprint of the Taylor & Francis Group, an informa business*

First issued in paperback 2018

Copyright © 2012 Taylor & Francis

This book is a reproduction of *Race Ethnicity and Education*, Volume 14, Issue 1. The Publisher requests to those authors who may be citing this book to state, also, the bibliographical details of the special issue on which the book was based.

All rights reserved. No part of this book may be reprinted or reproduced or utilised in any form or by any electronic, mechanical, or other means, now known or hereafter invented, including photocopying and recording, or in any information storage or retrieval system, without permission in writing from the publishers.

Notice:
Product or corporate names may be trademarks or registered trademarks, and are used only for identification and explanation without intent to infringe.

*British Library Cataloguing in Publication Data*
A catalogue record for this book is available from the British Library

ISBN13: 978-0-415-67302-0 (hbk)
ISBN13: 978-1-138-37720-2 (pbk)

Typeset in Times New Roman
by Taylor & Francis Books

**Disclaimer**
The publisher would like to make readers aware that the chapters in this book are referred to as articles as they had been in the special issue. The publisher accepts responsibility for any inconsistencies that may have arisen in the course of preparing this volume for print.

# Contents

Notes on Contributors     vi

1. The education of Black males in a 'post-racial' world
   *Jamel K. Donnor and Anthony L. Brown*     1

2. Boyz to men? Teaching to restore Black boys' childhood
   *Gloria Ladson Billings*     7

3. Toward a new narrative on Black males, education, and public policy
   *Anthony L. Brown and Jamel K. Donnor*     17

4. Escaping Devil's Island: confronting racism, learning history
   *Carl A. Grant*     33

5. From visuals to vision: using GIS to inform civic dialogue about African American males
   *William F. Tate IV and Mark Hogrebe*     51

6. Sociocultural knowledge and visual re(-)presentations of Black masculinity and community: reading *The Wire* for critical multicultural teacher education
   *Keffrelyn D. Brown and Amelia Kraehe*     73

7. Living the dream or awakening from the nightmare: race and athletic identity
   *Louis Harrison Jr., Gary Sailes, Willy K. Rotich and Albert Y. Bimper Jr.*     91

8. Research concerns, cautions and considerations on Black males in a 'post-racial' society
   *Tyrone C. Howard and Terry Flennaugh*     105

9. New possibilities: (re)engaging Black male youth within community-based educational spaces
   *Bianca J. Baldridge, Marc Lamont Hill and James Earl Davis*     121

*Index*     137

# Notes on Contributors

**Bianca J. Baldridge**
Graduate Student, Sociology and Education, Teachers College, Columbia University, New York, NY, USA

**Gloria Ladson Billings**
Kellner Family Chair in Urban Education and Professor of Curriculum and Instruction and Educational Policy Studies, Department of Curriculum and Instruction, University of Wisconsin–Madison, WI, USA

**Albert Y. Bimper Jr.**
Graduate Student, Department of Curriculum and Instruction, The University of Texas at Austin, TX, USA

**Anthony L. Brown**
Assistant Professor, Department of Curriculum and Instruction, The University of Texas at Austin, TX, USA

**Keffrelyn D. Brown**
Assistant Professor, Department of Curriculum and Instruction, The University of Texas at Austin, TX, USA

**James Earl Davis**
Interim Dean, College of Education, Professor, Education Leadership, and Policy Studies, Temple University, Philadelphia, PA, USA

**Jamel K. Donnor**
Assistant Professor, Curriculum and Instruction, The College of William and Mary, Williamsburg, VA, USA

**Terry Flennaugh**
Assistant Professor, College of Education, Michigan State University, East Lansing, MI, USA

**Carl A. Grant**
Hoefs-Bascom Professor of Education Department of Curriculum and Instruction, University of Wisconsin–Madison, Madison, WI USA

**Louis Harrison Jr.**
Professor, Department of Curriculum and Instruction, The University of Texas at Austin, TX, USA

NOTES ON CONTRIBUTORS

**Marc Lamont Hill**
Associate Professor of English Education, Teachers College, Columbia University, New York, NY, USA

**Mark Hogrebe**
Instiutional Graduate Student, Department of Education, Washington University in St. Louis, MO, USA

**Tyrone C. Howard**
Professor, Graduate School of Education & Information Studies, University of California, Los Angeles, USA

**Amelia Kraehe**
Graduate Student, Department of Curriculum and Instruction, The University of Texas at Austin, TX, USA

**Willy K. Rotich**
Assistant Professor, Department of Physical Education, St. Bonaventure University, St. Bonaventure, NY, USA

**Gary Sailes**
Associate Professor, School of Health, Physical Education, and Recreation, Indiana University, Bloomington, IA, USA

**William F. Tate IV**
Department Chair, Edward Mallinckrodt Distinguished University Professor in Arts & Sciences, Department of Education, Washington University in St. Louis, MO, USA

# The education of Black males in a 'post-racial' world

Jamel K. Donnor and Anthony L. Brown

For many in the United States and abroad, the 2008 presidential election of Barack Obama denotes a watershed moment. With the election of the first African American president, many individuals have enthusiastically declared that America entered a new era where race is no longer a determinant in shaping the life fortunes and experiences of people of color. Because the current President of the United States is an African American male, many have used this moment of accomplishment to craft the larger social narrative that race is no longer a barrier in the social advancement of the African American male. While there is an increased presence of African American males in various sectors of American life, such as law, academia, and politics, to posit that race is no longer a relevant factor in the lives of males of African descent is misguided.

Consider, for example, the circumstances surrounding the arrest of Harvard Professor Henry Louis 'Skip' Gates. Upon returning home from filming a documentary for the Public Broadcasting Station (PBS) entitled 'Faces of America', Professor Gates and his cab driver were identified by his white female neighbor, Lucia Whalen, as breaking into his home. Responding to Ms. Whalen's 911 call to the Cambridge Police Department that 'two Black males with backpacks' were forcing their way into a residence, Officer James Crowley, a white male, asked Professor Gates to exit the home. After declining the request to exit the premises, Officer Crowley informed Professor Gates that he was 'investigating a report of a break in in progress' (Cambridge Police Department 2009, 1–2). Responding to Officer Crowley's statement, Professor Gates remarked, 'why, because I'm a [b]lack man in America?' (Cambridge Police Department 2009, 2). Crowley proceeded to ask Professor Gates 'if there was anyone else in the residence' (Cambridge Police Department 2009, 2). Professor Gates replied 'that is none of [your] business' (Cambridge Police Department 2009, 2). Informing Professor Gates that he was responding to a 'citizen's call to Cambridge Police,' Officer Crowley asked for identification despite 'believing [Professor Gates] was lawfully in the residence' (Cambridge Police Department 2009, 2). Upon providing the officer with his Harvard University identification card and Massachusetts driver's license, Professor Gates asked Crowley for his name and his badge number. Failing to furnish the professor with the requested information, Crowley proceeded to leave the premises. Professor Gates repeated his request for the officer's badge number. Determining that Professor Gates' behavior had become 'tumultuous,' Officer Crowley arrested the professor for disorderly conduct (Cambridge Police Department 2009, 2). Although the charges against Professor Gates were dropped, and he along with Officer Crowley met with President Obama to quell the negative publicity associated with the arrest, this example illustrates how race remains an underlying and salient component in the lives of African American males regardless of social status. Despite his prominent status as a public intellectual and professional affiliation with the most prestigious university in the United States,

Professor Gates did not 'escape the prism of race' (Ladson Billings and Donnor 2005, 279). Further, this example illustrates that being 'Black' and 'male' irrespective of societal position recapitulates the historically and ideologically informed racial imaginary of Black male deviance and criminality. This existential marking of the Black male body, we argue, has direct and indirect implications for education (Holt 1995).

The goal of this special issue of *Race Ethnicity and Education* is to contribute to the education literature's understanding of the contemporary challenges in the schooling of African American males. The contributors to this special themed issue discuss, in varying ways, the constant and dynamic interplay between ideology, history, space, policy, and structure in configuring the education of African American males. Further, the contributors to this special issue of *Race Ethnicity and Education* respond to the mainstream, curricula, theoretical, and methodological discourses that continue to construct Black males as a 'unique' population with dispositions and proclivities that are inherently contradictory to societal norms. Lastly, the articles in this special issue highlight the structural, institutional, and discursive practices that define, constrain, and adversely affect the material and existential lives of African American males.

The first article in this issue entitled, 'Boyz to men? Teaching to restore Black boys' childhood,' by Gloria Ladson Billings describes the current state of education for Black male students. She contends that many individuals, including teachers, view the teaching of African American boys as a 'daunting task.' The result, according to Ladson Billings, is a gender-specific emphasis on maintaining order and discipline, rather than academic achievement or learning. Hence, in many instances by the time most Black boys reach the third or fourth grade their teachers and other school personnel no longer treat them like children, but rather, like men en route to prison. Ladson Billings posits that educators need to develop and utilize pedagogical strategies to learn about the interests and course taking patterns of boys to ensure that they are taught in intellectually, socially, and culturally appropriate ways so schools can function as centers of change, rather than as places that perpetuate racial inequity.

Next, in our article, 'Toward a new narrative on Black males, education, and public policy,' we argue that the dominant social narrative of the Black male crisis perpetuates a discourse of Black male pathology. Analyzing mainstream trade publications and reports from private foundations on the status of Black males, we conclude that many of the solutions to address the Black male crisis de-emphasize the historical importance and structural role race plays as a life opportunity shaping variable. We assert that this omission not only renders an incomplete understanding on the social and educational status of Black males, more importantly, the policies and programs informed by the discourse of Black male pathology are unlikely to create meaningful change. We suggest that a new and fluid narrative is needed to account for the multifarious ways the social and educational status of Black males in the United States are systematically constructed.

In crafting a new social and educational narrative on Black males in America, the following articles examine how various institutions configure the life chances of African American males. In 'Escaping Devil's Island: confronting racism, learning history,' Carl A. Grant argues that African Americans, especially males living in urban communities, are physically and mentally trapped. Similar to the penal colony off the coast of French Guiana, Devil's Island, Grant asserts that African American males in urban schools are closed off from opportunities in part, due to a lack of historical knowledge. For Grant, the significance of historical knowledge, in the advancement of African American males is essential to deciphering the broader social world around them. While social movements of the twentieth century, such as the Civil Rights Movement, have produced racial progress, according to Grant, none of them has generated enough progress to eliminate the racism that keeps Black males on Devil's Island. Grant contends that this historical 'sin of omission' markets racism as prejudice in personal preferences. The paradox in framing racism as an isolated phenomenon or individual act is that white supremacy remains intact. Grant posits, that for African American males to successfully escape Devil's Island a resiliency informed by a history of self-determination and social justice must be taught to develop and maintain a sense of agency in order to promote social change.

The fourth article, by William F. Tate IV and Mark Hogrebe entitled, 'From visuals to vision: using GIS to inform civic dialogue about African American males,' argues that a key step toward building opportunity in urban communities is the development and support for a visual political literacy project. Tate and Hogrebe discuss the significance of Geographic Information System (GIS) as a psychological and political tool in supporting civic engagement and capacity related to improving the status of African American males and their communities. Using the city of St. Louis as a case study, Tate and Hogrebe's visual political literacy project of spatial maps calls for a greater investment in funding and human development resources to support sustained research related to African American males. In addition, they call for the utilization of insights gleaned from geospatial arrangements to improve opportunities for Black male academic advancement and job potential. The methodological approach and conceptual knowledge advanced in this article are cutting edge.

The next two articles in this special issue by Keffrelyn D. Brown and Amelia Kraehe, and Louis Harrison Jr., Gary Sailes, Willy K. Rotich, and Albert Y. Bimper Jr., discuss the sociocultural construction of African American males in two important mainstream institutions in the United States-popular media and sports. Beginning with 'Sociocultural knowledge and visual re(-)presentations of Black masculinity and community: reading *The Wire* for critical multicultural teacher education,' Brown and Kraehe discuss the implications of using popular media situated around representations of Black masculinity as a pedagogical tool for white teachers. Conducting a textual analysis of the critically acclaimed Home Box Office (HBO) series *The Wire*, Brown and Kraehe explain how visual media and popular culture play an important role in crafting societal knowledge about Black males as learners and as people. Highlighting the historical, psychological, and global power of visual media, Brown and Kraehe argue that *The Wire* renders a nuanced and complex image of Black males and the communities they call home. Yet, while *The Wire* provides a more nuanced depiction of Black male life, the authors illustrate how the show might serve to perpetuate and reify long-standing tropes of deviance and difference as it relates to the Black male and his place within the 'Black' community. Brown and Kraehe suggest that *The Wire* and similar critical media projects can offer the requisite conceptual spaces for teachers to transform themselves from mere depositors of information into engaged pedagogues who understand and 'authentically teach' about the confluence of exogenous forces that shape the educational lives of African American males (Freire 1997). They, however, also recognize and caution about the challenges of using visual media in teacher education. Thus, they maintain that when using visual media in teacher education classrooms instructors must do so in a critical, non-decontextualized way that challenges, rather than reinforces problematic perspectives about people of color.

Louis Harrison Jr., Gary Sailes, Willy K. Rotich, and Albert Y. Bimper Jr.'s article 'Living the dream or awakening from the nightmare: race and athletic identity' examines the relationship between race and athletic identity. Discussing their findings from their study on the athletic identity of African American and white Football Bowl Subdivision (FBS) student-athletes, Harrison, Sailes, Rotich, and Bimper found that African American football student-athletes possess a stronger athletic identity compared to their Caucasian American counterparts. The authors discovered that African American male identification with the athlete role is more likely to intensify as they interpret their involvement with major college football as a conduit to playing professional football. Harrison et al. argue that educators and academic advisors who work closely with African American student-athletes are vital in the development of other identities, particularly students. Thus, it is important that African American student athletes do not over-identify or foreclose themselves to being just an athlete at the expense of other pertinent aspects and possibilities in their development.

Next, Tyrone C. Howard and Terry Flennaugh in their article entitled, 'Research concerns, cautions and considerations on Black males in a "post-racial" society,' examine the research literature on Black males and discuss its implications for schooling within the context of 'post-racialism'. According to Howard and Flennaugh, much of the research on Black males focuses on observed behavior, which is absent of the factors that might contribute to the behaviors under observation. They posit that any attempt to dismiss or overlook race as a key variable in the ways that Black males experience school further marginalizes them collectively. For Howard and Flennaugh, Black male identity is multifaceted, and thus studies must consider the intersectionality of race, class, and gender to fully understand how each marker, respectively, influences identity construction and meaning making within the context of education and academic achievement. Like any population of students, the authors contend that Black males possess multiple identities that are profoundly shaped by race, socioeconomic status, and gender in all of their complex manifestations. Moreover, Howard and Flennaugh warn that research on Black males at its core is controversial and must be transformative if it is to humanize a dehumanized population.

Finally, Bianca J. Baldridge, Marc Lamont Hill, and James Earl Davis in 'New possibilities: (re)engaging Black male youth within community based educational spaces' discuss the findings from their qualitative study on Empower Youth (pseudonym), a nationally federally-funded youth community development program, that serves over 10,000 youth in low-income urban and rural communities. An out-of-school designed to provide youth with supplemental education, job training, and life skills, Empower Youth as a youth community development program focuses on issues facing low-income neighborhoods, including housing, (un)employment, crime prevention, and leadership development. Conducting a series of interviews with 24 African American male participants of Empower Youth, Baldridge, Hill and Davis discovered that the program's incorporation of work opportunities, emphasis on applied knowledge and responsive adult–youth relationships helped Black males navigate difficult experiences in traditional school settings. The authors contend that youth and community development programs, such as Empower Youth, can serve a broader societal function by providing young Black males with the support and skill-set needed to offset larger undesirable outcomes in education, such as disaffection, underperformance, and dropping out. Baldridge, Hill and Davis conclude that out-of-school programs that reframe African American males as valued members of society not only respond their distinct educational and social needs, but also serve as templates for traditional learning environments to model.

The articles in this special issue of *Race Ethnicity and Education* fundamentally shifts the conversation on education and Black males in the twenty-first century from crisis mode to a more holistic approach. By expanding the field's understanding of how unequal access to productive opportunities and quality resources converge to systemically create disparate experiences and outcomes for African American males, these articles remind us that race *still* matters in 'post-racial' America.

## Acknowledgements

We are grateful to our invited reviewers whose support made the double-blind peer review process for this special issue a success. Thus, we would like to recognize the following scholars for participating in the peer review process: Laurence Parker, Lawson Bush, Michael J. Dumas, Adrienne D. Dixson, Sabina Vaught, Kmt Shockley, Eddie Comeaux, James W. Satterfield and Pedro Noguera.

We are particularly thankful to David Gillborn for considering and supporting this special issue of *Race Ethnicity and Education* on the education of Black Males in a 'post-racial' world.

## References

Cambridge Police Department. Incident report # 9005127. http://www.0721docket_redacted _revised__1248200728_6644.pdf.

Freire, P. 1997. *Pedagogy of the oppressed.* New York: Continuum.

Holt, T.C. 1995. Marking: Race, race-making, and the writing of history. *The American Historical Review* 100: 1–20.

Ladson Billings, G.J., and J.K. Donnor. 2005. Waiting for the call: The moral activist role of critical race theory scholarship. In *Handbook of qualitative research,* 3rd ed., ed. N.K. Denzin and Y.S. Lincoln, 279–301. Thousand Oaks, CA: Sage.

# Boyz to men? Teaching to restore Black boys' childhood

Gloria Ladson Billings

*Department of Curriculum and Instruction, University of Wisconsin–Madison, Madison, USA*

> Many schools see teaching African American boys as a daunting challenge. However, in many schools the primary focus of Black male children's educational experience is maintaining order and discipline rather than student learning and academic achievement. By the time Black boys reach the 3rd or 4th grade their teachers and other school personnel no longer treat them like children, but rather like men. This paper will describe the current state of education for Black male students and propose ways to ensure that we teach all children, particularly Black boys in intellectually, socially, and culturally appropriate ways.

I begin this discussion with a disclaimer – I am a mother of African American sons. Granted they are now adults, but their experiences as children, adolescents, and young adults have had a profound impact on how I read the scholarly literature and make sense of education policy and practices regarding Black[1] boys. No discussion of African American males is complete without the litany of statistical woes that beset them. And, while I will reference those numbers, my aim is to move beyond a mere delineation of the problems to looking at how African American male students' schooling actually functions to exacerbate their problems and to discuss how we might become agents of change that help to alleviate the problems.

First, it is important to start with the things we already know and have heard repeatedly about the situation of Black men in the United States – and that situation does show some improvement. In 2000 a mere quarter of the 1.9 million Black men between 18 and 24 attended college (33.8%). In contrast, 35% of Black women in that same age group and 36% of all 18–24 year olds were attending college. Between 2003 and 2005 college participation among African American males increased from 37.8% to 38% (American Council of Education 2007).

The American Council of Education (2007) further reports that the graduation rate of Black males is the lowest of any population. Only 35% of the Black men who enrolled in NCAA Division I schools graduated within six years. White men graduated at a rate of 59%; Latino men, 46%; American Indian men, 41%; and Black women, 45%. But it is not merely college graduation rates that foreshadow a poor outcome for African American males. Their life chances are markedly different than that of other groups.

Ronald Mincy, editor of *Black Males Left Behind* (2006), reported 'There's something very different happening with young Black men and it's something we can no longer ignore. Over the last two decades, the economy did great and low-skilled women, helped by public policy latched onto it. But Black men were falling farther back.' (Eckholm 2006)

In 2005, 65% of Black male high school dropouts in their 20s were jobless – that is, unable to find work, not seeking it, or incarcerated. By 2004, the share of jobless in this category had grown to 72% compared with 34% of White and 19% of Latino dropouts. Even when high school graduates were included, half of Black men in their 20s were jobless in 2004, up from 46% in 2000.

In the current economic recession Black male unemployment rates for those 20-years-old or older has risen from 15.4% to 17.2% (US Bureau of Labor Statistics 2009). For young Black males, aged 16–19 the unemployment rate is 49.4% (US Bureau of Labor Statistics 2009). These numbers rival depression era figures.

Incarceration rates climbed in the 1990s and have reached historic highs in recent years. In 1995, 16% of Black men in their 20s who did not attend college were in jail; by 2004, 21% were incarcerated. By their mid-30s, six out of ten Black men who had dropped out of school had spent time in prison. In the inner city, more than half of all Black men do not finish high school.

A 2004 study by the Schott Foundation found that although Black males make up only 8.6% of public school enrollment, they represent 22% of expulsions and 23% of suspensions. Polite and Davis (1999) found that for the same offense, suspension days ranged from two to 22 days – intimating that school personnel use a fair amount of discretion in determining how to sanction students. Of Black boys who enter special education, only 10% return to regular classrooms permanently and only 27% ever graduate. In addition to the numbers, research has found that Black boys often do not feel cared for in their school communities (Rawls 2006). Yet, the single most important thing in turning lives around according to Noddings (1992) 'is the ongoing presence of a caring adult' (cited in Varlas 2005, 1).

Just listing the social facts concerning Black male students is depressing and distressing. Our tendency is to do one of two things – either wring our hands in despair or point our fingers in blame. Unfortunately, sometimes we do both (at the same time) but rarely do we take a more measured and systematic approach to parsing out the part of the students' problems that we as educators have some control over. For the sake of this discussion I want to frame our (i.e. adults associated with schooling) responses into a few sets of behaviors and thoughts that govern what we do with African American male students that, for the most part, we do not do with other groups of students. These behaviors have to do with thoughts and behaviors that describe tensions between love versus hate, fear and control, and infantilization versus criminalization.

**The love–hate relationship with Black males**

Perhaps more than any other group in our society, America (indeed the world) has a love–hate relationship with Black males. The 'love' aspect of the relationship is exhibited in the way mainstream Americans embrace a variety of cultural forms that are either designed or dominated by Black males. In his provocative film, *Do the Right Thing* (1989), director Spike Lee confronts the White racist son of the neighborhood pizza store owner with the fact that although he despises Black people, his favorite recording artist is Michael Jackson and his favorite athlete is Michael Jordan. The son, Pino, struggles to explain the paradox and finally mutters something about Jackson and Jordan not actually being 'Black.' Somehow their super star qualities have allowed them to transcend the pedestrian notions of everyday Black men. Lee's inclusion of that scene may have been designed to help America see its own confusion and ambivalence about Black people, Black males in particular.

No cultural form is more marketable than Black male youth culture (Price 2006). The clothes, the style, the language, and the effects of young, Black, urban males are visible throughout the nation and the world. It has left an indelible mark on Madison Avenue, Hollywood, and most forms of media. Everywhere I have traveled recently, Australia, Japan, the Caribbean, London, Paris, Ghana, and even Sweden have presented examples of this culture to me. The young people wear baggy pants, professional sports team jerseys, baseball caps, expensive sneakers and have tattoos. The international youth heroes are music makers like P. Diddy, 50 Cent, Jay-Z, L'il Wayne and athletes like LeBron James, Allen Iverson, and Shaquille O'Neal.

The symbolic message attached to these young Black men is that they are seductive and intriguing. Perhaps what one must begin to unravel is the construction of Black men as both dangerous (taboo, forbidden) and sensual. Clearly we have no shortage of images of Black men as simultaneously appealing and repulsive.

When we look at the 'hate' aspect of this dichotomy, we see African American males as 'problems' that our society must find ways to eradicate. We regularly determine them to be the root cause of most problems in schools and society. We seem to hate their dress[2], their language, and their effect. We hate that they challenge authority and command so much social power. We seem convinced that if they wouldn't act so... 'Black,' they would not be problems. While the society apparently loves them in narrow niches and specific slots – music, basketball, football, track – we seem less comfortable with them than in places like the National Honor Society, the debate team, or the computer club. When Black men do show up in these places we consider them oddities and exceptions. Like the character Pino in Spike Lee's film, these 'exceptions' are often not considered truly Black. An interesting take on this notion is the response to Barak Obama early in the US Presidential race as not being 'Black enough.' However, when the one exception does end up in those unexpected spaces the society is quick to announce his or her exceptionality to everyone, especially their peers, to further re-inscribe the notion that these individuals are 'special.' Their specialness can serve to alienate them from other Black people and place them in what might be described as psychological danger. This lifting up of one individual ignores the fact that all students need peers and being placed in an exceptional category leaves one without support or social moorings. We set that individual up for failure at some level in some aspect of his life. This treatment is especially detrimental to the social and emotional development of Black male students (Spencer 2008).

**Fear and control**

The love–hate relationship that we have with Black males is buffered by two equally strong sentiments – fear and the need for control. For example, I cannot think of very many young Black men who have not had the experience of having some woman – of any race – cross the street to avoid contact with them. This behavior coupled with things like women clutching their purses, people stepping out of elevators when Black males step in, or having taxi drivers routinely pass Black male passengers on the street are a part of daily experiences of Black men in this society (Shields 1999). Perhaps if these incidents occurred on a more random basis we could attribute them to male–female inequality. But when they happen almost exclusively to Black men – any Black man (regardless of class, education status, and age) – we know that there exists a widespread fear of them throughout the society. My experience with these kinds of incidents comes first hand as a mother of adult sons. Despite working hard to raise smart, courteous, kind, law-abiding citizens, I am faced with the reality of the many times the incidents described previously have happened to them. While my sons laugh the incidents off as ignorance on the part of the other people and share stories of Black male comedians who joke about similar experiences, I will confess that it makes me angry. My sons have done nothing to deserve this kind of treatment but the society has projected its wholesale fear on them.

In schools the response to this fear is manifested in exhibiting increasing levels of control. We feel compelled to control Black male bodies at all times (Enteman and Rojecki 2001). About a year ago I went into four schools in a city of about 700,000. The first school had mostly White students and I was amazed at how freely students were permitted to walk the halls and move about the classroom. It was only in the places where safety was an issue, where the children's bodies were tightly controlled (e.g. there was a portion of the play yard where cars were permitted to drive to drop off students). However, when I made my way to schools serving large numbers of Black students (and in one case the entire student population was Black) I could not help but notice the degree to which every aspect of the students' activities were regulated – not just what they were taught, but also how their bodies were controlled. They were required to wear uniforms; they had to line up in particular ways, they were prohibited from talking in social spaces like hallways and the cafeteria. There is only one analogy to this kind of regulation – prison.

A few years ago I witnessed another other example of this tight regulation. An elementary principal proudly took me to see her 'restitution room.' In it were several rows of children, all Black and all male, sitting absolutely silent with their hands folded. The classroom was presided over by an instructional aid and there were no books or reading materials in the room. There were no displays on the bulletin boards, no cute and colorful pictures of school children or animals, no admonitions about how to be a good student. It was just a bare room with four walls. The principal turned to me and asked what I thought. My response was probably impolite but I replied, 'I think it's fine if you're training them for prison.'

**Infantilization versus criminalization**

The paradox of Black boys' experiences in school and society is that mainstream perceptions of them vacillate between making them babies and making them men. When they are somewhere between the ages of three and six years they are acknowledged as cute but rarely as intellectually capable. They rarely are held to high academic standards or expected to be academic leaders in the classroom (Kunjufu 2005). Some may focus on their cuteness but not on their cognition. We may think they are sweet but rarely particularly smart.

This notion of little Black boys as cute does not last long. Before long they are moved to a category that resembles criminals. Their childhood evaporates before they are eight or nine-years-old when teachers and other school officials begin to think of them as 'men.' The fear and control previously referenced appears to be activated and the once 'cute' boys become problematic 'men.'

I recall sitting in a classroom of 3rd graders observing a student teacher. The classroom was filled with a diverse group of students – Latinos, Asian Americans, African

Americans, and White students. One little boy, an Asian American student I will call 'Stanley' kept getting up out of his seat. Repeatedly, the student teacher said things such as, 'sit down Stanley,' 'go back to your seat Stanley,' and 'not now Stanley,' while she was attempting to work with another group of students in a reading group. I documented nine times that she spoke to Stanley about getting out of his seat. Some time later a Black boy I will call, 'Larry' got up out of his seat to ask the student teacher a question and immediately she snapped, 'what are you doing out of your seat? You're out of here!' In a few minutes he was on his way to the principal's office.

During our post-observation conference I pointed out the disparity between her responses to the two boys. I showed her each time I had documented her repeated warnings to Stanley and her one sanction issued to Larry. When she looked at my log she was shocked at what she had done and at a loss for words to explain why she had treated the two boys so differently. Hers was a classic example of how her fear of losing control (after all her supervisor was observing her and she wanted everything to go smoothly) fostered criminalization.

In another instance a colleague was doing professional development work with a middle school that historically served a White, upper middle-class community. More recently the school began to receive a number of low- to moderate-income families within its boundaries and the teachers, administrators, and White parents began to complain about how badly behaved the Black students were. My colleague made an unannounced visit to the school a few days before the scheduled professional development session. On the day of the professional development session my colleague began by saying, 'You have some serious problems in this school.' The staff members began nodding their heads in agreement. 'You have some students here who think they do not have to follow the rules,' she continued. And once again the heads nodded. 'You have some students who have no regard for authority.' Heads continued to nod and a few muttered, 'yes.' Finally, the professional developer said, 'And they are the White, male students!' At that moment a look of shock and disbelief came over the faces. Nowhere in the staff's minds were White boys seen as the problem even though the professional developer had spent a day watching White boys mouthing off to teachers and other adults, disrupting classes with smart aleck comments, and generally having their way in the school. The professional developer had also seen the notorious 'big, bad Black boy' the staff had talked about – all 98 pounds of him. The incongruity between what the teachers described as the problem and what the outside observer witnessed underscores the way that Black boys can go from students to criminals in the minds of the their teachers and other adults.

The instances I have described are bad enough as isolated events. However, they are more often than not a pattern of behaviors and responses that Black boys regularly face in school. Two cases in the US, The Jena 6 and that of Genarlow Wilson underscore the widely different treatment that Black boys can expect from both schools and the justice system. In Jena, Louisiana, the African American boys who assaulted a White student were treated criminally while the White boys who initially maintained a 'White' tree and then hung a noose there when the principal indicated that Black students were permitted to sit under it were given short school suspensions. In Georgia, Genarlow Wilson, a 17-year-old high school student who maintained a 3.2 GPA and was looking forward to a promising college career was arrested and charged with sexual assault for a consensual sexual encounter with a teenage girl.

Wilson was convicted and sentenced to 11 years – ten years mandatory jail time and one year of probation. Wilson also would have to register as a sex offender. As his case wound its way through the justice system Wilson ended up spending almost three years in prison. He was released in late October 2007 at the age of 21. For those of us who are parents of teenagers the thought of them having sex may seem criminal but clearly we do not think they deserve to go to jail because of it. Wilson engaged in behavior that countless teenagers do every day. Why did the young Black man, with no criminal record, end up in prison?

**Schools as the source of the problem**

Perhaps we could rest easier if the site of Black boys' problems were their homes with their parents and siblings, or the streets with the police and law enforcement But one of the primary places where Black boys' problems appear is in school. From the moment Black boys enter school who and how they can be is predetermined. When my daughter began kindergarten I noticed that there was one Black boy in her classroom. Within a few weeks I began to hear my daughter say, 'Christopher is a bad boy.' Knowing that Christopher was the only Black boy in the class I asked my daughter to explain what she meant by her statement. She responded, 'Oh, he's always in trouble. He's a bad boy!' When I began to serve as a parent volunteer in the classroom I noticed that Christopher was one of the brightest students in the class. Regularly he completed assigned tasks before anyone else in the classroom. He quickly grew bored and began to wander around the room. He would look at other children's work and remark, 'Are you still working on that, you must be stupid!' That kind of remark immediately got him a reprimand and before long he was being referred to the principal's office. Of course, five-year-old Christopher was speaking in an inappropriate way and the teacher needed to deal with that. But he needed to receive a reprimand that allowed him to stay in the classroom. He also needed the teacher to acknowledge his superior intellect, encourage him as a student, and design appropriate instructional activities so that he would have less time to get bored and begin pestering other students. Instead what Christopher was beginning to learn from his kindergarten experience was how to be a 'bad boy.'

Years later I went into a high school where I happened upon a middle-aged White male teacher who was in a serious argument with a White male student. The two were shouting at each other when the student let out a major profanity calling the teacher a 'M-F' (the student actually said the obscenity). The shocked teacher looked at the student and said to him, 'Why are you talking like that, you're not Black?' I looked with amazement at the other adult present, the custodian who was a Black man. He just shook his head and walked away. This was a jarring instance that reminded me that there is a perception of who Black male students are that persists even when there are no Black males present. The teacher did not tell the student that he had no right to speak to him using a profanity. He also did not attribute the student's bad behavior to him. Instead, he attributed such behavior to the influence of some imagined Black student who apparently is crude, obscene, and disrespectful.

Martin Haberman (1991) points out that students in urban classrooms regularly strike a deal with their teachers. This deal is particularly apparent among Black male students and involves teachers and students negotiating the following deal: 'You don't require any work from me and I won't disrupt your class.' We see that this particular deal has been struck every time we walk into classrooms and see Black male students sitting in the back with their heads down on their desks. They do not do any work or contribute to the intellectual activity of the classroom but they are keeping their end of the bargain. The teachers appreciate their 'integrity' and keep their end of the bargain by failing to include them in the learning environment or demanding any academic work from them.

The ability to strike such a deal with students is emblematic of the incredibly low standards schools set for Black boys. They are regularly expected to participate in what Haberman (1991) calls the 'pedagogy of poverty.' Haberman identified 14 specific acts that traditionally constitute the core functions of urban teaching: giving information, asking questions, giving directions, making assignments, monitoring seatwork, reviewing assignments, giving tests, reviewing tests, assigning homework, reviewing homework, settling disputes, punishing non-compliance, marking papers, and giving grades.

There are times when any one of these activities might have a beneficial effect, but, Haberman writes, 'taken together and performed to the systematic exclusion of other acts, they do not work.' This pedagogy of poverty is 'sufficiently powerful to undermine the implementation of any reform effort because it defines the way pupils spend their time, the nature of the behaviors they practice, and the basis of their self-concept as learners. Essentially, it is a pedagogy in which learners can "succeed" without becoming either involved or thoughtful.'

Further, Haberman (1991) asserts that the pedagogy of poverty appeals to those who did not do well in schools themselves. It appeals to those who rely on common sense rather than thoughtful analysis. It appeals to those who fear poor children and children of color and as a result they often are obsessed with control. It appeals to those who are unaware of the full range of pedagogical options.

Schools also contribute to the problem by 'creating' infractions that will apply primarily to Black boys (Majors and Bilson 1992). So, Black boys find themselves excluded from academic opportunities because of arbitrary and capricious school rules (e.g. hat wearing inside a building, wearing baggy pants, giving an adult a disapproving or surly look). The magnification of these kinds of minor infractions is especially targeted toward Black boys as a method of control.

Another way that schools contribute to the problems that Black boys experience has to do with what some scholars identify as the 'feminization of learning' (Gurian and Stevens 2004). This concept refers to the way that schooling, its personnel, and its activities are linked to more stereotypical feminine spheres. Many boys are deeply influenced by the messages the society send about what a 'real man' is and as a consequence they reject schooling. This is true, not only of Black boys, but increasingly of all boys. However, schools have been slow to respond to this perception of themselves as overly feminine. Clearly, the teaching population reinforces this notion and the kinds of learning activities schools encourage rarely tap into boys' interests.

Few early childhood classrooms have workbenches with tools. Few middle grade classrooms give students an opportunity to build models or learn to play drums. Seemingly, it is only in the vocational tracks of our high schools that students have the opportunity to learn about automobiles – one of the most significant inventions of modern life. Interestingly, in a West Philadelphia high school known for its failing academic profile, a teacher organized a group of mostly Black boys to prepare them to compete in the 'Tour d' Sol' a contest for building solar powered automobiles (http://www.progressiveautoxprize.org/teams/west-philly-hybrid-x-team, accessed February 13, 2010). To most people's surprise the team beat all of their suburban competitors – both high school and college level. Once they won the competition, the students and their teacher put together a template for replicating success in subsequent years and they won the contest again. By the third year, when the school was attracting lots of attention for its achievement in the auto building contest the administrators began talking about shutting it down because it was 'draining too many resources.' Fortunately, some private monies were found to keep the project going. Because activities like this are missing from the typical school curriculum we find ourselves regularly trying to maintain peace and order in the school rather than trying to develop and challenge minds.

While it is important to avoid gender stereotyping in the development of school curriculum we do have a responsibility to use available data to learn more about the interests and course taking patterns of boys in our schools. In programs like Brooklyn's El Puente we see that boys regularly choose aspects of its hip hop curriculum that focus on DJ'ing, graffiti art, spoken word, and dancing, and girls are more likely to focus on dance, spoken word and clothing design. While there is some overlap, there are clear gender distinctions in student interest and smart teachers will capitalize on those differences to support student learning.

Eastside Preparatory Academy in East Palo Alto, California, has decided to create a focused mission in which students are challenged to do exceptionally high quality work (similar to that of elite prep schools) and the faculty, staff, and administrators surround the students with plenty of support to help students achieve. In its ten-year existence Eastside, which serves a 100% low income and minority community, has posted a 100 high school graduation rate and a 100% four-year college-going rate. The students take four years of English, college preparatory mathematics, science, social studies, and participate in the arts and service learning.

The boys in the settings listed above are treated like students and they respond favorably to that treatment. They are encouraged to, as the late Ted Sizer says, 'use their minds well' and see school as a place where they can experience success. Ultimately, they can see school as a place where boys can become young men.

## Notes

1. Throughout this paper I use the terms, 'Black' and 'African American' interchangeably.
2. National Basketball Commissioner, David Stern imposed a dress code on athletes in 2005 that was thought to be specifically directed toward Allen Iverson.

## References

American Council of Education. 2007. *Twenty second annual status report on minorities in higher education: 2007 supplement.* Washington, DC: American Council of Education.

*Do the Right Thing.* Directed by Spike Lee. New York: Forty Acres & A Mule Productions, 1989.

Eckholm, E. 2006. Plight deepens for Black men, studies warn. *New York Times*, March 20. http://www.newyorktimes.com/2006/03/20/national/20blackmen.html.html?_r&equals;3&th=oref=slogin&emc=th&pagewanted=print&oref=slogin (accessed November 4, 2007).

Enteman, R., and A. Rojecki. 2001. *The Black image in the white mind: Media and race in America.* Chicago: University of Chicago Press.

Gurian, M., and K. Stevens. 2004. With boys and girls in mind. *Educational Leadership* 62, no. 3: 21–6.

Haberman, M. 1991. The pedagogy of poverty vs. good teaching. *Phi Delta Kappan* 73, no. 4 290–94.

Kunjufu, J. 2005. *Keeping Black boys out of special education.* Chicago: African American Images.

Majors, R., and J.M. Bilson. 1992. *Cool pose: The dilemma of Black manhood in America.* New York: Touchstone.

Mincy. R., ed. 2006. *Black males left behind.* Washington, DC: The Urban Institute.

Noddings, N. 1992. *The challenge to care in schools: An alternative approach to education.* New York: Teachers College Press.

Polite, V., and J. Davis, eds. 1999. *African American males in school and society: Practices and policies for effective education.* New York: Teachers College Press.

Price, E. 2006. *Hip hop culture.* Santa Barbara: ABC-CLIO.

Rawls, Jesse, Jr. 2006. School identification: How young African American males in an urban elementary school come to identify with school. *Dissertation Abstracts International* 67, no. 07A: 135.

Schott Foundation. 2004. *Public education and Black male students: A state report card.* Cambridge, MA: Schott Foundation.

Shields, D. 1999. *Black planet: Facing race during an NBA season.* New York: Three Rivers Press.

Spencer, M.B. 2008. Lessons learned and opportunities ignored post-Brown v. Board of Education: Youth development and the myth of a colorblind society. *Educational Researcher* 37, no. 5: 253–66.

United States Bureau of Labor Statistics. 2009. Economic news release. http://www.bls.gov/news.release/empsit.t02.htm (accessed December 9, 2009).

Varlas, L. 2005. Bridging the widest gap: Raising the achievement of Black boys. *Education Update* 47, no. 8: 1.

# Toward a new narrative on Black males, education, and public policy

Anthony L. Brown[a,1] and Jamel K. Donnor[b]

[a]Department of Curriculum & Instruction, University of Texas–Austin, Austin, USA;
[b]Department of Curriculum & Instruction, The College of William and Mary, Williamsburg, USA

> This article examines the Black male crisis thesis promulgated by the social science literature, public policy, and mainstream discourse, respectively. The authors contend that the stock-story that the majority of African American males are 'at-risk' for engaging in self-destructive behavior or on the verge of extinction perpetuates a discourse of Black male pathology, which leads to over-emphasis of behavior modification as a strategy for their collective improvement. Subsequently, de-emphasis on the historical and structural role of race as a life opportunity-shaping variable occurs, which renders an incomplete understanding of the social and educational status of Black males in the United States. As a result, public policies and social programs guided by this deficit discourse are unlikely to create meaningful change for this population, because society's existing political economic structures are left unchallenged. The article concludes with the assertion that a 'new narrative' is needed in order to rethink the complex and systematic ways the social and educational status of Black males in the United States are constructed.

'A key question about stories, as with other situation-defining symbolic forms like metaphors, theories, and ideologies, is whether they introduce new and constructive insights into social life.'

W. Lance Bennett and Murray Edelman (1985)

## Introduction

The quote above by Bennett and Edelman suggests that stories are not only useful for conveying particular viewpoints, they are particularly powerful in explaining the human condition. Indeed, the manner in which a social problem is framed not only determines the scope of its stakeholders, but more importantly, its solutions (Doherty 1998). One of the most dominant and persistent social narratives in the United States is that young African American males are in a perpetual state of crisis. From the mainstream media's frequent portrayals of Black[2] youth as criminals to the education literature's regular reporting on the academic shortcomings of the nation's young Black men, such stories have increased the public's awareness of the disparities and inequalities this social group disproportionately endures. The reoccurring accounts on the marginal status of young African American males has led to a proliferation of targeted responses in the form of public forums, academic symposiums, philanthropic reports, and trade publications portending to address the crisis.

While the Black male crisis narrative has generated a significant amount of mainstream and scholarly attention, it has not necessarily led to systematic improvement for the group (Trammel et al. 2008). A reason for the lack of measurable progress, we argue, is that the young Black male crisis narrative overlooks the significance of the historical and structural interrelationship between race and social inequity. Thus, programs, policies, forums, and trade publications asserting to address the young Black male crisis are unlikely to produce meaningful outcomes because they lack a structural critique and historical analysis of racial inequity. As a result of this omission, targeted responses to the young Black male crisis narrative inadvertently recapitulate a larger societal discourse of African American males as a population needing to be saved from themselves.

The purpose of this article is to explain how articulations and responses to the Black male crisis circuitously perpetuate a racialized understanding of this population. The goal of this article is twofold. The first is to disrupt the Black male crisis narrative by identifying its analytical and conceptual shortcomings. The second goal of this article is to expand the policy discourse concerning young African American males by discussing how race is engendered informally through language, ideology, habit, and practice.

The first section of this article discusses the historical context of social policies targeting African American males. The second section explains the framework for analyzing social policy and public discourse regarding African American males. The third section discusses the proliferation in advocacy trade books on African American males. We conclude by calling for a rethinking of the Black male crisis narrative.

## Historical context of the social policy about the African American male

The policy discourse from the mid-1960s through the 1990s, concerning the social and educational conditions of Black males provides the historical backdrop for contemporary policy discussions about African American males. It is important to note that the attention given to this history also encapsulates the nuances and contours of African American male policy discourse in relation to the most recent proliferation of concern about the African American male. Each period points to larger sociopolitical contingencies (e.g. poverty, unemployment, single mother home etc.) that informed the social milieu of both young and adult African American male life. We contend that there are three distinct periods of policy discourse about African American males from the 1960s to the present.

The first period emerged in the mid-1960s amid growing concerns of urban poverty and the development of social policy in the era of the pre-Great Society policies and the civil rights acts. The second period resurfaced in the mid-1980s, a period of rapid de-industrialization and alarming rates of urban unemployment. The third and most recent instantiation surfaced in the last ten years in an era when African American men can be found working and succeeding within every sector of society, including the presidency of the United States which occurred simultaneously with the growing number of African American men suffering from unprecedented numbers of unemployment, health-related deaths, incarceration, violent death and educational underachievement.

By the mid-1960s, there had been three decades of secondary attention given to the social conditions of African American males (Fultz and Brown 2008). The policy discourse about African American males was often secondary to larger concerns about the African American family. From the 1930s to the 1960s, researchers constructed the African American man as an unknown and unidentified subject within empirical research studies and policy discussions. Eliot Liebow's (1967, 6) words illustrate this sentiment:

> Neglect of the lower-class male is a direct reflection of his characteristic 'absence' from the household, leaving behind him the 'female-based' or 'female-centered' households, so that one comes away with a picture of the low-income urban world as one peopled mainly with women and children. The adult male, if not simply characterized as 'absent,' is depicted as a somewhat shadowy figure who drifts in out of the lives of family members.

Contrary to Liebow's assertion, this was not the case by the mid-1960s. While much of the policy discourse about African Americans focused on the African American family as the face of urban poverty, researchers and policy makers began to pay closer attention to the social and psychological contexts of both young and adult African American males. The growing attention given to the Black male was most visible via the controversial and widely read federal policy document 'The Negro Family: The Case for National Action,' also known as the 'Moynihan Report.' Published in 1965 by then Assistant Secretary of Labor Daniel Patrick Moynihan, the objective of the report was to make public the social context of American poverty and promote social policies that advocated for families in poverty – what was also referred to the 'Moynihan strategy.' Moynihan attempted to paint a sociological portrait of Black life. To do this he had drawn from theories and research about African Americans that had been in existence since the late 1930s. He was particularly influenced by the work of E. Franklin Frazier and Kenneth Clark.

The 'absent father' and its effects on Black boys was now the central focus of the discussion about the African American family. Moynihan posited that because young Black males did not have access to masculine norms, this affected Black boys' ability to develop normally and find motivation to achieve. Thus, he recommended that Black male youth gain compensatory masculine norms via programs outside of the home, most notably the military (Moynihan 1965/1967). Moynihan in particular felt that the military would be an ideal space to instill compensatory masculinity. Moynihan (1965/1967, 88) states:

> There is another special quality about military service for Negro men: it is an utterly masculine world. Given the strains of the disorganized and matrifocal family life in which so many Negro youth come of age, the Armed Forces are a dramatic and desperately needed change: a world away from women, a world run by strong men of unquestioned authority, where discipline, if harsh, is nonetheless orderly and predictable, and where rewards, if limited, are granted on the basis of performance.

While different methodologies and approaches to make sense of the cultural context of African American males emerged from the 1960s through the 1970s, the policy narrative of the impoverished Black family and the emasculated Black male remained the fundamental belief among scholars concerned with promoting policies to address African American poverty.

Then from the 1980s through the 1990s, a full-blown national debate emerged that focused on the context of the African American male in a de-industrialized economy. The metaphor used to describe the social, psychological and educational conditions of African American males was to refer to them as an 'endangered species' and on the precipice of peril due to illness, incarceration, and violent death. Jewell Taylor Gibbs here (1987, 1–2) defines the endangered Black male:

> ...an endangered species is, according to Webster, 'a class of individuals having common attributes and designated by a common name... [which is] in danger or peril of probable harm or loss.' This description applies, in a metaphorical sense, to the current status of young black males in contemporary American society. They have been miseducated by the educational system, mishandled by the criminal justice system, mislabeled by the mental health system, and mistreated by the social welfare system.

William Legette (1999, 291) also referred to this period of policy discourse as the *crisis of the black male thesis*, which he defines as a 'consensus that social and economic problems in the black community [were] the result of black men not being able to perform the roles expected of men in a patriarchal society.' Within this policy era, the African American boy was now also an explicit subject of inquiry. Much of this discussion was also made visible within widely-circulated public discourse because of the work of educational advocate Jawanza Kunjufu, specifically his four-volume, self-published *Countering the Conspiracy to Destroy Black Boys*. Another significant feature of this period of research was the focus on African American men to serve as role models and mentors to historically underserved African American male students. This recommendation is striking because from the 1930s to 1970s the policy discourse about African American boys generally blamed Black men for either being absent or peripheral fathers or serving as negative male role models.

By the late 1990s, however, much of the discussion about African American males had slowed down. Then for approximately the last eight years, society has witnessed the most significant attention given to African American males. This surge in attention grew exponentially with the nomination and election of Barack Obama, the first African American male president of the United States. The questions that many ask are whether the election of Barack Obama settled the race question for African Americans en masse and whether his presence in the White House will have an impact on how African American males make sense of their own life chances and identities.

During this period, politicians, comedians, educators, actors, social scientists, journalists and newscasters have all joined the discussion about the social and educational conditions of the African American male. What is unique about this era of discourse is the implicit belief that African American male social problems were no longer informed by race and racism, given that African American men are now represented in almost every facet of society including CEOs of Fortune 500 companies and now the presidency of the United States. The next section of this paper explores this era's construction of African American male social problems via policy reports and popular trade books.

## The framing of the young Black male problem

Two presuppositions guide our analysis of policy discourse and popular responses to the young Black male crisis narrative. The first is that both mechanisms portray young Black males as culturally and psychologically damaged (Scott 1997). The notion of psychological damage has taken on different instantiations since the 1960s, which in some instances refers to Black males as powerless individuals who fall victim to self-fulfilling prophesies of defeat and failure to more recent analyses concerned with how racial stereotyping produces an internalized negative self-concept, or what Claude Steele (1997) refers to as stereotype threat. The second is that policy discourse and popular responses to the young Black male crisis narrative are rooted in contested notions of respectability (Higginbotham 1993), which emphasize individual behavior and attitudinal modification as the primary strategy for collective improvement. The confluence of both constructs, we argue, perpetuates a dual understanding of Black males. The first is through its behavioral assumption that presumes young African American males rely on a set of 'decision heuristics' or non-traditional decision-making schematas, such as 'cool pose,' which produces attitudes and behaviors that are antithetical to individual success in a democratic society (Schneider and Ingram 1990, 517). The second way is by minimizing race as a life opportunity-shaping variable (Gordon 1997). Stated differently, contemporary policy discourse and public responses to the young African American male crisis narrative conveys a meta-narrative, postulating that the existing structural organization of American society is fair, equal, and blind to race. We define meta-narratives as totalizing or mythical stories that provide the foundational context and knowledge about people and racial groups (Pride 2002; Somers and Gibson 1994)

## *Black males as damaged*

The notion that young Black males are culturally and psychologically damaged is one of the oldest and most common approaches used to craft social policy and elicit public action (Scott 1997). This deficit view of African American males is buttressed by America's noxious legacy of chattel slavery, Reconstruction, and Jim Crow segregation. As a result of the foregoing racial formation projects, contemporary conceptions of young African American males as acutely susceptible to engaging in self-destructive behavior is used to argue on behalf of public policies and social programs that purport to improve their collective status (Omi and Winant 1997). Indeed, the idea that people of African descent are psycho-culturally deficient is not a recent phenomenon. Utilized by racial conservatives and racial liberals, the notion that African Americans are damaged has been employed to justify *de jure* racial discrimination and racial integration, respectively (Scott 1997). According to Scott (1997, xii):

> Between 1880 and 1920, the period in which conservatives instituted de jure segregation and disenfranchisement, the experts who dominated the image of black people depicted African Americans as incapable and undeserving of participation in a modern society...As the South codified segregation, the experts believed that the separation of the races, far from damaging blacks, was healthful. During the interwar years, liberals replaced conservatives as the hegemonic group of experts on African American life, history, and personality. Many liberals shared the view that blacks were psychologically damaged, including the assumption that in race relations proximity rather than distance was more damaging to blacks.

In essence, African Americans have been socially constructed through politics, culture, and the social sciences as a target population in which society's well-being is directly affected – good and bad (Schneider and Ingram 1993). With respect to young African American males, however, what is unique about the crisis narrative is its lack of rigorous analysis and overemphasis on modifying behaviors, attitudes, and culture – all non-structural factors.

As a target population for public policy, young African American males have been constructed through the social scientific literature of the mid-twentieth century as endangered and disconnected from mainstream society. Subsequently, philanthropic reports, policy initiatives, and trade publications have tried to link the group's social status to the public interest by articulating a dire situation. For example, in *Stepping Up and Stepping Out*, a report for the Association for Black Foundation Executives, public awareness on the collective status of the young Black male crisis is sought by highlighting the practices of funders that have 'stepped up to the significant task of seeking to improve the life chances and opportunities of black males; and in doing so have stepped out on the proverbial limb' (Littles, Bowers, and Gilmar 2008, 9). The invoking of the metaphors 'stepping up' and 'stepping out' is intended to evoke cognitive structures that not only articulate the social status of young Black males in America, but also point out the burden or significance of the actions taken to address the crisis. For instance, A Legacy of Tradition (ALOT), The Chicago Community Trust (CCT), and The Schott Foundation for Public Education organizations are respectively profiled in the report as private agencies involved with attending to the supply-side of the young Black male crisis through fundraising and grant-making.

In providing financial inducements and capacity-building instruments, such as grants, these funding organizations assume that the conditional transfer of money to community agencies will elicit action or lead to the development of a knowledge-base or set of competencies that will improve the collective status of young Black males (Elmore 1987; McDonnell and Elmore 1987). Clearly, there are benefits of both policy instruments. For example, ALOT's 'giving circles' seek to expand members' understanding of issues facing Black males, as well as recruit older professional African American men who otherwise would not participate in philanthropy (Littles, Bowers, and Gilmar 2008). Similarly, CCT provides grants to agencies in the Chicago metropolitan area with a strong record and interest in Black males, such as the Center for the Study of Race, Politics, and Culture at the University of Chicago and the Intergovernmental Committee at the University of Illinois. Likewise, the Schott Foundation for Publication Education awards grants to public schools that 'successfully' closed the achievement gaps in graduation rates for African American male students.

Unfortunately, the benefits of supply-side strategies, such as inducements and grants, are diffuse and limited to recipient agencies, rather than the target population (Elmore 1987; McDonnell and Elmore 1987). For example, while capacity-building tools are useful for encouraging the adoption of non-traditional programs, they also encourage short-term responses to structural problems (Schneider and Ingram 1990; Legette 1999). A notable example of a short-term response to the young Black male crisis narrative is all-male schools. Particularly popular in urban communities, single-sex schools are viewed as viable mechanisms for addressing the low graduation rates of young Black males, because they portend to provide needed discipline and limit distractions (Brown 2003). However, the success of such authoritarian mechanisms are mixed given that curricula and teacher instruction at these schools are prescribed by the No Child Left Behind Act of 2007 (NCLB), which emphasizes high-stakes testing over higher order cognitive skills, such as reasoning and interpretation (Donnor and Shockley 2010). Moreover, because African American males are more likely to attend schools guided by NCLB, they are less prepared for college and more prepared to participate in the military (Brown 2003; Lipman 2004; Donnor and Shockley 2010). On the surface, all-male schools may appear as a viable response to the crisis narrative, below the surface, however, students may be further marginalized, unwittingly. Lastly, grants and similar incentive instruments presume that awardees are 'utility maximizers' that possess the capacity to recognize opportunities and 'choose higher valued alternatives' (Schneider and Ingram 1990, 515). Instead, students who are viewed as damaged or in crisis are further stigmatized, because requirements for participation in programs involve affirming the target population's pathological deservingness (Scott 1997).

## Advocacy trade books and the African American male

Since the mid-1980s when concerns about African Americans males surfaced as a national crisis, there have been countless numbers of books published to address their conditions. While many of these books are edited or single-authored full-length books published within the academic literature, a more significant number of trade books have been published with the intention of reaching the wider public. These books address different topics such as education, the criminal justice system, gangs, relationships, fatherhood, masculinity, mentorship, HIV and AIDS, suicide, and drug abuse and rehabilitation. Oftentimes the audience of these books is wide in terms of readership, but the focus is generally intended to speak directly to African American men and youth. In recent years, a number of trade books published within major publishing presses and readily available within major book distributors such as Amazon, Barnes and Noble, and Borders have surfaced. The importance of trade books is significant given the wide readership of these texts. Our analysis will give attention to five books published in recent years: *Letters to a Young Brother: MANifest your Destiny* (Hill Harper 2006); *Being a Black Man: At the Corner of Progress and Peril* (staff of the *Washington Post* 2007); *The Black Male Handbook: A Blueprint for Life* (Kevin Powell 2008); *What Black Men Should Do Now: 100 Simple Truths, Ideas, and Concepts* (K. Thomas Oglesby 2002); *Come on People: On the Path from Victims to Victors* (Bill Cosby and Alvin Poussaint 2007).

In our analysis of trade books, we found three overarching meta-narratives about African American males. The first is that African American males instigate their own problems by embodying an autonomous Black male subculture of apathy and disrespect, which we call the 'politics of disrespectability and apathy.' We define the 'politics of disrespectability and apathy' as the belief that African American males possess a defined racial ontology or way of being that is antithetical to mainstream norms of society as well as apathetic to the histories of political struggles that advocated for their civil and human rights. In addition, Black males intentionally portray the 'politics of disrespectability and apathy' even when issues of poverty or racism are no longer perceived as a defining factor. The second meta-narrative present in trade books about African American males is the implicit construction of the African American male as irresponsible, destructive, oversexed, agnostic, unhealthy and adverse to schooling and work. Said differently, we posit that the self-help discourses found within trade publications, while seeking to provide a blueprint for African American males to change their lives, implicitly reify negative and essentialized constructions of an autonomous African American male subculture. The third and final meta-narrative that often surfaces within these trade books is the ideological belief that race and racism are no longer factors in African American male problems.

## Looking closely at trade books

All of the books we reviewed either implicitly or explicitly worked from the premise that African American males fashion their own problems by embodying a 'politics of disrespectability and apathy.' In each of the texts reviewed, the authors provide a clear description of the deleterious statistics of African American males, followed by a discussion of a Black male culture trapped by materialism, affected by father absence and handcuffed by an existing script of manhood. While four of the five texts analyzed employed the narrative of the Black male crisis as a way to provide a more holistic and complete picture of African American males, Cosby and Poussaint's book *Come on People* – particularly their opening chapter, 'What's going on Black men?' – takes a slightly different approach, suggesting that entrenched African American problems are anchored by an aberrant Black male culture of coolness and detachment. Here Cosby and Poussaint (2007, 11) make this point about Black male coolness:

> To be cool is to be emotionally detached, at least on the surface. For some, showing emotions is uncool, unmanly. Expressing the kind of emotions that any good father should express – like warmth, love, caring, and grief – is almost impossible for someone who has spent his whole life stuck on being cool. Many who feel abandoned by a parent protect themselves from being hurt by putting on a cool detachment. Better to put on those bad shades and shut off the world.

What underpins the discussions on coolness or the cool pose is the belief that African American males suffer from a damaged psyche (Scott 1997, 15) that prohibits them to take responsibility for their mental and physical health, economics, spirituality, and relationships. For example, one of the authors in the text *The Black Male Handbook* argues that Black males suffer from feelings of '[a]lienation, marginalization, and isolation [causing] them to adopt a "me against the world" mentality.' In another instance, the text *What Black Men Should Do Now: 100 Simple Truths, Ideas and Concepts,* 17 of the 100 'simple truths' focus on the socio-psychological conditioning of Black males' inability to love, to commit, to work hard, to express affection and to have an overall positive self-concept.

What is striking about these texts is how they inadvertently help reify long-standing constructions about the African American male. The idea of African American males' lack and deficiency is foundational to many of the texts. Within the self-help genre of trade books, the author will first outline the Black male problem or manhood problem and then offer a myriad of corrective practices, philosophies, meditations, beliefs and anecdotes that Black males must do to change their lives. Texts such as *Letters to a Young Brother, What Black Men Should Do Now, Come on People* and *The Black Male Handbook* each provide explicit advice to African American males and their families.

While these anecdotes and self-help philosophies may seem innocuous or even helpful, such narratives are problematic for two reasons. First, they help to reify a standard prop taken from policy discourse that suggests that Black males are an autonomous pathological subculture. Second, by only focusing on self-help ideologies much of the historical legacy of race and racism in this country goes unexamined, leaving only a Black male subject for us to examine his flaws, insecurities and subcultures.

This leads us to our final concern with trade texts. In these texts few discussions account for the structural and institutional implications of race and racism to Black males' lives. For example, the editor of *The Black Male Handbook* states: 'Yes, racism is alive and well in America, and we will forever challenge and critique it, no question. But if black males are going to be empowered, that empowerment has to be proactive – and holistic' (xxii). In many cases race and racism is mentioned in passing or, as in the case Cosby and Poussaint's *Come on People*, racism is acknowledged but the authors can only provide a limited explanation of why Black men are not doing well in society. Here Cosby and Poussaint (2007, 8) state:

> Black Americans fought to open doors of opportunity – and now black immigrants are walking through those doors while too many of us [Black males] are hanging out on street corners. There certainly is institutional racism – particularly ask black men – but racism doesn't explain everything.

This was an explicit and implicit sentiment for each of the trade text reviewed. Racism is either slightly recognized or it is seen as only a partial explanation to the social and educational conditions of Black males. Again, in looking across these texts, the 'politics of disrespectability and apathy' emerged, suggesting that African American males writ large – regardless of class, region, sexuality – are a group of men who are deeply troubled by personal, psychological, social, spiritual and educational inadequacies that transcend the structural and institutional factors that help to reproduce the conditions of Black males' lives.

## *Making respectable Black men*

When crafting less formal responses to the young Black male crisis narrative, many organizations, popular media outlets, and trade publications focus on addressing behaviors and characteristics deemed counterproductive to the group's advancement. In this instance, enhancing the public image of young African American males becomes the site for collective improvement (Cohen 1997). Because young African American males are publicly defined as a population in a perpetual state of crisis, organizations and individuals responding to the narrative proffer programs and advice for altering behaviors and attitudes considered deleterious. For example, African-centered Rites of Passage programs seek to provide participants with the foundational understanding of African and African American history and culture, as well as life skills and character development necessary to help young Black males better assimilate into society (Alford, McKenry, and Gavazzi 2001). According to Alford and others (2001, 141), African American Rites of Passage programs (AA-RITES) serve to 'increase the self-esteem and ethnic pride of adolescent Black males, helping them to be better fit, both mentally and socially, to receive the academic regimen placed before them.' Here, the engendering of culturally specific attributes is framed as a pathway for reshaping the collective fortunes of young African American males. Furthermore, individual reform is tacitly advanced as leading to racial and social equality for African Americans as a whole (Legette 1999).

For historically oppressed groups, such as African Americans, adherence to behaviors and traits generally accepted as respectable is intended to counter racist images and establish 'common ground on which to live as Americans with Americans of other racial and ethnic backgrounds' (Higginbotham 1993, 188). According to Higginbotham:

> ...[r]espectability demand[s] that every individual in the black community assume responsibility for behavioral self-regulation and self-improvement along moral, educational, and economic lines. The goal [is] to distance oneself as far as possible from

images perpetuated by racist stereotypes. Individual behavior...[will] determine the collective fate of African Americans. It [is] particularly public behavior that [is] perceived to wield the power either to refute or confirm stereotypical representations and discriminatory practices. (196)

In the search to define what it means to be a young male of African descent in the United States, responses to the young Black male crisis narrative do not avail themselves to systematic critiques of the political economic structures responsible for racial and social inequities, because social change is sought by reforming the individual not society. Hence, responses to the young African American male crisis narrative are often hortatory and symbolic (Schneider and Ingram 1990). As a traditionally underserved population, responses and recommendations for the young Black male crisis are authoritarian in focus because they advance 'certain goals without the need for coercive or incentive-driven government intervention' (Schneider and Ingram 1990, 519). Paradoxically, there is an inadvertent recapitulation of the group's marginalization because members of the target population are not recognized as possessing the autonomy or capacity to contribute to their betterment. This 'population reasoning' (Popkewitz 1998, 26) normalizes society's understanding of young Black males as being in a constant state of crisis, because they are defined and redefined in a manner that separates them from their 'immediate historical situation' (Popkewitz 1998).

## Discussion and implications

In working toward a new narrative, it is important to point out that no single story or counter-story can accomplish this task. Rather, a new narrative requires an examination of historically contingent narratives informed by the social and epistemic forces of place and time. Otherwise, future policy discourse concerning African American males will fall into the conceptual trap of moving from one grand narrative to another (Brown in press). Thus, we argue that a melding of methodological approaches and analytical tools is required to fully articulate why the life opportunities, experiences, and outcomes of African American males are disparate from other social groups.

### *History and the structure of inequality in education*

Given that social inequality, racism, and racial discrimination in the twenty-first century occurs through a 'subtler series of screens,' rather than overt and *de jure* methods deployed during the nineteenth and twentieth century, we argue that understanding and improving the collective educational opportunities and social experiences of African American males requires a historical perspective and a sociopolitical understanding of public education, including its connections to shifts in the US economy (Holt 1995; Omi and Winant 1997; Katz, Stern, and Fader 2005, 76–7; O'Connor, Lewis, and Mueller 2007).

Because many of the concerns and problems facing African American males in education and society are *not* new, we contend that contemporary responses to the Black male crisis narrative must reference history to avoid inaccurate descriptions and incomplete solutions. Used as a method for comparison, history links the past to the present by allowing for a comprehensive understanding of trends and patterns, including, how and why conditions have changed or remained constant over time (Katz 1993). For instance, in analyzing the 'historical continuities and discontinuities' of racial inequality in the American public education system, Walters (2001) discovered that the 'distributional processes' in education, specifically, school funding arrangements (e.g. property taxes), are the most durable over time (36). According to Walters (2001):

> ...the system of distributing education that is in place at any given time is the product of the past: The institutional mechanisms available to the state to implement change, available to threatened groups to resist change, and available to disadvantaged groups to foment change are constrained in critical respects by policy decisions made in earlier periods. State policies instituted in one era, even for egalitarian purposes, may work at cross-purposes to equalizing attempts in later periods (36).

In essence, history requires one to think holistically and continuously about inequality in education. Moreover, given that students, especially African American males, schools, and opportunities are enmeshed within a particular set of discourses, processes, and hierarchies regarding purpose and functionality, existing structural arrangements, collective outcomes and disparities must be viewed as products of a cumulative interrelationship between competing ideologies, institutions, and human behavior (Apple 1995; Mickelson 2003). Indeed, a 'paradox of inequality' is the 'coexistence of structural rigidity with individual and group fluidity' (Katz, Stern, and Fader 2005, 77). According to Katz and others, the continuance of structural inequality in conjunction with individual and group mobility 'highlights the limitations of policies that focus only on access to education without addressing the factors that structure and reproduce inequality' (107). In short, inequality in education is contextual according to place and time.

Consider for example, that since the Kennedy administration, the tax rate for the richest 1% of Americans has declined from 85.5% in 1963 to 22.45% in 2007 (Anyon 2005, 52; Henchman 2009). During the same period, federal, state and local taxes paid by corporations have declined from 40% in 1940 to 9.2% in 2000. More recently, the Government Accountability Office (2008) reported that two out of every three United States corporations did not pay federal income taxes from 1998 through 2005 (Browning 2008).[3] Conversely, the payroll taxes for middle and low-income families have increased dramatically during the same time period (Anyon 2005).[4] For instance, the tax rate for middle-class families rose from 5.3% in 1948 to 24.63% in 1990, while payroll taxes paid by middle-class families rose from 6.9% in 1950 to 31.1% in 2000 (Anyon 2005, 53). What this means is, the burden for funding public goods and services, such as schools, is disproportionately paid for by the middle- and lower-class. Thus, the current American tax structure places a premium on residential locations with quality goods and services, including schools, thus causing for an aversion to share or equally reallocate resources. Subsequently, racial inequity becomes geographically locked-in according to where one lives. Much of the literature on school quality and neighborhood capacity indicates that race and class are proxies for which schools fail (Briggs 2005a, 2005b; Powell 1997). Hence, additional analytical queries informed by geography and performance are needed (see Tate and Hogrebe, this issue).

As a matter of equity, we recommend a 'split-rate taxation' method to remedy structural deficiencies (Brunori 2003, 13). This method of taxation places a premium on the value of the land, rather than the improvements made on the property, which is difficult to tax (Brunori 2003). Moreover, it allows local governments to generate the revenue necessary to provide basic services and not make decisions based on the free market or redistributing wealth, because the tax base is stable (14). More importantly, it would allow local governments to spend as much as they want on education and to monitor the school system, rather than being dependent on inter-governmental allocations, which often comes with mandates that determine the curriculum and teacher pedagogy. Most important, the public benefit to reforming the current tax structure would provide municipalities with the funds necessary to invest in the public education of African American males. According to Levin and others (2007), 'simply [equalizing] the high school graduation rate of Black males with that of white males would yield approximately $256,700 per graduate or $167,600 in additional tax revenue, save $33,500 in public health costs, and save a minimum of $55,500 in costs associated with the criminal justice system. They estimate that the aggregate net public benefit would range from $3.27 billion to $4.74 billion, with a median figure of $3.98 billion. Further, such an approach would not only increase Black male employability, but also reduce their participation in illegal activities and reliance on state and federal government social services (Sum et al. 2007).

## *The global political economy of American education*

Schools are a microcosm of society. Thus, the social, political, and economic implications for education and traditionally marginalized groups, such as Black males, are inextricably linked to the exogenous and macro-level forces that shape American society (Burbules and Torres 2000; Green 2001; Lipman 2004; Waks 2006). In this particular instance, both African American male social and educational inequality, and advancement must be situated in the context of globalization. By globalization, we are referring to the restructuring of the US economy, along with members of the Group of 8 (e.g. United States, France, Germany, Italy, Canada, United Kingdom, Japan, and Russia), in which the exchange and movement of capital, ideas, labor, culture, and commerce for the world are reliant upon information technology, and premised on free market principles (Green 2001, Lipman 2004). At the core of globalization, is the processing information and generation of knowledge efficiently at high speeds to create goods and services for consumption worldwide (Lipman 2004; Nembhard 2005).

Concomitantly, the nature of work and the skills necessary for sustainable productive employment opportunities have been fundamentally altered (Burbules and Torres 2000; Green 2001; Lipman 2004; Nembhard 2005; Waks 2006). In the global economy, international economic competitiveness is contingent upon the productivity of well-trained people and the steady stream of scientific and technical innovations they produce. Globalization has not only altered the types of products required for international competitiveness, more importantly, the requisite skills needed to ensure workforce participation have been altered (Waks 2003). Hence, the purpose of education in the global economy has changed (Hargreaves 2003). In moving toward a new narrative, questions about why African American males are underachieving in schools must be buttressed against various global forces that define and inform social and economic opportunity in America. In other words, researchers, policy makers, and educators must not only explore questions that account for how Black males are experientially positioned within education, but also, how the broader American political economy defines and constrains the educational experiences of Black males (Donnor and Shockley 2010).

Hence, future studies on Black males and education must build on the works of scholars, such as Howard (2008), Ferguson (2002), and Noguera (2008) who illustrate how the educational experiences of African American males are constrained by teachers' and school officials' conceptions of race and achievement, which result in higher school expulsion and suspension rates, and a disproportionate placement in special education. There are two conceptual lessons learned from this body of research. The first is that when Black males are given an opportunity to speak candidly about their educational experiences, a much more nuanced narrative surfaces, which accounts for the structural and discursive constructs that constrain their lives. The second is that by focusing on structural constraints of race, class and gender, researchers and educational advocates can better grasp the multitude of institutional and stereotypical discourses that reproduce the educational experiences of Black males and enable policy discourse to move beyond what Brown (in press) refers to as the *same old stories*. Finally, we argue that policy analysts and researchers must reveal the racialized nature of education policy and its implications to the public construction of Black males' lives. In addition, educational policy analysis must reveal the racialized nature of educational policy and its implications to Black males. This kind of work has been poignantly expressed through the work of David Gillborn (2005, 2009) in the UK.

## Concluding thoughts

The question underpinning much of the policy and public discourse about African American males is whether Black males are responsible for their own actions or whether there are real structural constraints that affect their life chances and outcomes. Our analysis of policy reports and trade books, uncovered that African American male behaviors, dispositions and culture receive greater attention than the institutional and structural contingencies that shape their life chances. While such attention might be rooted in altruistic efforts to solve Black male inequality, we argue, that this focus is more of a reflection of the *power* of the Black male crisis narrative in America. While there were varying degrees of attention in the policy reports and trade books examined in this article, across each of the texts we found that race as a structural variable was ignored or mentioned cursorily.

As we have discussed throughout this article, part of the problem is inherent in the process of promoting and stimulating social and educational policy. As several policy scholars (O'Connor 2001; Schneider and Ingram 1993; Scott 1997) have explained, a key element in the process of promoting social and educational policies is the manner in which the narrative about a social problem is dramatized. Meaning, in order to evoke public attention and legislative action the narrative must be compelling. As such, narratives used to frame policy discourse regarding traditionally underserved populations are often over-determined socially and psychologically in order to render them and their respective issues visible. According to O'Connor (2001), this approach toward policy discourse framing of social inequality is *poverty knowledge*, which 'reflects a central tension within liberal thought about the nature of inequality...whether it is best understood and addressed at the level of individual experience or as a matter of structural and institutional reform' (9).

In the context of education, Brown (2009) theorizes that the logic behind identifying particular individuals, student groups and populations as more likely than others to experience undesired outcomes is framed within a discourse of risk. According to Brown (2009) the different sociological, psychological and anecdotal logics employed to make sense of and redress the educational experiences of historically underserved students, most notably African Americans, while often well-intentioned re-inscribe and over-determine the broader societal categories that position groups as deviant. While there have been some shifts in the discourse about African American males in recent years, in many respects it is the same old stories (Brown in press) of deficits, deviance, and cultural pathology. In essence, Black males create their own problems and that programmatic change can only come via the human capital of Black male role models, while institutional and structural mechanisms shaped by race are left unscathed (Brown 2009).

In thinking about new ways to redress the social and educational conditions of African American males, one must be mindful that Black males' experiences are not isolated instantiations of social and educational inequalities tucked away in dark American ghettos, but rather the metaphorical and symbolic canaries in the mineshaft alerting us that something larger is fundamentally wrong with the body politic (Guinier and Torres 2002). More importantly, the racial injustice experienced by Black males is symptomatic of the unequal and unjust arrangements of power and privilege in America.

## Notes

1. This paper was fully co-authored and the authors listed are ordered alphabetically.
2. The authors use 'Black' and 'African American' interchangeably throughout the manuscript.
3. The study covered 1.3 million corporations of all sizes, most of them small, with a collective $2.5 trillion in sales. It includes foreign corporations that do business in the United States (*New York Times* http://www.nytimes.com/2008/08/13/business/13tax.html).
4. The tax share at the federal level has declined from 40% in 1940 to 9.2% in 2000. The tax rate for middle-class families rose from 5.3% in 1948 to 24.63% in 1990. Payroll taxes paid by middle class families rose from 6.9% in 1950 to 31.1% in 2000 (Anyon 2005, p. 53).

## References

Alford, K., P. McKenry, and S. Gavazzi. 2001. Enhancing achievement in adolescent black males: The rites of passage link. In *Educating our black children: New directions and radical approaches,* ed. R. Majors, 141–56. London: RoutledgeFalmer.

Anyon, J. 2005. *Radical possibilities: Public policy, urban education, and a new social movement.* New York: Routledge.

Apple, M.W. 1995. *Education and power.* New York: Routledge.

Bennett, W.L., and M. Edelman. 1985. Toward a new political narrative. *Journal of Communication* 35, no. 4: 156–71.

Briggs, X.D. 2005a. Introduction. In *The geography of opportunity: Race and housing choice in metropolitan America,* ed. X.D. Briggs, 1–16. Washington, DC: The Brookings Institution.

Briggs, X.D. 2005b. More pluribus, less unum? The changing geography of race and opportunity. In *The geography of opportunity: Race and housing choice in metropolitan America,* 17–44. Washington, DC: The Brookings Institution.

Brown, A.L. 2009. 'O brotha where art thou?' Examining the ideological discourses of African American male teachers working with African American male students. *Race Ethnicity and Education* 12, no. 4: 473–93.

Brown, A.L. In press. "Same old stories:" The black male in social science and educational literature, 1930s to the present. *Teachers College Record* 113, no. 9.

Brown, E.R. 2003. Freedom for some, discipline for "others:" The structure of inequality in education. In *Education as enforcement: The militarization and corporatization of schools,* ed. K.J. Saltman and D.A. Gabbard, 127–52. New York: RoutledgeFalmer.

Brown, K. 2009. Is this what we want them to say? Examining the tensions in what U.S. preservice teachers say about risk and academic achievement. *Teaching & Teacher Education* 26, no. 4: 1077–87.

Browning, L. 2008. Study tallies corporations not paying income tax. New York Times. http://www.nytimes.com/2008/08/13/business/13tax.html.

Brunori, D. 2003. *Local tax policy: A federalist perspective.* Washington: The Urban Institute Press.

Burbules, N.C., and C.A. Torres. 2000. Globalization and education: An introduction. In *Globalization and education: Critical perspectives*, ed. N.C. Burbules and C.A. Torres, 1–26. New York: Routledge.

Cohen, C.J. 1997. *The boundaries of blackness: AIDS and the breakdown of black politics*. Chicago: University of Chicago Press.

Cosby, B., and A. Poussaint. 2007. *Come on people: On the path from victims to victors*. Dallas: Thomas Nelson.

Doherty, K.M. 1998. Changing urban education: Defining issues. In *Changing urban education*, ed. C.N. Stone, 225–49. Lawrence: University Press of Kansas.

Donnor, J.K., and K. Shockley. 2010. Leaving us behind: A political economic interpretation of NCLB and the miseducation of African American males. *Journal of Educational Foundations*, Summer-Fall, 43–54.

Elmore, R.F. 1987. Instruments and strategy in public policy. *Review of Policy Research* 7, no. 1: 174–86.

Ferguson, A.A. 2001. *Bad boys: Public schools in the making of Black masculinity*. Ann Arbor, MI: University of Michigan Press.

Fultz, M., and A.L. Brown. 2008. Historical perspectives of African American males as subjects of education policy. *American Behavioral Scientist* 51: 854–71.

Gibbs, J.T. 1988. *Young, Black, and male in America: An endangered species*. New York: Auburn House.

Gillborn, D. 2005. Education policy as an act of white supremacy: Whiteness, critical race theory and education reform. *Journal of Education Policy* 20, no. 4: 485–505.

Gillborn, D. 2009. *Racism and education: Coincidence or conspiracy?* Abingdon: Routledge.

Gordon, E.T. 1997. Cultural politics of black masculinity. *Transforming Anthropology* 6, nos. 1–2: 36–53.

Green, C. 2001. *Manufacturing powerlessness in the black diaspora: Inner-city youth and the new global frontier*. Walnut Creek: Altamira Press.

Guinier, L., and G. Torres. 2002. *The miner's canary: Enlisting race, resisting power, transforming democracy*. Cambridge, MA: Harvard.

Hargreaves, A. 2003. *Teaching in the knowledge society: Education in the age of insecurity*. New York: Teachers College Press.

Henchman, J. 2009. *A review of significant State tax changes during 2009*. Tax Foundation. http://www.taxfoundation.org/publications/show/25641.html (accessed December 25, 2009).

Higginbotham, E.B. 1993. *The righteous discontent: The women's movement in the black Baptist church, 1880–1920*. Cambridge, MA: Harvard University Press.

Holt, T.C. 1995. Marking: Race, race-making, and the writing of history. *American Historical Review* 1–20.

Howard, T.C. 2008. Who really cares? The disenfranchisement of African American males in preK–12 schools: A critical race theory perspective. *Teachers College Record* 110, no. 5: 954–85.

Katz, M.B. 1993. Reframing the 'underclass' debate. In *The 'underclass' debate: Views from history*, ed. M.B. Katz, 440–78. Princeton: Princeton University Press.

Katz, M.B., M.J. Stern, and J.J. Fader. 2005. The new African American inequality. *The Journal of American History* 75–108.

Kunjufu, J. 1985. *Countering the conspiracy to destroy Black boys*. (Vols. 1–4). Chicago: African American Images.

Legette, W.M. 1999. The crisis of the black male: A new ideology on black politics. In *Without justice for all: The new liberalism and our retreat from racial equality*, ed. A. Reed, 291–324. Boulder, CO: Westview.

Levin, H., C. Belfield, P. Muennig, and C. Rouse. 2007. The public returns to public educational investments in African American males. http://www.cbcse.org/media/download_gallery/Public%20Returns%20Feb07.pdf (accessed April 2, 2007)

Liebow, E. 1967. *Tally's corner: A study of Negro streetcorner men*. Boston: Little, Brown and Company.

Littles, M., R. Bowers, and M. Gilmar. 2008. *Stepping up and stepping out: Profiles of philanthropy responding to an American crisis*. Association for Black Foundation Executives. http://www.abfe.org/pdf/Stepping_Up_and_Stepping_Out.pdf (accessed August 1, 2009).

Lipman, P. 2004. *High stakes education: Inequality, globalization, and urban school reform*. New York: RoutledgeFalmer.

McDonnell, L., and R.F. Elmore. 1987. Getting the job done: Alternative policy instruments. *Educational Evaluation and Policy Analysis* 9, no. 2: 133–52.

Merida, K., ed. 2007. *Being a Black man: At the corner of progress and peril.* Jackson, TN: Publicaffairs.

Mickelson, R.A. 2003. When are racial disparities in education the result of racial discrimination? A social science perspective. *Teachers College Record* 105, no. 6 1052–86.

Moynihan, P. 1965/1967. The Negro family: The case for national action. In *The Moynihan report and politics of controversy*, ed. R. Rainwater and W. Yancey, 47–132. Cambridge, MA: MIT.

Nembhard, J.G. 2005. On the road to democratic economic participation: Educating African American youth in the postindustrial global economy. In *Black education: A transformative research and action agenda for the new century*, ed. J.E. King, 225–40. Mahwah.

Noguera, P. 2008. *The trouble with black boys: And other reflections on race, equity, and the future of public education.* San Francisco: Jossey-Bass.

O'Connor, A. 2001. *Poverty knowledge: Social science, social policy, and the poor in twentieth-century U.S. history.* Princeton, NJ: Princeton University Press.

O'Connor, C., A. Lewis, and J. Mueller. 2007. Researching 'Black' educational experiences and outcomes: Theoretical and methodological considerations. *Educational Researcher* 36, no. 9: 541–52.

Oglesby, K.T. 2002. *What black men should do now: 100 simple truths, ideas, and concepts.* New York: Kensington.

Omi, M., and H. Winant. 1997. *Racial formation in the United States: From the 1960s to the 1990s.* New York: Routledge.

Popkewitz, T.S. 1998. *Struggling for the soul: The politics of schooling and the construction of the teacher.* New York: Teachers College Press.

Powell, J.A. 1997. The 'racing' of American society: Race functioning as a verb before signifying as a noun. *Law and Inequality* 15: 99–125.

Powell, K., ed. 2008. *The black male handbook: A blueprint for life.* New York: Atria Books.

Pride, R. 2002. *The political use of racial narratives.* Urbana: University of Illinois Press.

Schneider, A., and H. Ingram. 1990. Behavioral assumptions of policy tools. *The Journal of Politics* 52, no: 2: 510–29.

Schneider, A., and H. Ingram. 1993. Social construction of target populations: Implications for politics and policy. *American Political Science Review* 87, no. 2: 334–47.

Scott, D.M. 1997. *Contempt and pity: Social policy and the image of the damaged black psyche, 1880–1996.* Chapel Hill: University of North Carolina Press.

Somers, M., and G. Gibson. 1994. Reclaiming the epistemological "other": Narrative and social constitution of identity. In *Social theory and the politics of identity*, ed. C. Calhoun, 35–99. Oxford: Blackwell.

Steele, C. 1997. A threat in the air: How stereotypes shape intellectual identity and performance. *American Psychologist* 52, 613–29.

Sum, A., I. Khatiwada, J. McLaughlin, and P. Tobar. 2007. *The educational attainment of the nation's young black men and their recent labor market experiences: What can be done to improve their future labor market and educational prospects?* Boston: Northeast University, Center for labor Market Studies.

Tate, W.F., IV, and M. Hogrebe. 2011. From visuals to vision: Using GIS to inform civic dialogue about African American males. *Race Ethnicity and Education* 14, no. 1: 51–71.

Trammel, M., D. Newhart, V. Willis, and A. Johnson. 2008. *African American male initiative.* The Kirwan Institute for the Study of Race & Ethnicity, The Ohio State University. http://4909e99d35cada63e7f757471b7243be73e53e14.gripelements.com/publications/AAMale Initiative_KelloggReport_April2008.pdf (accessed June 1, 2009).

Waks, L.J. 2003. How globalization can cause fundamental curriculum change: An American perspective. *Journal of Educational Change* 4: 383–418.

Waks, L.J. 2006. Rethinking technological literacy for the global network era. In *Defining technological literacy: Towards an epistemological framework*, ed. J.R. Dakers, 275–96. New York: Palgrave Macmillan.

Walters, P.B. 2001. Educational access and the state: Historical continuities and discontinuities in racial inequality in American education. *Sociology of Education* Extra Issue, 35–49.

# Escaping Devil's Island: confronting racism, learning history

Carl A. Grant

*Department of Curriculum & Instruction, University of Wisconsin–Madison, Madison, USA*

> This article argues that African Americans, especially males living in urban areas, are physically and mentally trapped on a Devil's Island. The penal colony on the coast of French Guiana is a metaphor for the boundaries and constraints that close off opportunities and constrain African American historical knowledge. The article argues that although African Americans have struggled to learn their history (e.g. economic, political and social), the goal of critically using that history to decipher their social world eludes them. While social movements of the twentieth century produced some racial progress, none of them generated enough progress to eliminate the racism that keeps Blacks on Devil's Island – racism that includes widely accepted mantras such as 'the United States is a Nation of Immigrants,' a historical 'sin of omission' that markets racism as merely prejudice within the context of pluralism and makes it more difficult for Whites to address the privilege their skin color provides and to acknowledge the structures in society that keep racism in place.

Escape or graduation from an urban school or an urban area by African American males, while not impossible, is nevertheless akin to escape from Devil's Island, the penal colony on the coast of French Guiana. Some African American males, like some of the prisoners on Devil's Island, are fortunate enough to escape from the brutality and oppression. However, many African American males, living in urban areas and attending urban schools, like many prisoners who attempted to escape from Devil's Island, are unsuccessful. They are killed during gang and drug violence, or for just trying to get from home to school (Hill 2009). On Devil's Island, prisoners whose attempts to escape were foiled, were then [re]imprisoned and placed in solitary confinement. Thus, most prisoners on Devil's Island decide not to attempt escape, just like many African American males in urban schools who drop out and hang around, waiting for time and conditions of urban poverty to take their toll.

Whereas I don't wish to prolong relating the relationship of the historical and present day status of African American males living in urban areas to prison life on Devil's Island, I did observe a metaphorical connection during my reading of René Belbenoit's (1938) *Dry Guillotine: Fifteen Years Among the Living Dead*. As I write this article, I use the metaphor Devil's Island to refer to the physical space, particularly urban sites, where African American males live and go to school and their bounded thinking created and supported over time by the racist, biased, truncated knowledge they receive from the school curriculum and other social spaces.

To those who do not recall the story, let me explain the metaphorical connections. *Alfred Dreyfus*, the most famous prisoner sentenced to Devil's Island was a Jewish French army captain wrongfully convicted of treason. Dreyfus and several other prisoners unjustly sentenced to Devil's Island remind me not only of African males abducted from Africa, enslaved and sent to the Americas; barracks and cells with tainted air, humidity, hookworms, and malaria are commonplace to the inhabitants of Devil's Island and are metaphorically akin to the housing and living conditions in urban areas where many contemporary African Americans live (Kotlowitz 1991; Kozol 1991; The Leadership Conference 2010).

Escape from Devil's Island, like escape from a ghettoized urban area, is exceedingly difficult. There are two ways to leave the island: by boat or through the dense, mosquito-infested jungle. Leaving by boat is usually reserved for prisoners who have completed their sentence. A convict leaving Devil's Island by boat is analogous to African American males completing their high school education and leaving the urban area to attend college or to pursue a vocational opportunity. Successful escape from Devil's Island via the dense jungle and across the piranha-infested Moroni River, however, was rare and is analogous to some African American males' attempts to escape the hardship of urban areas through drugs and gang activity. Living a lifetime in urban poverty with little chance to break out from under the yoke of oppression is like a life sentence on Devil's Island.

**Introduction to argument**

Devil's Island is not only the physical space for poor Black urban youth; it is also the psychological spaces that defines and (tries to control) how African Americans should think and what they should think about. It keeps ideas, ambitions, and identity construction by African American males psychologically castrated within the economic, political and social areas of life that Whites have historically dominated (Majors and Billson 1992). Devil's Island in such an ideological sense then is applicable to all African American males, and for urban males, the physical and material nature of life in the segregated inner city represents one more layer of imprisonment. In a sense, this is true for all African Americans, but it takes on a special urgency for African American males: Whether looking at incarceration rates (44% of the prison population [Harawa and Adimora 2008), school dropout rates (50% [Editorial Projects in Education 2008]), or unemployment (17% [Martin 2009]), African American males occupy a particularly marginalized place in American society as racism remains brutal and demonstrable. The metaphor 'Devil's Island' represents the boundaries and constraints that close off opportunities and constrain the historical knowledge made available to African American males of all circumstances.

I write this article from the perspective of an educator who has visited a good number of schools across the US. A month ago while observing in a classroom, I relived a memory from 1977 of African American middle school students in a multiracial class ducking under their desks as the teacher showed the scene of the Middle Passage from the movie *Roots*. Although this memory is more than 30-years-old and race relations have seemingly improved (CBS NY Times 2009), this recent showing of the Middle Passage scene from *Roots* generated similar embarrassment among African American students to the embarrassment I observed years before.

As I remember both groups of African American students, I recall two connected observations: One, the weight of the world seemed to fall on students' shoulders as they observed the dehumanization of enslaved Africans during the Middle Passage scene. Two, I discovered they had a limited knowledge of their history and seemed to lack a strong racial identity that would allow them to be saddened and angered about the brutality of the Middle Passage, but not ashamed or embarrassed. The students seemed not to know that African Americans have for centuries stood strong and achieved in the face of racial adversity; they did not seem to understand that being smart and pursuing knowledge was not a 'White thing' but a human thing and that African Americans have a rich history in that area; and they did not seem to understand the significance of knowing African American historical knowledge or that history supports their 'self-fashioning and self-emancipation' (Holt 1994).

In general, I argue that African American males must learn their history in order to develop the capacity (knowledge, skills and dispositions) to disrupt the systemic racism and negative social construction of racial identity they face and that seeks to control them. I am not saying this is the panacea to eradicating racism or inequality, but it is an essential first step, a precursor to being able to take action *against* brutality and injustice. I point out that schools do a poor job of teaching African American history (Wynter 1990; Quarles 1987); and that social movements and/or approaches have been ineffective in providing the tools to rescue African Americans from Devil's Island. Also, I argue that the metaphor the 'US as a nation of immigrants' – a metaphor that defines and frames much of the school curriculum and other social spaces – distorts and inaccurately reports American history, keeping African Americans in a place of subordination, and normalizing and marketing a systemic pattern of racism (e.g. Grant and Grant 1981; Wynter 1990; Quarles 1987; Brown and Brown 2010).

I borrow my framing of the significance of history from Southgate (2000) and Holt (1994) and my definition of identity from Hoover (1997) and Oyserman and Harrison (1998). Southgate (2000) argues, '[H]istory – the memories of things past – is of supreme importance in maintaining a sense of identity (4), while Holt (1994) contends, 'Historicity is crucial both in the sense of personal and collective memory and in terms of the constructs of the "non-self" that take shape with its space. One cannot conceptualize an individual consciousness, a self continuous from one time point to another, without a concept of history or memory' (9).

Regarding identity, Hoover (1997) contends it 'is a thread that binds self and society' (46). In the case of African American youth, Oyserman and Harrison (1998) state, '[A]nswers to the "who am I?" question are likely to include both distinctive, unique features of the self one will become and also representations of oneself as a black person in America. That is, the self-concept is likely to contain both personal identity and also racial identity – a sense of what it means to be both American and of African heritage' (282).

My theoretical framing is guided by a theory of self-determination and social justice (Smith 1999), particularly as articulated by Du Bois (1960): 'What I have been fighting for … is the possibility of black folk and their cultural patterns existing in America without discrimination; and on terms of equality…' (150). This framing supports my argument that African Americans must learn their history in order to develop the self-awareness and group knowledge that are critical to self and group identity and academic and social achievement. In addition, they must learn their history because it serves as a compass to help them to find their way on the map of human geography. Here, I am paying attention to African American movements (e.g. settlement) and cultural development (e.g. customs), including language and religion in different regions (e.g. New Orleans, Chicago) and their quality of life and how they get/got along in these regions (Fellman, Arthur, and Judith 2007). Also, a knowledge of history helps African Americans to pay attention to human geography that concerns human relationships, between and among different groups of people (Knox and Marston 2004). It 'tells a people where they have been, where they are; and more importantly, history tells a people where they still must go and what they still must be' (Clark cited in Jenkins 2006, 30). Furthermore, a knowledge of history helps cultivate a sociological imagination (Mills 2000), which is significant for helping African Americans to imagine themselves away from both the physical and conceptually bound notions of Devil's Island.

**African American students' historical knowledge**

I am writing this article from the perspective that many African Americans do not have a thorough knowledge of their historical legacy and that their identity is located too much in the here and now (Gee 2000). There are a variety of structural, systemic, and individual reasons why African American students have a limited knowledge of their history:

(1) Discussions in school often skirt around the horrors of slavery and suggest that slavery existed in only Southern states. For example, a state and a city like New York are not usually included in discussions of states and cities where enslavement took place. In addition although students may reference slavery as 'a horrible thing done to Black people,' what students, including the African American students, learn is a weak understanding of enslavement. Brown and Brown (2010) state, '[T]extbook narratives generally position the slave trade and the practice of slavery as devoid of institutional/structural ties and characterize the perpetrators of violence against enslaved Africans and Africans American as individual actors, or "bad men," who behaved in ways that were deviant and not necessarily supported by larger social, economic and political structure.'

(2) As long as African American history is mainly taught during the month of February, dependence on the school to teach African American history is misplaced. During February, pictures of Martin Luther King and Rosa Parks are recycled from the previous years, along with an entertainment celebrity. Added to this will be the telling of the Rosa Parks story, often done using abridged, partial truths (Kohl 1991), and the reciting of King's 'I Have a Dream' speech.

(3) According to Lois Weiner (1999), teachers do not teach an inclusive history because they lack the resources. Writing to beginning urban teachers, Weiner states: 'Don't be surprised if the school has no books you want to use or not enough books for you to assign one to each student!' Weiner adds, 'This might be a blessing because you won't be forced to use a boring, outdated textbook' (38).

(4) African Americans have often been considered an important part of history only when their presence had an impact on European American politics.

(5) Finally, African American students do not learn an inclusive history when they engage in a 'Cool Pose.' Majors and Billson (1992) contend that African American males, particularly those who live in the inner city, have adopted

and used cool masculinity – or 'cool pose' – as a way of surviving in a restrictive society and they don't wish to be seen engaging in serious academic learning. This 'cool pose' can be seen as a rational response to the distorted and anemic history African American students are taught in school.

## Ineffective approaches and social movements for Black equality

It is useful here to briefly describe four approaches/movements developed during the twentieth century to influence social conditions (e.g. race, employment and education) and ways of thinking about African Americans: Rigid Competitive Movement; Intercultural Movement; Melting Pot/Intergroup Movement; and Cultural Racism. Whereas in each of these movements there is some racial progress, none of the movements generated enough progress to eliminate the racism that keeps the Black males on Devil's Island.

### *Rigid Competitive Movement*

Farley (2000) contends that the period from the end of the Civil War to World War II can be described as rigid competitive race relations (159). During the 1920s and 1930s as social scientists, other academics and civic leaders were offering this thesis to explain the Black–White relations, employment became a major source of division between the races. Dual pay scales, denial of skilled position to Blacks, refusal to allow Blacks to join labor unions and segregation in federal employment, among other factors, stiffened racial division between poor Blacks from the south and poor Whites from the east. Du Bois (1920), in *Of Work and Wealth*, describes the competition for employment in East Saint Louis between Black and White, and in doing so underscores how skin color, not jobs, was the primary point of resistance between the two races. Du Bois (1920) states, 'They [White workers] saw something [the Black man] at which they had been taught to laugh and make sport ... the distortion of every speech and book had taught them [that the Black man] was a mass of despicable men, inhuman; at best, laughable; at worst, the meat of mobs and fury' (88). Maintaining this belief about Blacks along with White bosses perpetuating racial distrust and hatred between the two racial groups caused Whites not to accept poor Blacks as allies in management–labor struggle over jobs. Whereas, solidarity between Black and Whites would have been useful in acquiring employment for both groups; and for helping African Americans to escape their psychological and physical imprisonment on Devil Island (see Wright 1941). Wright states, 'If we had been allowed to participate in the vital process of national growth, what would have been the texture of our lives, the pattern of our traditions, the routine of our customs, the state of our arts, the code of our laws, the function of our government! Whatever others may say, we black folks say that America would have been stronger and greater!' (145).

### *Intercultural Movement*

Starting in the 1930s and on into the 1950s, some (e.g. Mary L. Riley, Lily Edelman; see Banks 2005) began to argue that increased attention should be given to ease the transition of White immigrants into US society and to develop tolerance among ethnic groups who were not the best of friends in Europe. This stepped-up attention is commonly called the Intercultural Movement, which grew out of the idea of

'Americanization.' One goal of the Intercultural Movement was to make the American Creed and the values ascribed within it meaningful to new arrivals from Europe while also teaching the importance of ethnic group history and pride and instilling allegiance to the US (Banks 2005). Allegiance was instilled through programs in schools, settlement houses, and newspapers published in immigrants' native language. The curriculum of these programs celebrated the immigrants' history, culture, and contribution to society and helped them to understand that whereas the US wanted them to assimilate, it was not attempting to erase their cultural memory. Arguably the Intercultural movement contribution to improving race relations between Blacks and Whites was minimal, however of significance is that during this period attention to the significance of ethnic relations, and the sociological understanding of nature of prejudice flourished (see Allport 1954).

## *Intergroup Movement*

The Intergroup Movement came about at the end of World War II and the beginning of the Cold War. It was a reaction to the Intercultural Movement that mainly supported European immigrants and ignored Black and White relations. The Intergroup Movement took issue with the strategy of the Intercultural Movement to use the schools and media to shape the values and beliefs of Americans to line up with northern European Whites and took issue with how the Intercultural Movement advocated European superiority. The Intergroup Movement stressed reduction/elimination in racial bias between Blacks and Whites and elimination of prejudice among ethnic groups in general. It advocated theories of assimilation and amalgamation and argued for the application of these theories to social and educational policy.

A major voice in the Intergroup Movement was the returning African American soldiers who had fought to bring freedom to Europeans. Veterans demanded their civil and human rights, and their demands caused uproar on the international stage. Advocates of the Intergroup Movement contended that the rise of fascism and the Cold War between the Soviet Union and the US demanded that the US live up to its democratic ideals with all of its citizens. Tushnet (1987) explains:

> [T]he ideological rationale for the war against Nazi Germany and the ongoing ideological competition with the Soviet Union made segregation increasingly anomalous ... Whenever the State Department accused Communist regimes of violations of human rights ... they responded 'with great ease': 'You tell us about forced labor in Russia – what about the lynching of Negroes in Alabama? You tell us about undemocratic elections in Bulgaria – what about the poll tax in Mississippi?' (188).

## *The Civil Rights Movement*

Starting with the Montgomery Bus Boycott and *Brown*, there was a resurgent demand by African Americans for equity and equality in all social institutions. African Americans wanted off Devil's Island. During the 1960s Civil Rights Movement, major Civil Rights legislation was passed and President Johnson's Great Society programs were initiated to counteract poverty. During the mid-1970s, as life for African Americans improved and racial conflict between Blacks and Whites decreased – because of Civil Rights legislation – many African Americans began to adopt assimilationist thinking (Ashmore 1994; Farley 1984). However, by the mid-1980s, many African Americans began to question this thinking as they realized that assimilation, especially in schools and housing, was not taking hold, and the goal of equality and social justice seemed to be slipping away. African Americans saw that there were consistent applications of racial subordination and discrimination in the practice of law and the implementation of social policy with the exception of 'interest-convergence' issues, in which both the White majority and minorities profit from the expansion of rights (see Bell 1980). Public debate and ongoing controversies over affirmative action programs, and other policy programs, including school programs (e.g. Headstart) to challenge the racist legacy in public policy programs were resisted within the context of the role of government, individual freedom and alternative concepts of social justice. In addition, conservative federal officials and many in the US public were becoming annoyed with hearing about race and racism and began to develop new theories (e.g. cultural racism), strategies (putting welfare moms to work), and a new language (e.g. colorblind) to counter and turn back Civil Rights gains. Ashmore (1994) states, 'The civil rights movement had provided Blacks with the visibility long denied them, but for the most part they were viewed by Whites through the mass media. This meant that while they could achieve wide recognition and be admired, even idolized, the social gap that divided the black and white communities remained largely intact' (305).

In sum, the Civil Rights Movement had an impact on all Americans and it changed the consciousness of society at large. Overt forms of racial discrimination and government-supported segregation of public facilities came to an end; but despite the civil rights gains of the 1960s, racial discrimination remained a significant factor in American life and many African Americans, especially those living in urban areas who were still trapped on Devil's Island. Looking back, Ashmore (1994) states, 'There is reason to wonder, certainly, whether the American political system as it has evolved under the impact of the expanding cities is anywhere giving us the kind of public and private leadership our age demands' (408) to eliminate racism.

## Cultural racism

As the Civil Rights Movement lost its currency another form of racism, cultural racism, became prevalent and effective in keeping African American males both physically and conceptually on Devil's Island. According to Halstead (1988) cultural racism 'involves prejudice against individuals because of their culture' (140). Halstead (1988) argues, 'This term (cultural racism) is being used with increasing frequency to draw attention to a shift in the focal point of much racism from physical characteristics such as social customs, manners and behavior, religious and moral beliefs and practices, language, aesthetic values and leisure activities. Whereas, post-reflective gut racism seeks to explain and justify racist attitudes in religious or scientific terms, cultural racism attempts the same thing in cultural terms' (140).

The culture of people of color is seen as flawed and thus standing in the way of progress. They are encouraged to adopt mainstream culture and norms and embrace compensatory education programs to achieve academic success and shake off the 'at-risk,' 'cultural disadvantaged label.' The acting White thesis (Fordham and Obgu 1986; Buck 1954) supports cultural racism ideology in that African American students who are high achievers are informed by their peers and other classroom interactions that they selling out – acting White, implying that Black culture does not support academic success (Buck 2010).

Several social scientists (e.g. Feagin 1972; Frankenberg 1993; Schuman 1975; Kluegel 1990) contend that cultural racism is pervasive among Whites – 'even those who consider themselves unprejudiced – and that it is specifically used by many whites to explain black poverty; and allow other whites to escape owning up to the responsibility for causing minority poverty through discrimination and exploitation' (Farley 2000, 164). According to Pettigrew (1985) and Kluegel (1990), cultural racism places the blame for poverty on people of color, is unwilling to examine the working of White privilege, thus leading to symbolic racism which is marked by unwillingness to make the changes that are needed to eliminate the disadvantages that Blacks in society experience. Thus cultural racism causes African American students' ambition and identity construction to be psychologically castrated within social areas of life that Whites dominate (Majors and Billson 1992) – and thus to keep African American students trapped on Devil's Island.

In sum, with the increasing influence of cultural racism – especially since, on paper (legally) at least, discrimination and institutionalized racism does not exist; but because patterned inequalities still exist, those who are privileged explain these patterned inequalities based in the 'flaws' of those who are 'failing' and their cultures. Thus, to combat racism today means to combat *cultural racism* ... and to do so, students themselves have to move beyond internalized oppression and internalized cultural racism. They have to understand a history and a legacy that have created these patterned inequalities and that obscure those inequalities through a legal system that makes these inequalities appear to have nothing to do with structures. African American youth have to understand that the struggle for agency within the world is predicated on the fact that race is ideologically defined by Whites; however, for Whites, that same notion of race, unless one is thinking from a critically conscious perspective, refers only to people of color. Because of reigning social norms within mainstream society, Whiteness holds the position of colorlessness, and the very ubiquity of that position constitutes not only automatic privilege for White people but also the established norm against which all else is measured. Such sensibilities hold true in our legal system and also in our nation's classrooms (Isaksen 2009).

**No blame game**

I am not blaming students about their lack of knowledge of African American history. If blame must be assigned, it is more my generation's fault than today's students. I am reminded of the old man in James Baldwin's (1959/1985) essay, 'Nobody Knows My Name.' In it, Baldwin speaks of an old Black man in Atlanta who, in giving him directions, directs Baldwin toward a segregated bus, which is his first ride on a racially segregated bus. In reflecting on this ride, Baldwin discusses not only the Black man who directed him to the bus but also other old Black men he encountered in the South – Black men who had borne the humiliation and dehumanization of racism. This humiliation is not only derived from the effects of racism on themselves but rather how it affected their loved ones. For example, the look in the old man's eyes as he directed Baldwin toward the bus conveys, in my reading of it, a sense of emasculation because he, like others in his generation, was unable to eliminate racism and thus had to stand by and watch as racism is passed on to the next generation of African Americans. Like the old man in Baldwin's essay, I too (along with many of my generation), am humiliated and angry at racism not being eliminated on our watch.

## The need for history and identity formation

There are numerous reasons why African American males need to know their history (e.g. social, political, economic): it informs them about the role of the legal system in the creation, maintenance, and transformation of racial identity as well as how the different government/social systems are implicated in the creation of racial categories and inequality (e.g. Goldberg 1993; Jacobson 1998); it informs them how law, politics, economy and education exert a pervasive influence on the conceptions and practices of identity and how categories of difference (e.g. race) shape Black males' daily lives, their health and welfare, the spaces and places where they live, and the relationships between social groups (e.g. Bennett 1964; Drake and Cayton 1945/1993; Du Bois 1978; Holt 1995).

Bembry (2002 argues, 'African American youth need to learn, to understand, and to appreciate the struggles their parents, their grandparents ... right up the line to their original African ancestors, brought to America against their will had to endure' (2). In addition, African American history informs African Americans about who they are not, as identity involves defining 'who one is not' (Grant and Sleeter 1996, 150). Further, knowledge of history helps African Americans to understand that while identity is developed in and can be limited by social contexts (e.g. urban environment, school curriculum), they are not psychological and physical prisoners to these structures. They have agency to resist and change; history shows that precedent (Du Bois 1903; Woodson 1933).

African American males today have a difficult time responding to questions such as 'Who am I?' 'Where am I going as I strive to become a productive citizen?' Arguably, many youth of all colors may find these questions challenging, but African American youth – because they are physically and mentally prisoners of Devil's Island – may find the questions much more challenging and with more dire consequences given the nature of systemic racism. When Grant and Sleeter (1996) asked male teenagers of color, including African American males, 'Where do you see yourself ten years from now or what work will you be doing as an adult?' responses from the students were vague, unrealistic: often as a professional athlete. Baldwin (1965) argues:

> For history ... is not merely something to be read. And it does not refer merely, or even principally, to the past, on the contrary, the great force of history comes from the fact that we carry it within us, are unconsciously controlled by it in many ways, and history is literally present in all that we do. It could scarcely be otherwise, since it is to history that we owe our frames of reference, our identities, and our aspirations. (47)

The search for identity by African American men has a long, tumultuous history (White and Parham 1990; Woodson 1933). White and Parham (1990) state, '[H]istory, anthropology, and many other fields of study have fallen victim to attempts by many to both (a) destroy and/or otherwise erase its historical connection to ancient Africa, and (b) transplant its roots into European civilization' (3). Because of such actions, many African American males of my generation did not fully answer the identity question nor did we know our history. We have struggled to take inventory of how identity grows and is 'nurtured or frustrated in a complex bonding of self and society' (Hoover 1997, 21), and how it is contested (Hoover 1997, 61) and intertwined with power. We know that our identity is not fully shaped by enslavement but comes out of and is shaped by many experiences: the Civil War, Reconstruction, the Black Codes, World Wars I and II, *Brown*, the Civil Rights Movement, and the election of

Barack Obama. Nevertheless, we are still developing a complete taxonomy of our experiences as a people, particularly in the US; thus, learning our history is of primary importance in developing that taxonomy and giving us a historical foundation to resist racism and promote social change.

## Learning your history does not automatically happen

Learning one's history is not a given; it is a struggle, especially for oppressed people, because it is not seen as central to the social fabric of society. Oppressed people are denied access to their history through omissions, distortions and inaccuracies in the mainstream narrative. It is difficult for them to actively seek out and/or have access to their history because knowing it is not made important in textbooks and the media (Dines and Humez 2003). Kent (1971) states that Richard Wright's biographer claims that at the age of 32, Wright had not read Booker T. Washington's *Up from Slavery:* 'In a footnote to Chapter 13, Miss Webb [Wright's biographer] states: "Wright was almost ashamed to admit that he had never read *Up from Slavery. .*"' (17). Similarly, Professor Joyce King (cited in Cornbleth and Dexter 1995), who as a member of the California Curriculum Commission played a major role in the California textbook controversy, states that she did not learn about the heritage and achievements of Black people until her junior year at Stanford's study abroad program in Italy. It was then that she learned about the Harlem Renaissance and read the poetry of Countee Cullen and Claude McKay in Italian. Similarly, Derrick Bell (1992) states:

> Slavery was barely mentioned in the schools and seldom discussed by the descendants of its survivors, particularly those who had somehow moved themselves to the North. Emigration, whether from the Caribbean islands or from the Deep South states, provided a geographical distance that encouraged and enhanced individual denial of our collective, slave past. We sang spirituals but detached the songs from their slave origins (1).

I too can add to this testimonial. I did not really learn about African American history until I was a graduate student at the University of Wisconsin–Madison. The following statement by Woodson (1933) – which I believe is still relevant today – helps to explain, perhaps, how and why Joyce, Derrick and I (and many others) did not learn our African American history in school:

> The same educational process which inspires and stimulates the oppressor with the thought that he is everything and has accomplished everything worthwhile, depresses and crushes at the same time sparks of genius in the Negro by making him feel that his race does not amount to much and never will measure up to the standards of other peoples ... Negroes are taught to admire the Hebrew, the Greek, the Latin and the Teuton and to despise the African ... The thought of the inferiority of the Negro is drilled into him in almost every book that he studies ... This crusade is much more important than the anti-lynching movement – because there would be no lynching if it did not start in the classroom. Why not exploit, enslave or exterminate a class that everybody is taught to regard as inferior. (2)

## The school curriculum

African American students are in a curriculum quagmire. They are caught in an historical system of rules that supports a system of reason that keeps and maintains them in an oppressed condition. The system of rules that I am referencing is the policy and practice manifested both implicitly and explicitly in P/K-12 textbooks. This system of rules has a long racist legacy and, although modified at times, does not ever really give in to social pressures and other actions to eliminate racism. (See for example, 'Arizona House of Representatives passing the Senate-amended version of HB2281, banning racial and ethnic studies from the curricula of state-funded K-12 schools' [Mullins 2010; Alterman 2004]). Frederick Douglass (1849/1991) rightly noted that, 'Power concedes nothing without a demand. It never did and it never will...' (2). Douglass's statement about power conceding nothing becomes explicitly clear when you examine the continuous struggles against the inferiority thesis, the immigration/melting pot thesis and incrementalism thesis (Alterman 2004) to correct and/or change the bias, inaccuracies, omissions, and distortions of African Americans in P/K-12 curriculum and textbooks.

## Inferiority thesis in textbooks and society

African Americans have been subjugated to Devil's Island for centuries. The supposed inferiority of African Americans and the superiority of European Americans have dominated American ideology and behavior since the arrival of European colonists in the sixteenth century and African Americans in 1619 as enslaved people (Quarles 1987). The inferiority thesis persisted even after the Civil War and during Reconstruction. Quarles (1987) argues that during this period, White Southerners took every opportunity to perpetuate the inferiority thesis. They vigorously disagreed with teachers from the North who had come to the South to teach African Americans. For example, they protested when, during mealtime, the Northern teachers and the Blacks would eat together and when the Whites would address Blacks as 'Miss' or 'Mr.' (128–9).

Textbooks, the documents of 'official knowledge' (Apple 2000) and the 'Guardians of Tradition' (Elson 1964), were primary sources for proclaiming the inferiority of African Americans. Ruth Elson's (1964) study of nineteenth century textbooks illuminates the use of the 'inferiority' thesis to control curriculum knowledge. Elson states, 'From the description in all Geography books, the African Negro is clearly regarded as the most degraded of the races. Southerners, who by 1830 justified slavery on the grounds that the Negro was incapable of improvement, could find ample evidence for their attitudes in the schoolbooks used at the times in both North and South' (87). Black's (1967) examination of textbooks supports Elson's. Black states:

> While the white man was portrayed as the superior race, the Negro throughout the nineteenth century was described as the most inferior .Young minds were exposed to such sentiments as the Negroes' 'mental powers, in general, participate in imbecility of their bodies' in an 1815 reader, and Negroes are 'destitute of intelligence' in an 1851 geography. (85–6)

Describing African Americans as 'destitute of intelligence' made it easy to marginalize or omit them from being contributors to the development of America and to exclude them as full citizens. Whereas over the years, the portrayal African American in textbooks has improved, in other words you don't see the blatant notion of inferiority as reported by Elson (1964) and Black (1967); nevertheless African Americans are still portrayed as inferior by way of representation, contribution to society and role group characterization (Brown and Brown 2010; Grant and Grant 1981; Grant and Sleeter 1996; Wynter 1990. In addition, the inferiority thesis still remains active in the 'cultural deficit' and cultural racism approach to teaching African American students (e.g. Ladson Billings 2006)

## The United States: a nation of immigrants?

America as a 'nation of immigrants' is an icon/mantra that many White Americans find acceptable because it describes their ethnic group's entrance to the US and does not call attention to the 'sins of omission' as it relates to other non-immigrant ethnic groups. The immigrant story markets racism as merely prejudice within the context of pluralism and therefore makes it less difficult for Whites to deal with the privilege their skin color provides and to acknowledge the structures in society that keep racism in place. Wynter (1990) argues that:

> ... the representation [e.g. backgrounding and misequating race] with the reality is not accidental. It is essential to the textbook's central strategy of backgrounding the issue of *race* and misequating it with secondary immigrant issues of 'prejudice.' That enables structural *racism* as experienced by ... Blacks ... to be backgrounded into the derivate phenomenon of 'prejudice' ... experienced by Euro-ethnic immigrants. Once backgrounded and misequated with 'prejudice,' the phenomenon of race and racism on the basis of whose correlated cultural belief system, the very structure of the polities of the post-Columbus Caribbean and Americas was to be based, can therefore be represented as the empirical effect of pluralistic 'cultural difference' and the cost of 'cultural pluralism.' ... The tragic dynamics of the relation between non-Immigrant and Immigrant America, and its historical continuum, is hereby obliterated ... (75).

Referring to the US as a nation of immigrants puts in place a cultural myth 'that shapes the way we [Americans] think, [and] it tells us what makes sense' (Colombo, Cullen, and Lisle 1995, 3). In addition, such a mantra selectively blinds us and prevents us from critically examining it as cultural myths (Colombo, Cullen and Lisle 1995, 3). Peterson (2006) argues, '... once we accept the mantra we are "a nation of immigrants" as a "truism," we no longer examine or think about what those words actually say or mean' (1). Further, African Americans who do not believe in and accept the nation of immigrants myth, are nevertheless subject to the 'double consciousness' thesis that Du Bois identified. Du Bois (1903) argued that the African American experience of self was unstable and dualistic, which caused them to see themselves both as American citizens but also as a racially subordinated minority group that was excluded politically and socially.

## The fallacy of the immigrant mantra

The immigrant American Story of History cannot correctly include African Americans, American Indians and Mexican Americans because their entrance into the US was not by way of immigration. African Americans are not immigrants; they came to the country as enslaved people. Telling US history by way of the immigrant story makes the history of African Americans 'a secondary add-on and supplement to the real, i.e. the generic history of America' (Wynter 1990, 32). Besides being dehumanizing, it downplays the suffering and brutality African slaves suffered during the Middle Passage and the horrors of enslavement in US; it facilitates ways of reasoning that support bias, distortion, omission and inaccuracies in US history; and it negatively affects students' self-esteem and challenges their efforts to bring about social change.

Such distorted, inaccurate and biased descriptions of African American history infuriated Carter G. Woodson, who in response founded the Association for the Study of Negro Life and History (ASNLH). In 1915, Woodson argued that the history of African Americans – their significant contribution to the making of the US – was being distorted, omitted and/or reported inaccurately in order to sell the immigrant story of American history. In 1927, Woodson wrote to Thomas H. Barnes advocating the need to establish a Home Study Department. Woodson wrote:

> Recently a Negro instructor in a college was asked to give a course in Negro history. He treated the request as a joke. He has been well instructed in the story of the Hebrew, the Greeks, and the Romans. He has made a special study of the achievement of Europeans and Americans. He has been taught that these nations accomplished all. The perpetuation of the immigrant story of American history similarly is an exercise of power in which the African American male history and culture is set aside by the master ... and the will and wishes of the master ... are what prevails view, therefore, there is no other history worth considering. The fact is that the so-called history teaching in our schools and colleges is downright propaganda, an effort to praise one race and to decry the other to justify social repression and exploitation. The world is still in darkness as to the actual progress of mankind. Each corner of the universe has tended to concern itself merely with the exploits of its own particular heroes. Students and teachers of our time, therefore, are the victims of this selfish propaganda. (Association for the Study of Negro Life and History, Oct 1, 1927, 1).

Being taught history that includes the Black man's struggle for self-determination and social justice and his challenge to resist and escape from enslavement and Jim Crow is ignored. And doing so perpetuates internalized oppression.

## Conclusion

I have argued that African American male adolescents living in urban areas and attending urban schools and African American males in general are akin to prisoners on Devil's Island. Both are trapped conceptually and some physically in a harsh, violent, poverty-stricken environment and are oppressed by a racist ideology. I believe that for African American students to successfully leave (escape) Devil's Island – physically and mentally – with a positive identity, a resiliency that serves them in tough times and with agency, that keeps them motivated and active at both the personal and collective level; and that encourages them to become agents of social change they need a comprehensive understanding of their historical legacy.

I contend that Africans in America, first as enslaved people and now as US citizens, have for years been in search of their history, which is continually denied to them in the mainstream teaching of US history (Douglass 1849; Woodson 1933; Wynter 1990). Mainstream teaching across the decades has taken advantage of numerous applications of power to keep African American history distorted, inaccurate and filled with bias (Black 1967; Cornbleth and Dexter 1995; Elson 1964; Wynter 1990). The iconic mantra, 'America is a Nation of Immigrants,' is one such example as it continues to not only marginalize Black people but also does not encourage White people from thinking about how well the mantra represents all Americans (Wynter 1990). In addition, the silence by many Whites about America as a Nation of Immigrants position the mantra as a form of cultural racism in that it promotes 'dysconscious racism' or the lack of consciousness about White privilege (King 1991).

I have argued that it is not uncommon for educated African Americans to not know their history (e.g. Bell 1992; King 1995). To this end, I have argued that history –particularly as portrayed in the school curriculum – becomes a form of consciousness raising against internalized oppression; and I have also stressed why knowing history is critical and invaluable to identity formation of African American adolescent males. James Marcia states that individuals, who construct their identity, modifying or rejecting some conferred elements, also possess a sense of having participated in a self-initiated and self-directed process. They know not only who they are, they know how they became that and that they had a hand in the becoming. Furthermore, they have developed skills useful in the adaptive process of further self-construction and self definition (34) which are significant to a flourishing life. I have argued, borrowing Carl Becker's words, that 'Everyman ... reaches out into the distant country of the past' to inform his future (Becker 2000). 'Without this historical knowledge, this memory of things said and done, his today would be aimless and his tomorrow without significance.' This 'aimlessness' and 'lack of significance' is what I observe in urban areas and urban schools. In addition, I learned as Martin Luther King, Jr. stated, 'The job of arousing manhood with a people that have been taught for so many centuries that they are nobody is not easy' (Washington 1991, 702). Simply put, I contend that African Americans need to receive a comprehensive study of their history in order to, 'keep the wolf of insignificance at the door' (Bellows 2004, 156); and because students' knowledge of their history (e.g., racism, collective struggle) served to contribute to their agency and facilitate academic motivation (O'Connor 1997).

Finally, I am writing to give today's African American male a communication that is similar to the one given to James Baldwin (1985) by the old man on the bus. Like the old man, I too am saying to today's African American males that I regret that my generation did not eliminate racism on our watch. In addition, I am angry that we did not reform a school system that ignores our history but instead demands that our children be educated by means of high stakes tests and accountability in run-down buildings (Johnson and Johnson 2006). That said, I am arguing that African American males must continually seek an understanding at both the individual and group level of their 'complex personhood' and be willing to be 'haunted' by the horrors and brutality of social and political events of the past and present (Gordon 1997) in order to eliminate racism. Maya Angelou's (1993) words are significant here, 'History, despite its wrenching pain, cannot be unlived but, if faced with courage, need not be lived again.'

**Acknowledgements**
The author wishes to generously thank Melissa Gibson, Anthony Brown and Keffrelyn Brown for their suggestions and editorial work on this paper.

**References**
Alterman, E. 2004. *What liberal media? The truth about bias and the news.* New York: Basic Books.
Allport, G. 1954. *The nature of prejudice.* Reading, MA: Addison-Wesley Publishing Company.
Angelou, M. 1993. On the pulse of morning: An inaugural poem. In *On the pulse of morning,* 97. New York: Random House.

Apple, M. 2000. *Official knowledge: Democratic education in a conservative age.* New York: Routledge.
Ashmore, H.S. 1994. *Civil rights and wrongs.* New York: Pantheon.
Association for the Study of Negro life and History. 1927. *Annual report of the director of the Association for the Study of Negro Life and History, Incorporated.* Washington, DC: Association for the Study of Negro Life.
Baldwin, J. 1965. Unnameable objects, unspeakable crimes. http://www.blackstate.com/baldwin1.html (accessed December 9, 2009).
Baldwin, J. 1985. Nobody knows my name. In *The price of the ticket*, 183–94. New York: St. Martin Press.
Banks, C. 2005. *Improving multicultural education.* New York: Teacher College Press.
Becker, C. 2000. Quoted by David Lowenthal in "Dilemma and Delights of Learning History," In *Knowing Teaching and Learning History*, P. Stern et al. New York: New York University Press.
Belbenoit, René. 1938. *Dry guillotine: Fifteen years among the living dead.* Reprint. New York: Dutton.
Bell, D. 1980. In Brown v. Board of Education and the Interest-Convergence Dilemma. *Harvard Law Review* 93: 518–33.
Bell, D. 1992. *Faces at the bottom of the well: The permanence of racism.* New York: Basic Books.
Bellows, S. 2004. *Mr. Sammler's planet (1970).* New York: Penguin Classics.
Bembry, R. 2002 Why black history month is important. http://www.helium.com/items/810116-why-black-history-month-is-important (accessed March 15, 2010).
Bennett, L., Jr. 1964. Before the Mayflower: A history of Black America. Chicago: Johnson Publishing.
Black, H. 1967. *The American schoolbook.* New York: William Morrow.
Brown, K.D., and A.L. Brown. 2010. Silenced memories: An examination of the sociocultural knowledge on race and racial violence in official school curriculum. *Equity and Excellence in Education* 43: 139–54.
Buck, P. 1954. *My several worlds: A personal record.* New York: John Day Co.
Buck, S. 2010. *Acting white.* New Haven: Yale University.
CBS NY Times. 2009. Most blacks and whites say race relations are good. CBS NY Times Survey. www.cbsnews.com/stories/2009/04/27/.../polls/main4972532. (accessed December 4, 2009).
Clark, J.H. 2006. Quoted by Toby Jenkins in Mr. Nigger: The challenges of educating black males within American society. *Journal of Black Studies* 37: 127–55.
Colombo, G., R. Cullen, and B. Lisle. 1995. *Rereading America.* Boston: Bedford.
Cornbleth, C., and W. Dexter. 1995. *The great speckled bird.* Mahwah, NJ: Lawrence Erlbaum.
Dines, G., and J. Humez, eds. 2003. *Media studies: Policy, management and media representation,* Vol. 2. London: Routledge.
Douglass, Frederick. 1849. Gavitt's original Ethiopian serenaders. Originally published in *The North Star,* Rochester, June 29, 1849. Online in Stephen Railton, *Uncle Tom's cabin* and American Culture, University of Virginia. Accessed December 9, 2009.
Douglass, Frederick. 1991. Letter to an abolitionist associate. In *Organizing for social change: A mandate for activity in the 1990s,* ed. K. Bobo, J. Kendall, and S. Max. Washington, DC: Seven Locks Press.
Drake, St. Clair, and H.R. Cayton. 1945/1993. *Black metropolis: A study of life in a northern city.* Chicago: University of Chicago Press.
Du Bois, W.E.B. 1903. *Souls of black folk.* New York: Bantam.
Du Bois, W.E.B. 1920. *Darkwater: Voices from within the veil.* New York: Harcourt, Brace & Co.
Du Bois, W.E.B. 1973. Whither now and why. In *The education of Black people: Ten critiques, 1906–1960,* ed. H. Aptheker, 151. New York: Monthly Review Press.
Du Bois, W.E.B. 1978. *On sociology and the black community.* Chicago: University of Chicago Press.
Editorial Projects in Education. 2008. Diplomas count 2008: School to college: Can state P–16 councils ease the transition? *Education Week* 27, no. 40: 6–9.

Elson, R.M. 1964. *Guardian of tradition: American schoolbooks of the nineteenth century.* Lincoln: University of Nebraska Press.
Farley, J.E. 2000. *Majority–minority relations*, 4th ed. Upper Saddle River: Prentice Hall.
Farley, R. 1984. *Blacks and Whites, narrowing the gap?* Cambridge, MA: Harvard University Press.
Feagin, J. 1972. Poverty: We still believe that God helps those who help themselves. *Psychology Today* 1: 101–29.
Fellman, J., G. Arthur, and G. Judith. 2007. *Human geography: Landscapes of human activities,* 10th ed. Boston: McGraw-Hill.
Fordham, S., and J. Ogbu. 1986. Black students' school success: Coping with the burden of acting white. *The Urban Review* 18, no. 3: 176–206.
Frankenberg, R. 1993. *White women, race matters: The social construction of whiteness.* Minneapolis: University of Minnesota Press.
Gee, J. 2000. Identity as an analytic lens for research in education. *Review of Research in Education* 99–125.
Goldberg, D.T. 1993. *Racist culture: Philosophy and the politics of meaning.* Cambridge: Blackwell.
Gordon, A.F. 1997. *Ghostly matters.* Minneapolis: University of Minnesota Press.
Grant, C.A., and G.W. Grant. 1981. The multicultural evaluation of some second and third grade textbook book readers–A survey analysis. *The Journal of Negro Education* 50, no. 1: 63–74.
Grant, C.A., and C.E. Sleeter. 1996. *After the school bell rings.* Philadelphia: The Falmer Press.
Halstead, M. 1988. *Education, justice, and cultural diversity: An examination of the Honeyford Affair, 1984–85.* London: Falmer Press.
Harawa, N., and A. Adimora. 2008. Incarceration, African Americans and HIV: Advancing a research agenda. *Journal of the National Medical Association* 100, no. 1: 57–62.
Hill, D. 2009. Teen attacked, beaten to death in melee. http://www.myfoxchicago.com/dpp/news/metro/video_derrion_albert (accessed December 5, 2009).
Holt, D., ed. 1994. *Assessing success in family literacy projects: Alternative approaches to assessment and evaluation.* Washington, DC and McHenry, IL: Center for Applied Linguistics and Delta Systems.
Holt, T.C. 1995. Marketing race, race-making, and the writing of history. *American Historical Review* 100, no. 1: 1–20.
Hoover, K. 1997. *The power of identity. Politics in a new key.* Chatham, NJ: Chatham House.
Isaksen, J. 2009. From critical race theory to composition studies: Pedagogy and theory building. *Legal Studies Forum* 24, no. 3: 4. http://tarlton.law.utexas.edu/lpop/etext/lsf/isaksen24.htm (accessed May 29, 2010).
Jacobson. M.F. 1998. *Whiteness of a different color.* Cambridge, MA: Harvard University Press.
Johnson, D., and B. Johnson. 2006. *High stakes*, 2nd ed. New York: Rowman & Littlefield.
Kent, G. 1971. Right wright: Blackness and the adventure of western culture. In *Black review 1*, ed. Mel Watkins. New York: William Morrow.
King, J. 1990. In search of African liberation pedadgogy: Multiple Contexts of Education and Struggle. *Journal of Education* 172, no. 2: 1–29.
King, J.E. 1991. Dysconscious racism: Ideology, identity, and the miseducation of teachers. *The Journal of Negro Education* 60, no. 2: 133–46.
Kluegel, J.R. 1990. Trends in whites' explanation of the black–white gap in socioeconomic status 1977–1989. *American Sociological Review* 55: 512–25.
Knox, P., and S. Marston. 2004. *Human geography: Places and regions in global context*, 3rd ed. New York: Prentice Hall.
Kohl, H. 1991. The politics of children's literature: What's wrong with the Rosa Parks myth? In *Rethinking our classroom* (2001). Milwaukee: Rethinking School.
Kotlowitz, A. 1991. *There are no children here.* New York: Nan A. Jalese.
Kozol, J. 1991. *Savage inequalities: Children in America's schools.* New York: Crown Publishers.
Ladson Billings, G. 2006. It's not the culture of poverty, it's the poverty of culture: The problem with teacher education. *Anthropology Education Quarterly* 37, no. 2: 104–9.

Majors, R., and J.M. Billson. 1992. *Cool pose: The dilemmas of black manhood in America.* New York: Simon & Schuster.

Martin, P. 2009. Black male unemployment comparable to 'great depression'. http://news.newamericamedia.org/news/view_article.html?article_id=7a2aa72d82d82727f405ef6b0c6dfb63 (accessed March 25, 2010).

Mills, C.W. 2000. *The sociological imagination,* 40th anniversary edition. Oxford: Oxford University Press. (Orig. pub 1959.)

Mullins, D. 2010. *Arizona legislature passes HB2281 banning ethnic studies.* http://www.thepostemail.com/2010/05/04/arizona-legislature-passes-hb2281-banning-ethnic-studies (accessed May 31, 2010).

O'Connor, C. 1997. Dispositions toward (collective) struggle and educational resilience in the inner city: A case analysis of six African-American high school students. *American Educational Research Journal* 34, no. 4: 593–629.

Oyserman, D., and K. Harrison. 1998. Implications of cultural context: African-American identity and possible selves. In *Prejudice: The target's perspective*, ed. J.K. Swim and C. Stangor, 281–300. San Diego, CA: Academic Press.

Peterson, D.G. 2006. Attention – We are NOT a 'nation of immigrants'. *American Chronicle*, http://www.americanchronicle.com/article/view/7272 (accessed November 20, 2009).

Pettigrew, T. 1985. New black–white patterns: How best to conceptualize them. In *Annual review of sociology*, ed. Ralph H. Turner and James F. Short, 329–46. Palo Alto, CA: Annual Reviews.

Quarles, B. 1987. *The Negro in the making of America.* New York: Collier Books.

*Roots.* Directed by Marvin J. Chomsky and John Erman, Calabasas, CA. David Wolper/Warner Bros, 1977.

Schuman, H. 1975. Free will and determinism in public beliefs about race. In *Majority and minority: The dynamics of racial and ethnic relations*, ed. Norman R. Yetman and C. Hoy Steele, 375–80. Boston: Allyn & Bacon.

Smith, S.J. 1999. The cultural politics of difference. In *Human geography today*, ed. Doreen Massey, John Allen and Philip Sarre, 129–50. Malden: Blackwell.

Southgate, B. 2000. *Why bother with history: Ancient, modern and postmodern motivation.* http://tachers.usd259.04g/pkitchen/Why%20History.Uses.htm (accessed October 9, 2009).

The Leadership Conference on Civil and Human Rights/The Leadership Conference Education Fund. 2010. Despite the promise of the Fair Housing Act, the rate of housing discrimination remains high. http://www.civilrights.org/publications/reports/fairhousing/discrimination-rate.html (accessed June 21, 2010).

Tushnet, M.V. 1987. *The NAACP's legal strategy against segregated education 1925–1950.* Chapel Hill: University North Carolina Press.

Weiner, L. 1999. *Urban teaching: The essentials.* New York: Teacher College Press.

Washington, J.M. 1991. *A testament of hope: The essential writings and speeches of Martin Luther King, Jr.* New York: HarperCollins.

White, J.L., and T.A. Parham. 1990. *The psychology of blacks: An African-American perspective*, 2nd ed. Englewood Cliffs, NJ: Prentice Hall.

Woodson, C. 1933. *The mis-education of the Negro.* Washington, DC: The Associated. Publishers.

Wright, R. 1941. *12 million voices.* New York: Thunder's Mouth Press.

Wynter, S. 1990. *'Do not call us Negros': How 'multicultural' textbooks perpetuate racism.* San Francisco: ASPIRE.

# From visuals to vision: using GIS to inform civic dialogue about African American males

William F. Tate IV and Mark Hogrebe

*Department of Education, Washington University in St. Louis, St. Louis, USA*

> There has been considerable attention in the sociology and public policy literatures to the relationship between spatial arrangements and opportunity structures in metropolitan America. This article attempts to address this issue in the context of Metro St. Louis, Missouri, a center of biotechnology development, where the majority population in St. Louis City is African American. More specifically, it does so by examining extant social science literature related to African American males in urban America. A focus is on highlighting developmental challenges and opportunities for intervention where spatial arrangements are a consideration. Next, it provides an argument that metropolitan regions attempting to intervene would benefit from Geographic Information Systems (GIS) as part of a visual political literacy project aimed to support civic engagement and capacity related to African American male life course development. The metropolitan region of St. Louis is used as a case to illustrate the possibilities of geospatial tools as information sources. The article concludes with a recommendation for greater investment in resources to support sustained community-based research designed to inform understandings of geospatial arrangements that are linked to social disparities.

The issue of how best to encourage widespread citizen participation around the issue of public education leaves us with a fundamental question in democratic theory. The need to confront the role of race does little, in and of itself, to help us see how this goal can be reached. Once again we need to stress that there is no simple or universal strategy ... It seems clear that meaningful participation must be more active than simple electoral politics. Political and community leaders must invest in an institutional framework that promotes a deeper level of engagement. (Henig et al. 1999, 292)

Henig and others (1999) use the term civic capacity to refer to the extent to which various sectors of the community have formed structures (both formal and informal) to define and implement common goals and objectives. They argued that in urban America the civic capacity associated with economic objectives is generally well mobilized as part of development regimes. In contrast, it is extremely challenging to generate civic engagement and sustained support for public education in urban cities in the United States. Hence, one must pose the following query: why can urban development regimes support the construction of sports stadiums, downtown remakes, and other physical infrastructure that attract young knowledge workers, yet struggle with preparing local youth in matters of human development and educational attainment?

Often these urban development regimes misuse public funding originally dedicated to create housing and other supports for poor, underserved neighborhoods (Luce 2003). Unfortunately, disadvantaged communities do not benefit as intended. That said, this represents only part of the problem.

Henig and others (1999) further argued that the educational needs of low-income and minority youth largely concentrated in underserved urban neighborhoods represents a different problem space than economic development. Educational reform requires different types of interest, actors, and institutional contexts. The costs and benefits of economic development regimes are material, relatively near-term, and likely to consist of a small and transparent group of actors; however, to develop human capital often presumes diffuse benefits that are slow to materialize. Further, investments in poor and minority youth are perceived to be part of redistribution policy (Henig et al. 1999; Stone 1993). Stone (1993) has argued that the perception of enriched education and improved transportation access for traditionally disadvantaged communities should not be viewed as redistribution or zero-sum, but rather the term 'opportunity expansion' through human investment policies has potential gains, both economic and social for targeted groups and the community at large. Stone further lamented that opportunity expansion as a regime type was merely a hypothetical idea in the urban context. His central argument is that there are rarely any organized and sustainable efforts across institutions (e.g. health, education, government, business) with the express purpose and intent to positively influence the opportunity structures for communities that are largely poor and spatially segregated by race and class.

In this article, we argue that an important role for education researchers seeking to inform the problem space related to opportunity in urban communities is the development and support for a visual political literacy project using Geographic Information Systems (GIS). Myron Orfield (2002) succinctly captured the engagement function of visual depictions of regional demographics. He argued for the need to develop the most accurate and complete visual representations of the region as possible. A practical method to accomplish this aim, he asserted was to use color maps to show patterns and trends. Visual representations provide politicians, news reporters, community groups, and other interested parties with an information source in an era when reports or speeches are not read. Orfield's argument was part of a larger discussion about the economic disparities in metropolitan America; which calls for using Geographic Information System (GIS) tools as a vehicle to stimulate community discussion about regional conditions including education. Orfield (2002) focused on social inequality in metropolitan America as a subject of study for community members, rather than as a topic strictly associated with a disciplinary treatment by and for academics. The goal was to increase dialogue among the interdependent institutions and community actors about the geospatial configuration of social, political, and economic factors in their region. Dialogue related to the geospatial configuration of important factors was hypothesized to be a step toward building the capacity to change. The central point of his book was in many respects a response to the concerns of Henig and associates (1999), Stone (1993), and others seeking to generate civic capacity related to matters of human development. Orfield's call for building visual tools to support community engagement and discussion will be expanded on in this article. A particular goal of this article is to examine how a visual political literacy project might inform and advance civic engagement and related capacity as part of an opportunity expansion regime aimed to support African American males in urban America.

This article is organized into four sections. The first section is a brief review of extant social science literature related to African American males in urban America. The review is provided to highlight developmental challenges and opportunities for intervention. The second section of the article describes the psychological and political value of GIS mapping as a tool to support civic engagement and capacity related to African American males. The third section is a description of how the application of GIS can support research focused on African America male attainment. The metropolitan region of St. Louis, Missouri, will be used as an example to illustrate a visual political literacy project. The final section of this article offers a set of recommendations. Specifically, it is a call for greater investment in funding and resources to support sustained research related to African American males that might provide new insight into geospatial arrangements and community factors that limit opportunities for academic advancement and job potential.

Why focus on a visual political literacy project and African American males? First, it is essential to be familiar with the geospatial distribution of African American males in the United States. The 2000 United States Census reported that the ten largest regions in total population and in black or African American population are urban cities – New York, Los Angeles, Chicago, Houston, Philadelphia, Phoenix, San Diego, Dallas, San Antonio and Detroit. (McKinnon 2001).[1] The same study made available the names of the ten municipalities of 100,000 or more in population with the highest percentage of blacks or African Americans. The municipalities categorized in order with respect to percentage of blacks are as follows: (1) Gary, IN; (2) Detroit, MI; (3) Birmingham, AL; (4) Jackson, MS; (5) New Orleans, LA; (6) Baltimore, MD; (7) Atlanta, GA; (8) Memphis, TN; (9) Washington, DC; and (10) Richmond, VA. The cities ranged from 85% to 58% in terms of their proportion of black residents. The demography of urban cities in terms of African American residential concentration suggests these communities should clearly be a target area for policies and programs to address African American male attainment. However the demographic dispersion of African Americans is more complex. McKinnon (2001) indicated that 64% of all counties (3141 counties) in the country were less than 6% black, but in 96 counties, blacks comprised 50% or more of the total county population. All but one of these counties was located in the southern region of the United States. Ninety-five counties were stretched across the coastal and lowland South in a loosely fashioned arc shape. Generally these counties are not urban metropolitan regions with two noteworthy exceptions – Baltimore City (a county equivalent) and Prince Georges County, MD. St. Louis City, Missouri (a county equivalent) on the other hand was classified within the Midwest and labeled as the only county equivalent outside the South where blacks surpassed 50% of the total population. More than one researcher has argued that Missouri is a part of the South (Morris and Monroe 2009; Wells and Crain 1997). Moreover, there are two urban metropolitan regions in the state (St. Louis and Kansas City). What is evident from the literature on demographics and regional affiliation is that there needs to be an attempt to investigate the factors influencing African American male educational attainment in towns and rural communities in the South as well as larger urban metropolitan communities within the United States. Jacobs (1992) reasoned that towns, cities, and suburbs are distinct with stark differences across municipality categories and size. This suggests there may be differences in terms of the character and impact of geographic factors on African American male educational attainment. In this article, the focus will be on African American males living in urban cities and metropolitan communities. There is sufficient historical and social science substantiation to propose that the experiences of African American males in rural southern counties require a separate investigation (Anderson 1988; Katznelson 2005; Margo 1990; Morris and Monroe 2009).

If improving African American male educational attainment and related psychosocial factors are a desirable social goal, then understanding their experiences in community is a pragmatic strategy. Improvement here is meant to convey a desire for increasing the number of developmentally mature individuals in terms of health, academic readiness, psychological stability, and educational attainment. Spencer, Fegley, and Dupree (2006) posited that social scientists have generally studied health as a linear model, with risk factors on one end and outcomes on the other, without clear discussions of the social milieu and life course in between. This also has been the state of affairs in the scholarship where educational processes are under consideration. Individual-level risk factors are typically incorporated into research that examines African American students (Nisbett 1998). Yet out of school factors such as neighborhood and community effects are rarely explored. Wilson (1998) argued that geographic factors such as neighborhood and community are a missing link in the prominent paradigm of individual-level analysis of narrowly defined school outcomes:

> This individualistic framework is not designed to capture the impact of relational, organizational, and collective processes that embody the social structure of inequality. Included among these processes are the institutional influences on mobility and opportunity; the operation and organization of schools, the mechanisms of residential segregation and social isolation in poor neighborhoods; categorical forms of discrimination in hiring, promotions, and other avenues of mobility; ideologies of group differences shared by members of society and institutionalized in organizational practices and norms that affect social outcomes; unequal access to information concerning labor market, financial markets, apprenticeship programs, and schools; the activities of employers' associations and unions; government policies involving taxation, service, investment, and redistribution; and corporate decisions concerning the location and mobility of industries. (508)

If all of the problems associated with the education and related human development of African American males can be empirically validated as individually caused, then the need for generating civic capacity and collection cognition as part of a visual political literacy project is not an urgent priority. However, Wilson's (1998) argument counters the individualist paradigm of attainment and human development. Further, his position based on extant research literature suggests structural and environmental considerations are relevant to discussions of African American males (see for example Kain 1968). The authors will continue this line of discussion in the next section.

**Factors influencing African American male attainment**

If the aim is to improve African American male education attainment, then it is instructive to understand factors that influence this outcome. Both school and broader environmental factors affect African American male student performance and related outcomes. In this section, both school and environmental factors impacting African American males' educational attainment will be examined. The discussion focuses on teacher expectations and support, school opportunity, and neighborhood and community factors.

## Teachers' expectations and support factors

Ferguson (1998) documented one of the most vexing and challenging problems facing African American students – teacher expectations. His survey of the evidence found that teachers have lower expectations for blacks than for whites. Moreover, teachers' expectations have more of an impact on black students' performance than on white students' performance. The reason teachers expect less of blacks than whites is that black students' past performance and behavior are judged as worse. Establishing their expectations based on less favorable perceptions of African American children's past performance and behavior negatively influences the students' achievement and attainment. This phenomenon is uniquely problematic for African American males who are often seen as disruptive figures in school settings. National aggregates of African American risk ratios in the disability categories of mental retardation and emotional disturbance are 2.41 and 1.88 respectively (Klingner et al. 2005). The risk ratio provides a comparative index of risk of being placed in a particular disability category. Harry and Anderson (1999) argued that the difficulties African American males face in school are inappropriately constructed as learning, behavioral, and developmental deficits intrinsic to a majority of these students. It is reasonable to conclude that African American males are at great risk when teacher expectation and perceptions are negative. It is not totally clear why expectations are such a powerful influence on African American student outcomes. One explanation is that teachers' with low expectations withdraw help and support structures to students perceived in a negative light. Another explanation is that students who are viewed as deficient or troubled conform to the teacher's perception. Both explanations are linked to a socializing effect that is related to negative developmental and educational outcomes (Dupree et al. 2009). Sanders and Jordan's (2000) study provides additional insight. Using panel data drawn from the National Educational Longitudinal Survey of 1988, they examined the degree to which teacher–student relations, measured as teacher expectations and teacher supportiveness at grades 10 and 12, influence 12th grade students' educational investments and academic achievement. The study results indicated that 12th grade students who reported that their favorite teachers expected them to go to college also indicated being prepared for class, better behaved in school and less engaged in maladaptive behavior in and out of school than students who did not indicate high teacher expectations. The study also found that teacher support was significantly and positively related with student conduct and preparation for class, and negatively and significantly associated with maladaptive behavior (e.g. alcohol use). Expectations and support are critical teacher factors related to African American male attainment. The challenge with the expectation phenomena is that it is very difficult to intervene on an educator's expectation about a student or demographic group. In addition, many schools that serve African American males often have high concentrations of poor and minority students. These schools often lack the resources and personnel required to provide students with the high support and high expectation experiences they need for a consistent demonstration of adaptive behaviors, positive school engagement, and achievement. Schools with a high percentage of low-expectation teachers produce what Payne (2008) refers to as low mutual expectations. He argued that inner-city schools with low mutual expectations among the teaching staff are part of a social climate that is a product of structural challenges. His major point is that if more affluent suburban schools lost a large percentage of funding, its better teachers, and significant portions of its top-performing students, then teacher expectations would be more aligned with the low mutual expectations often found in inner-city schools where many African American males negotiate the learning experience.

What is clear from the literature is that teachers with high expectations who offer quality support represent an important protective factor for African American males while low teacher expectations and limited support is a risk factor (Thomas and Stevenson 2009). There is a need to address low-expectations and related support for African American males.

## *School opportunity factors*

High quality teachers and cognitively demanding instruction where the learner is central to the school enterprise are foundational to a positive educational experience. In a review examining democratic access to knowledge in US schools, Anderson and Tate (2008), found that there is a persistent difference in terms of access, availability, and entry to more rigorous college preparatory courses as well as consistent access to quality teachers when students are members of a minority group attending a resource poor, inner-city public school as compared to students in more affluent suburban communities (see Ferguson 1991; Lee 2004). For example, the availability of Advanced Placement decreases as the percentages of African American students in a school increases (Oakes, Muir, and Joseph 2000). This trend is not limited to the most advanced secondary coursework. Segregated minority high schools are less likely to offer courses that are prerequisite study for advanced coursework. Moreover, there is evidence that this difference in curriculum access extends to K-8 schools (Cogan, Schmidt, and Wiley 2001). This finding and the tracking literature more broadly suggests that cognitive demand is an important protective factor associated with school settings. The term cognitive demand is used here in two ways to describe learning opportunities (see Tate 2006). The first way is associated with curriculum policy and students' course-taking options – how much of a core subject (mathematics, science, language arts, history, etc.) and which courses. The second way relates to how much thinking is called for in the classroom (Bransford, Brown, and Cocking 1999). Routine memorization involves low cognitive demand, no matter how advanced the content. Understanding concepts involves high cognitive demand, even for basic content. Both types of cognitive demand are associated with student performance on achievement tests and other forms of attainment, but they are not substitutes for each other (Porter 2002; Tate 2006).

Teacher quality and cognitive demand are important factors in terms of influence on African American male achievement and attainment. There is a need for parents and community members to better understand the status of teacher quality and the nature of cognitive demand for African American males.

## *Neighborhood and community factors*

There are many factors that have a bearing on the experiences of African American males who inhabit urban cities in the United States. The discussion here will focus mainly on neighborhood factors directly associated with education attainment. Neighborhood circumstances have been linked to the college aspirations of African American children. Above and beyond individual-level attributes and neighborhood controls, living in an underserved and resource-poor neighborhood is a negative influence on the college aspirations of African American students (Stewart, Stewart, and

Simons 2007). Goldring and others (2006) reasoned that, in theory, neighborhood schools are expected to increase community connection to schools, incentivize resource sharing, and boost parent participation and social capital. Their research provides a contribution of consequence in finding that geographic proximity of school and neighborhood does not necessarily foster functional community support arrangements for students. Moreover, as desegregation oversight and related remedies are ended, African American youth are being reassigned to schools in high-risk neighborhoods (Hochschild and Scovronick 2003). Students residing in these neighborhoods negotiate substantial criminal activity, limited access to health professionals and health disparities, relatively low social capital, and high unemployment. Family formation, crime, housing patterns, and health are part of the production function related to the education attainment and life course development for African American males (Holzer, Raphael, and Stoll 2006; Sampson, Raudenbush, and Earls 2009). For example, one risk factor in both education and health is residential segregation and the associated geographic concentration of poverty. According to Williams and Collins (2001), racial residential segregation is a fundamental cause of racial disparities in health. Their review of evidence suggested that segregation is a primary cause of racial differences in socioeconomic status (SES) where the key determining mechanisms are access to education and employment.

Guinier (2003) posited that a variety of demographic, sociological, and economic factors have configured to make college attainment very challenging and the criteria for entry very stringent, in a manner that correlates with class, geography, and race. The link between a family's economic status and educational attainment has a lengthy record in the social sciences literature (Margo 1990). Miller (1995) contended that differences in academic achievement among racial groups reflect the fact that the variation in family resources is greater than the variation in school resources. His analysis of achievement patterns and resource allocations verifies that most high-SES students receive several times more resources that most low-SES students receive, and much of this resource gap is a result of family resources rather than schools. Miller argued further that African American (as well as other racial demographic groups') educational advancement is an intergenerational process. An intergenerational viewpoint suggests that education-related family resources are school resources accrued across multiple generations. On average, investments in the current generation of African American males in the form of intergenerationally accumulated education-relevant family resources are significantly less than comparable investments in White and Asian children. Family resources amassed over several generations positively influence educational opportunity and attainment (Katznelson 2005; Margo 1990; Turner and Bound 2003). This is a crucial point of emphasis as many studies that investigate the relationship between African American males, educational attainment, and economic factors characterize SES by income level rather than wealth (e.g. Primus 2006). Point of fact is that wealth passed across generational lines influences educational attainment (Shapiro 2004). To better understand the influence of wealth an assessment of African American families, rather than males only is informative. Shapiro (2004) modeled the variables that influenced changes in wealth from 1989 to 1999 separately for white and black households. Each racial group had different variables that significantly distinguished wealth-gainers from others. Change in family income was the most important factor for both demographic groups, but income translates into more wealth for whites than for blacks. For every dollar earned whites accrued $1.22 more wealth than blacks.

Differential wealth is both transformed into homeownership as well as secured by homeownership.

Wealth and poverty are heavily concentrated in metropolitan America. This concentration must be understood as part of a cycle of community growth that will be challenging to alter. Education attainment, neighborhood development, and business establishment are interrelated. Wheeler (2006) found that neighborhoods with larger percentages of highly educated residents (bachelor's degree or more) tend to attract a greater number of businesses. This relationship holds after accounting for a neighborhood's per capita income. This finding indicates that businesses prefer to have a ready pool of highly educated workers in close vicinity. Two possible reasons for this preference include the possibility of a strong supply of workers and because college graduates have a high propensity to consume. The bottom line is that highly educated residents and businesses in communities with robust economic activities are mutually reinforcing. More business activities and enterprise in a ZIP code tend to be coupled with lower rates of unemployment. It is rational to argue that many African American males would benefit from greater proximity to significant business activity. This is especially true if a region has limited transportation options; fewer jobs in a community may be associated with an individual resident's inability to find and secure jobs. Kain (1968) referred to this idea as the 'spatial mismatch' hypothesis. According to this theory, high rates of unemployment in the urban core, particularly among African Americans, are linked to jobs shifting from traditional downtowns to the suburbs. This shift in employment opportunities results in higher rates of joblessness among African Americans. There is evidence that job access for poor African Americans had improved in US metropolitan areas during the 1990s; however, job sprawl and variation in housing affordability remain as impediments to access to jobs for the poor (Covington 2009).

Since the St. Louis region will be discussed later in this article, some insight into the spatial mismatch phenomena in the region is order. Cummings (2004) argued that regional development disparities undermine the ability of community leadership to address spatial mismatch between St. Louis City residents needing jobs and the suburban business clusters where employment opportunities are being created. A great deal of the development efforts are focused on the biotechnology industry. He pointed out the mismatch between the current skill levels of those seeking jobs (young African Americans) and the requirements called for to realistically compete for the jobs being created in biotechnology and related industries. Cummings described a situation where corporate leaders and economic development planners have failed to agree upon the economic sectors that might be targeted for workforce development initiatives. One transparent area to establish workforce support is biotechnology. He posited that the workforce development reform is perceived as a black issue or a black program. Thus, the political debate over this topic has conformed to the class and racial discourse that have historically split the city and suburban interests in the metropolitan region. The issue of African American males, workforce development, and related matters associated with education attainment often produce uncomfortable silences or uninformed explanations. Indeed, both outcomes are unacceptable.

**A visual political literacy project**

Stone and others (2001) contended that collective cognition is of importance when the problem solving assignment is improving education attainment in urban America.

Elsewhere, Tate (2009) has argued that informed collective cognition and related civic engagement as part of a visual political literacy project focused on African American males in metropolitan regions was viable. Historically, geometrical and mechanical analogies have played an essential role in the development of models for the physical sciences (Farebrother 2002). This occurred because many objects under study could be seen and framed relatively inexpensively with existing technology. Yet, there was a trend by statisticians to turn away from this approach as the complexity of the field advanced. As a result, this loss was felt more so by the casual learner and practitioner. That said, today statistical findings and a wide range of other information related to African American males in urban communities can be conveyed visually to better inform community actors. New computing tools and capabilities have made data visualization more accessible to the public.

Why invest in the development of a visual political literary project? First, the cognitive science literature demonstrates from childhood through adulthood that images, illustrations, and graphic representations have an influence on learning as well as support reading. In particular, illustrated text supports delayed recall of information (Kulhavy, Stock, and Kealy 1993). Thus, visual literacy is a tool to support the type of collective cognition required in the problem solving efforts linked to increasing African American males' educational attainment in metropolitan America. If the challenges associated with this problem solving task can be portrayed pictorially there is a greater likelihood of learning and retention than if presented as written text only. Learning and retention are not the only benefits of visual modeling. Schwartz and Heiser (2006) posited that spatial representations capitalize on the perceptual system by enforcing and enabling spatial computations. The perceptual system is directly related to this discussion of visual political literacy. One function of perception is to provide an integrated, stable experience. According to the cognitive science literature, colors, motion, brightness, shape, location are processed in separate brain functions. Perception provides specialized abilities to more easily grasp the structure of complex arrangements represented in visual models. Another benefit to visual modeling is that perceptual structure is deterministic; at any one time, people only see one set of structures. Contrast the determinism associated with a visual model to language. For example, if we say, 'there have been a number of crimes committed near the school' the statement is somewhat vague about the crimes. Were the crimes committed in front, behind, or to the right or left of the school? How many crimes were committed? What types of crimes were committed? In contrast, a visual map of the situation can be very specific in terms of exact counts, placement, and nature. Moreover, visual computation tools are well suited to support inspecting, finding, zooming, rotating, and transforming representations. These operations are useful for generating plans and explanations in areas relevant to civic engagement. For example, the ability to transform a visual representation of a county allows the examiner to compare and contrast different geospatial units (street, business cluster, area around a school, or city) by factors of interest. The psychology literature focused on visual models suggests that graphic representation as a tool might help to inform our understanding of the geospatial conditions of African American males.

A second reason visual political literacy should be part of the African American male civic project is that maps and related representations have informed community debates about other regional development issues. Orfield (2002) chronicled the central role that GIS mapping played as a method to support regional planning in the Minneapolis–St. Paul metroplex as well as other communities in the United States.

Also, Gordon's (2008) historical examination of the St. Louis area incorporated GIS mapping to demonstrate how wealth transferred to the urban fringe while the central city experienced stark and downward trends in terms of resources to support human capital development. This process is arguable a part of larger economic transformations where manufacturing has declined in St. Louis as well as in other rust belt regions in the United States. In response, St. Louis has embarked on an effort to be a leader in biotechnology. This strategy is consistent with a pattern of shifting economic goals and related reconfigurations of urban spaces. Lipman (2006) argued that the changing structure of the world economy is transforming cities and the neighboring metropolitan regions. In particular, competition for corporate centers and strategically located business clusters are influencing the spatial dimension of cities and metropolitan areas. One direct implication of Lipman's argument is the need to better understand geospatial arrangements in metropolitan America.

The use of maps to inform regional planning appears basic at first glance. However, when considered in light of the cognitive benefits of visual modeling – learning, retention, and associated perceptual gains – GIS generated illustrations represent at least hypothetically a method to support collective cognition about African American males' education attainment. Perhaps an example will illustrate the potential political and psychological benefits of GIS tools. The Center for the Study of Regional Competitiveness in Science and Technology at Washington University in St. Louis has embarked on an effort to provide a GIS tool for the purposes of public engagement as well as analytical studies to inform policy debates.[2] The center's mission is to examine the alignment of people, policy instruments, and partnerships as well as other relevant factors associated with regional scientific and technological growth and production. One of the center's research projects focused on the geospatial distribution of the biotechnology industry in the St. Louis region. How the industry is clustered provides insight into who might benefit from the related business activity. The regional biotechnology clustering is noteworthy in light of the high degree of geopolitical fragmentation in metropolitan St. Louis. Orfield (2002) reported that metropolitan St. Louis ranks second in geopolitical fragmentation in a ranking of the 25 largest metropolitan areas in the United States. Metropolitan St. Louis consists of 312 local governments (12 counties and 300 municipalities and townships), with 13.8% of the population living in St. Louis City. There are 12.2 local governments per 100,000 residents in the metropolitan region. A high degree of geopolitical fragmentation is an indication that individuals and families who can afford housing elsewhere are moving out of the central city. This is in fact the situation in metropolitan St. Louis. Laslo (2004) estimated that during the period between 1950 and 2000, St. Louis City lost an average of 10,172 persons annually. Between 1950 and 1980, St. Louis County was the primary recipient of the out-migration. More recently, St. Charles County has been the main beneficiary, and as a result grew at one of the fastest rates in the nation between 1990 and 2000. According to Tate (2008), the geopolitical fragmentation and migration trends combined with a statistically significant, high degree of clustering by metropolitan St. Louis biotechnology organizations is an outgrowth of regional planning that has influenced the opportunity structures in the region. He estimated there was less than 1% likelihood that the dispersed pattern of biotechnology businesses and organizations was due to random chance. Tate argued that to better understand the region it was important to be able to visualize the political economy of biotechnology. Earlier it was stated that the city of St. Louis was the only county equivalent outside the South where blacks exceeded 50% of the total population. Thus, there is much to be learned about African American males from examining the nature and extent of opportunity and attainment in this city and the broader metropolitan region.

Tate (2008) conducted kernel density estimation (KDE) to assist in the visualization of the metropolitan St. Louis biotechnology clusters (see Figure 1). KDE is a method for calculating the density of events as a continuous field (Wang 2006). It turns discrete point data into a continuous surface of values and thus highlights the spatial patterns of the events. The 'events' in this case are biotechnology organizations. The kernel radius for each biotechnology organization was set at 2.8 miles. The methodology makes it feasible to analyze the region using the four biotechnology clusters as organizational frames of reference rather than the hundreds of municipalities and other governance arrangements in metropolitan St. Louis. He argued this methodological strategy was a useful tool to visualize the biotechnology enterprise and related opportunities in metro St. Louis. The GIS maps in this discussion will continue this strategy as a method to illustrate the geospatial arrangements of biotechnology clusters and the distribution of African American males categorized by education attainment. School district boundary lines will be displayed; however the unit of analysis will be the distinct biotechnology clusters in the region.

Opportunities to participate in the biotechnology industry require a quality K-12 education as well as post-secondary educational attainment. According to Slaughter (2009), historically African Americans were considered to be part of the population that neither had contributed nor were likely to contribute to science and technology

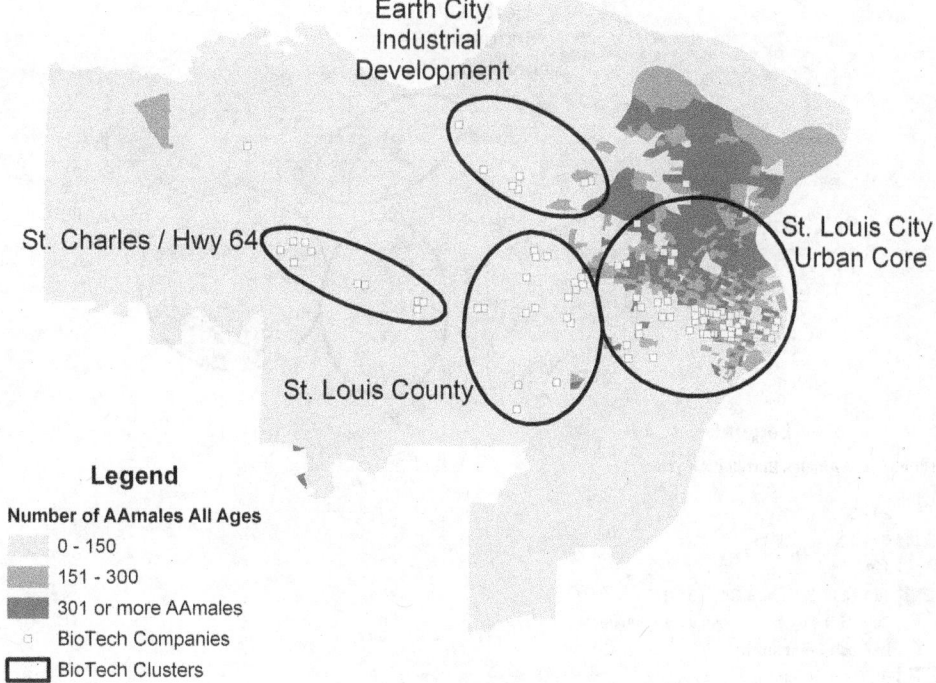

Figure 1. Year 2000 Census block groups showing number of African-American Males All Ages.
Note: Data are derived from the 2000 US Census, http://www.census.gov.

and, as a result little resources (intellectual or material) were afforded to efforts to increase their participation. Slaughter's argument is centrally concerned with expectations. Do families, educators, community leaders, and corporation leaders expect schools to prepare African American males to learn and ultimately participate in the local biotechnology economy of the St. Louis region? Geospatial tools can be used to generate interest in this question as well as to facilitate planning to support the development of high help and high expectation learning environments. To demonstrate the potential of GIS, data associated with African American males in the St. Louis region will be illustrated. A particular focus of the discussion will center on the African American male seniors enrolled in 2003–2004, because there is information about test performance for prior years of schooling. Specifically, the state of Missouri required this senior class to sit for both the mathematics and science assessments during 10th grade. The test performance information is limited since enrollments (in and out migrations) are constantly changing. However, with this limitation noted, for the purposes of community discussion and planning the test performance information is instructive.

Where are the African American males in relation to the biotechnology clusters? Figure 1 illustrates the distribution of African American males in the region by biotechnology cluster as estimated by the 2000 Census. Figure 2 displays the distribution of the African American males classified as seniors and enrolled throughout the 2003–2004 academic year by biotechnology cluster. The St. Louis City Urban Core biotechnology cluster as well as the communities north of this cluster has high concen-

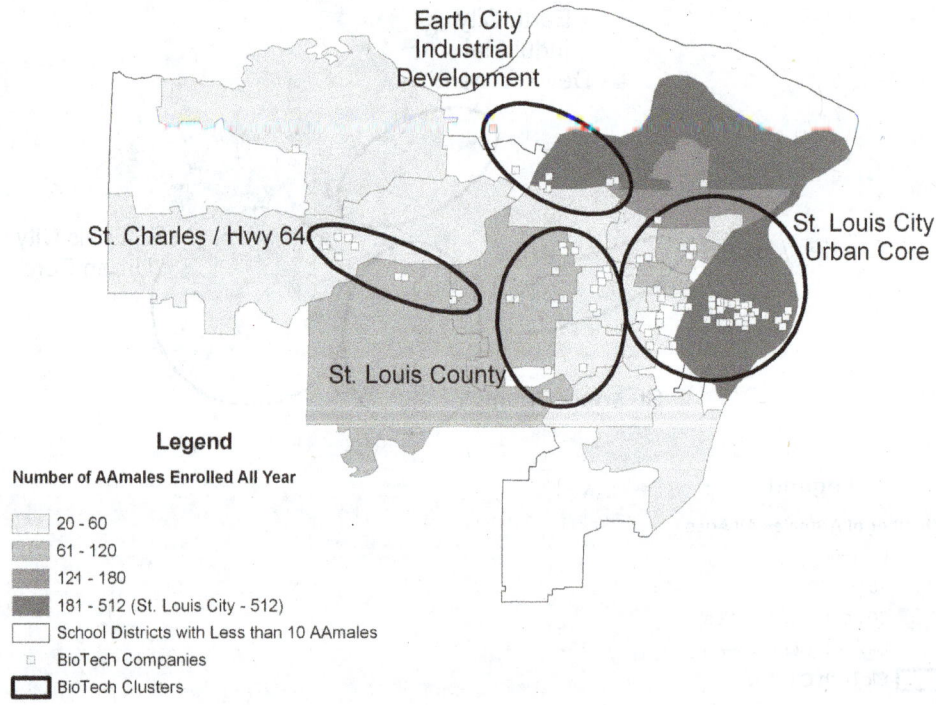

Figure 2. Number of African American male seniors enrolled in school districts throughout the 2003–2004 academic year.
Note: Data are derived from Missouri Department of Elementary and Secondary Education.

trations of African male residents. The St. Louis City Urban Core and Earth City Industrial Development clusters relative to the other biotechnology clusters have the largest number of African American males enrolled in schools located within their cluster boundaries. Also, just north of the St. Louis City Urban Core biotechnology cluster there are large numbers of African American male seniors enrolled in north St. Louis County school districts. This area is largely outside the boundaries of any biotechnology clustering. Both Figures 1 and 2 indicate that African American males are concentrated in St. Louis city and north St. Louis county.

What percentage African American male seniors enrolled in 2003–2004 graduated from high school by biotechnology cluster? Figure 3 provides a visual display of the percentage of African American male graduates by cluster. The St. Louis City Urban Core cluster has a high concentration of schools where 53% of the African American male seniors graduate. These schools are part of the St. Louis Public Schools. North and west of the St. Louis City Urban Core cluster there are consistently higher graduation rates. However, the number of African American males is relatively smaller in these clusters compared to St. Louis Urban Core cluster.

How many African American male seniors enrolled in 2003–2004 completed the state of Missouri's College Preparatory Studies Certificate (CPSC) by biotechnology cluster? To be eligible for the certificate, a student must meet three major requirements. The first requirement is that the student must complete the course of study in Table 1. This course of study represents the minimum course requirements. In addition, the English/Language Arts courses may include speech or debate, and

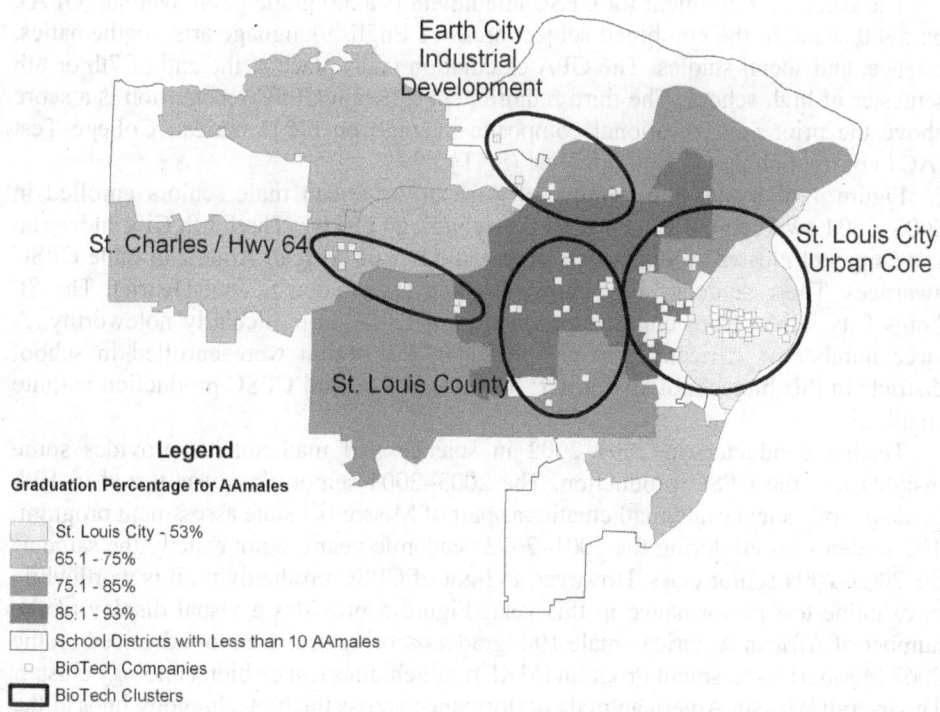

Figure 3. Percentage of African American male seniors in 2003–2004 completing high school graduation requirements.
Note: Data are derived from Missouri Department of Elementary and Secondary Education.

Table 1. Course requirements for College Preparatory Studies Certificate, Missouri Department of Elementary and Secondary Education.

| Subjects | Units |
| --- | --- |
| English/Language Arts | 4 |
| Mathematics | 3 |
| Science | 2 |
| Social Studies | 3 |
| Fine Arts | 1 |
| Practical Arts | 1 |
| Physical Education | 1 |
| Specified Core Electives | 3 |
| General Electives | 6 |
|  | Total 24 |

two units must be in courses emphasizing composition or writing skills. The mathematics requirements should include traditional college preparatory courses (e.g. Algebra I, Algebra II, plane geometry, etc.). Courses deemed less academically rigorous such as yearbook, drama, theater, photography, basic math, consumer math, pre-algebra, general math are unacceptable CPSC courses. The CPSC program of study is aligned with core curriculum required for college admissions in Missouri's state universities.

The second requirement for CPSC attainment is a 3.0 grade point average (GPA), on a 4.0 scale, in the combined subject areas of English/language arts, mathematics, science, and social studies. The GPA calculation takes place at the end of 7th or 8th semester of high school. The third requirement to attain CPSC recognition is a score above the prior year's national composite average on the American College Test (ACT) or the Scholastic Aptitude Test (SAT).

Figure 4 illustrates the number of African American male seniors enrolled in 2003–2004 awarded CPSC status by biotechnology cluster. The Earth City Industrial Development cluster produced the largest number of African American male CPSC awardees. These students were enrolled in the Hazelwood School District. The St. Louis City Urban Core cluster's production of CPSC is particularly noteworthy. A large number of African American males in the region were enrolled in school districts in this biotechnology cluster; however the overall CPSC production is quite small.

Testing conducted in 2001–2002 in science and mathematics provides some insights into the CPSC production. The 2003–2004 senior class was tested in 10th grade in both science and mathematics as part of Missouri's state assessment program. The students tested during the 2001–2002 academic year are not exactly the same as the 2003–2004 senior class. However, in light of CPSC productivity, it is worthwhile to examine test performance in this year. Figure 5 provides a visual display of the number of African American male 10th graders scoring proficient or advanced on the 2002 Missouri Assessment Program (MAP) mathematics test by biotechnology cluster. The overall African American male performance across the biotechnology hubs at the top two proficiency levels of the mathematics assessment ranged from 0 to 7 students per cluster. This visual provides a regional snapshot of the performance of African American males at 10th grade who demonstrated the skills and understandings aligned

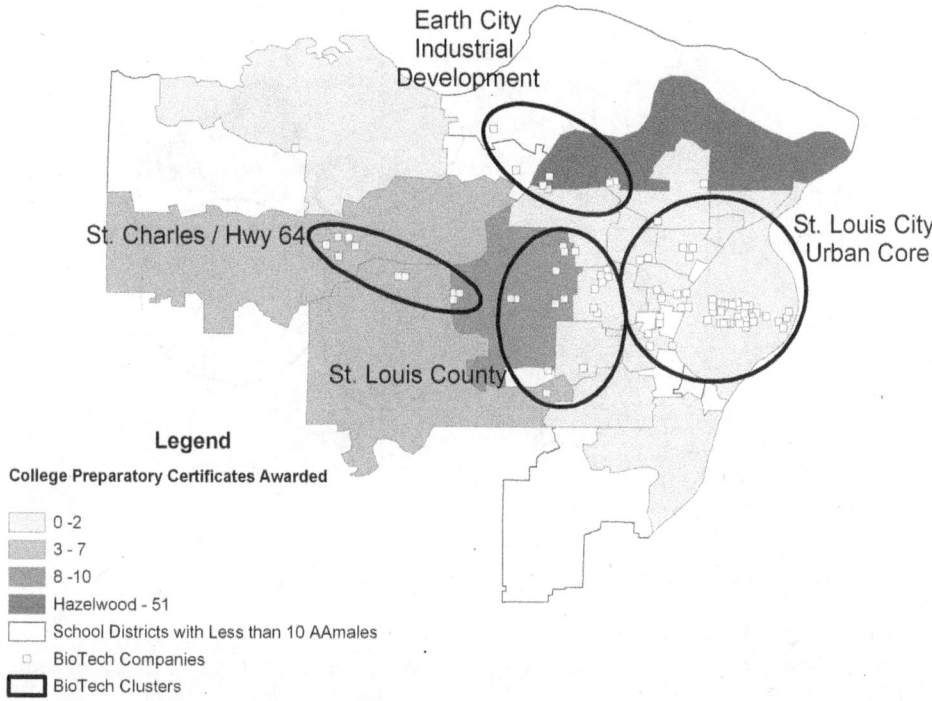

Figure 4. Number of African American male seniors completing Missouri's College Preparatory Studies Certificate in academic year 2003–2004.
Note: Data are derived from Missouri Department of Elementary and Secondary Education.

with the state of Missouri's mathematics standards. It follows that in fact a large majority of African American males were classified in the two lowest proficiency levels – Step 1 and Progressing.

Figure 6 shows the number of African American male 10th graders classified as proficient or advanced on the 2002 MAP science test by biotechnology cluster. The performance across the biotechnology clusters in the region is very similar to the mathematics outcome. Only a small number of African American males in the clusters performed at the two highest levels. A majority of the African American male students' test performances were classified in the two lowest proficiency levels – Step 1 and Progressing.

## Summary

The maps in the previous section provide snapshots of the political economy of St. Louis where African American males are prominent to the investigation. A majority of African American males reside in the St. Louis Urban Core biotechnology cluster or in communities to the north of this cluster. There are few concentrations of African American males residing in other biotechnology clusters. This residential pattern suggests the need for a quality transportation system if African American males are to have access to employment opportunities in the emerging industry of the community. The maps also provide a status report of the distribution of African American male students' college readiness as measured by graduation rates, course-taking patterns,

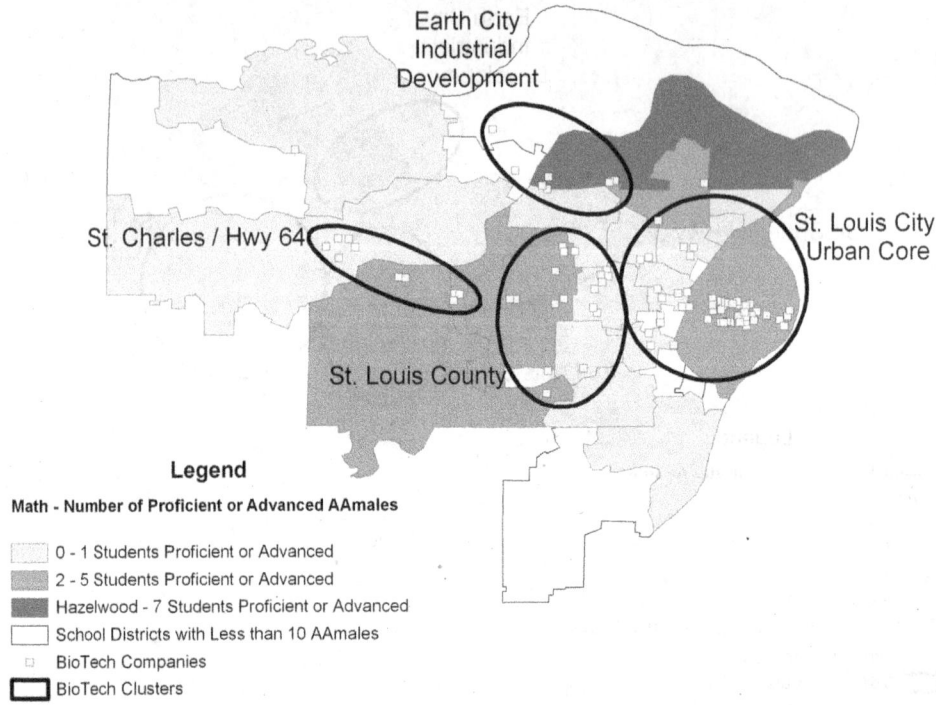

Figure 5. Number of African American males proficient or advanced in 10th grade math on Missouri 2002 MAP Test.
Note: Data are derived from Missouri Department of Elementary and Secondary Education.

grades, and testing performance (state and college entrance exams). This snapshot of college readiness suggests that many students lack the skills and understanding to fully participate in the biotechnology development regime. There is a clear need to examine this evidentiary base on an ongoing basis as well as to intervene directly.

The intent of this section is to offer a few examples of how a visual political literacy project might inform community discussions related to African American males. Knowledge about this demographic group is often limited to stock stories. The illustrations in the previous section provided enrollment figures, graduation rates, college preparation status, and mathematics and science proficiency by regional biotechnology cluster. Some important questions for the community to explore include:

- What can be done to improve the African American male graduation rate?
- What factors are influencing the college preparation status of African American males?
- What is happening in the Hazelwood School District in terms of producing African American males attaining Missouri's College Preparatory Certificates?
- Why are so few African American males developing proficiency in mathematics and science?
- How can the region produce more African American males (indigenous to the community) prepared to contribute to biotechnology?

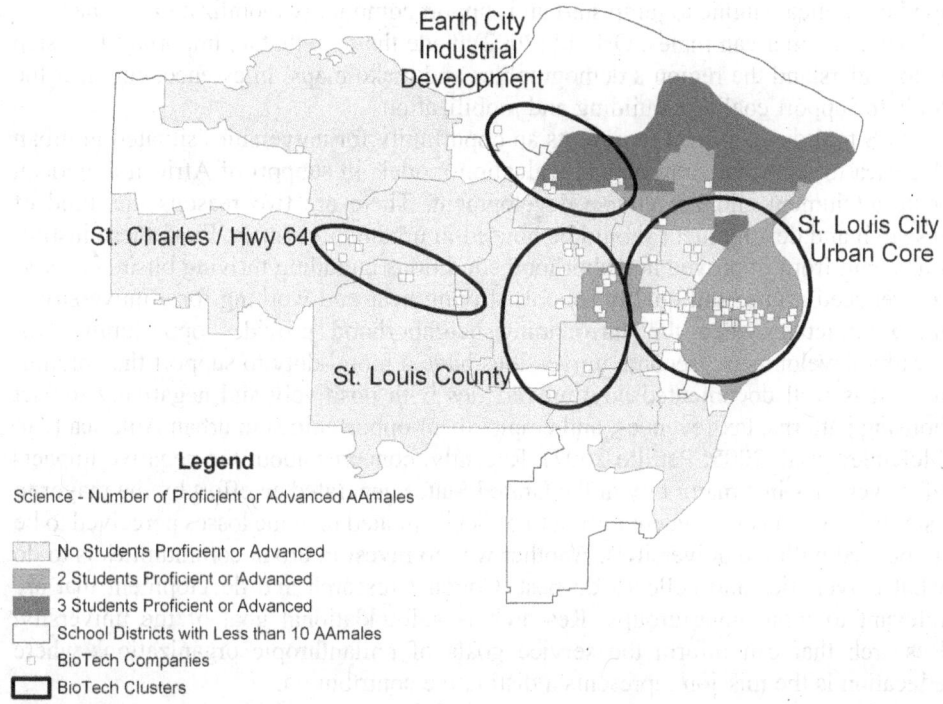

Figure 6. Number of African American males proficient or advanced in 10th grade science on Missouri 2002 MAP Test.
Note: Data are derived from Missouri Department of Elementary and Secondary Education.

These questions as well as others generated by the community at large are important. Unfortunately, there are very few communities where open discussions of these types of question have been normalized (Tatum 2007). Visual illustrations are not the solution. Rather, maps and related visuals are tools to help inform and promote sustained civic dialogue. Ultimately, there must be an engineer that agitates the status quo and generates conversations and action. More about engineering will be discussed in the final section.

## Engineering tools to support mobilization

It has been argued that contemporary evaluation relies on indicators that almost assure failure (Henig et al. 1999). For example, the dominant reliance on standardized tests creates a centralized command and control model that often does not accommodate community interaction. Henig and others (1999) recommended an evaluation framework that emphasizes community mobilization rather than strict sanction and school-level remediation strategies. In their view this alternative model would provide a variety of performance indicators as part of an aggressive communication system designed for the distribution of information to community members. A fully operating model would provide the community with a sense of the relative performance of schools and permits the identification of marginal gains on key measures. Henig and others (1999) theorized this approach might possibly promote community mobilization for reform efforts. In this article, it has been argued that GIS tools might be the methodological engine to jump start and support community mobilization on the topic of African American males. Orfield (2002) made the case that an important first step is to understand the region's demographics and make maps. In essence, engineer the tools to support coalition building and mobilization.

GIS tool development represents an opportunity for universities situated in urban America to contribute alternative evaluation models in support of African American male attainment and life course development. There are two reasons this kind of research and development should be housed in urban universities. First, these institutions gain from improved neighborhood conditions including thriving business activity, reduced crime, and quality schools. Living near and working for a university is more attractive when the surrounding neighborhood provides opportunities for healthy development. Second, universities have a moral duty to support the community. It is well documented how universities both positively and negatively impact housing patterns, tax revenues, and employment opportunities in urban America (e.g. McKinley et al. 2005; Pattillo 2007). Recently, concerns about the negative impacts of universities in a major city in the United States generated an effort by the mayor to establish a city tax on student tuition to offset estimated revenue losses perceived to be associated with the universities. Another way to invest in urban communities is to do what universities and colleges do best. Conduct research and development that are relevant to indigenous groups. Research is a foundational goal of the university. Research that can inform the service goals of philanthropic organizations where education is the mission represents a distinctive contribution.

Universities in New York, Los Angeles, Chicago, Philadelphia, San Diego, New Orleans, Atlanta, Houston, and Baltimore are especially situated to add GIS-based insights to discussions related to African American male attainment. Each city has a significant African American population as well as one or more universities classified as a member of the American Association of Universities, a leading university as ranked by the social science index, or top-rated in terms of research and development funding (Graham and Diamond 1997). Other cities including Phoenix, Dallas, Detroit and Washington, DC, are home to at least one university where significant research productivity is an organizational aim. These cities as well as San Antonio, Gary, Birmingham, Jackson, Richmond, and Memphis are situated to develop multi-institutional consortiums focused on African American male attainment. All the consortiums will need thoughtful integration into the planning activities of the region. This is feasible, as traditionally, universities have been active in regional planning.

The late John Hope Franklin in the preface to an essay appropriately titled *Visions of a Better Way: A Black Appraisal of Public Schooling* (Committee on Policy for Racial Justice 1989) identified three interconnected areas of education and community that are core to reform: (1) acknowledging the centrality of human relationships; (2) eliminating the obstacles to successful teaching and learning; and (3) mobilizing physical and political resources. The goal of this article has been to advance a method to support the development of a vision and related capacity in urban communities for African American male opportunity in education – a case for visuals to support the vision.

**Acknowledgements**

This article is based on research supported by the National Science Foundation under Award No. ESI-0227619. Any opinions, findings, and conclusions or recommendations expressed here are those of the authors and do not necessarily reflect the views of the National Science Foundation.

## Notes
1. The terms black and African American will be used throughout the chapter as categorical equivalents.
2. See http://artsci.wustl.edu/scienceandtechnology/ (accessed May 31, 2010).

## References
Anderson, J.D. 1988. *The education of blacks in the South, 1860–1935.* Chapel Hill: University of North Carolina Press.
Anderson, C.A., and W.F. Tate. 2008. Still separate, still unequal: Democratic access to mathematics in U.S. schools. In *Handbook of international research in mathematics education*, 2nd ed., ed. L. English, 299–318. New York: Routledge.
Baybeck, B., and E. Jones, eds. 2004. *St. Louis metromorphosis: Past trends and future directions.* St. Louis: Missouri Historical Society Press.
Bransford, J.D., A.L. Brown, and R. Cocking, eds. 1999. *How people learn: Brain, mind, experience, and school.* Washington, DC: National Academy Press.
Cogan, L., W. Schmidt, and D. Wiley. 2001. Who takes what math and in which track? Using TIMMS to characterize U.S. students' eighth grade mathematics learning opportunities. *Educational Evaluation and Policy Analysis* 23, no. 4: 323–41.
Committee on Policy for Racial Justice. 1989. *Visions of a better way: A Black appraisal of public schooling.* Washington, DC: Joint Center for Political Studies Press.
Covington, K.L. 2009. Spatial mismatch of the poor: An explanation of recent declines in job isolation. *Journal of Urban Affairs* 31, no. 5: 559–87.
Cummings, S. 2004. Racial inequality and developmental disparities in the St. Louis region. In *St. Louis metromorphosis: Past trends and future directions*, ed. B. Baybeck and E.T. Jones, 99–141. St. Louis: Missouri Historical Society Press.
Dupree, D., M. Gasman, K. James, and M.B. Spencer. 2009. Identity, identification, socialization: Preparation and retention of African American males in institutions of higher education. In *Black American males in higher education: Research, programs, and academe*, ed. H.T. Frierson, J.H. Wyche and W. Pearson, 1–20. Bingley, UK: Emerald Group.
Farebrother, R.W. 2002. *Visualizing statistical models and concepts.* New York: Marcel Dekker.
Ferguson, R.F. 1991. Paying for public education: New evidence on how and why money matters. *Harvard Journal of Legislation* 2: 465–98.
Ferguson, R.F. 1998. Teachers' perceptions and expectations and the Black–White test score gap. In *The black–white text gap*, ed. C. Jencks and M. Phillips, 273–317. Washington, DC: Brookings Institution Press.
Goldring, E., L. Cohen-Vogel, C. Smrekar, and C. Taylor. 2006. Schooling closer to home: Desegregation policy and neighborhood contexts. *American Journal of Education* 112: 335–62.
Gordon, C. 2008. *Mapping decline: St. Louis and the fate of the American city.* Philadelphia: University of Pennsylvania Press.
Graham, H.D., and N. Diamond. 1997. *The rise of American research universities: Elites and challengers in the postwar era.* Baltimore, MD: Johns Hopkins Press.
Guinier, L. 2003. Admissions rituals as political acts: Guardians at the gate of democratic ideals. *Harvard Law Review* 117, no. 1: 113–224.
Harry, B., and M.G. Anderson. 1999. The social construction of high-incidence disabilities: The effect on African American males. In *African American males in society and school*, ed. V.C. Polite and J.E. Davis, 34–67. New York: Teachers College Press.
Henig, J.R., R.C. Hula, M. Orr, and D.S. Pedescleaux. 1999. *The color of school reform: Race, politics, and the challenge of urban education.* Princeton, NJ: Princeton University Press.
Hochschild, J.L., and N. Scovronick. 2003. *The American dream and the public schools.* New York: Oxford University Press.

Holzer, H.J., S. Raphael, and M.A. Stoll. 2006. How do employer perceptions of crime and incarceration affect the employment prospects of less-educated young black men? In *Black males left behind*, ed. R.B. Mincy, 67–85. Washington, DC: Urban Institute.

Jacobs, J. 1992. *The death and life of great American cities*, 2nd ed. New York: Vintage Books.

Kain, J.F. 1968. Housing segregation, Negro employment, and metropolitan decentralization. *Quarterly Journal of Economics* 82, no. 2: 175–97.

Katznelson, I. 2005. *When affirmative action was white*. New York: W.W. Norton & Company.

Klingner, J.K., A.J. Artiles, E. Kozleski, B. Harry, S. Zion, W. Tate, G.Z. Durán, and D. Riley. 2005. Addressing the disproportionate representation of culturally and linguistically diverse students in special education through culturally responsive educational systems. *Education Policy Analysis Archives* 13, no. 38. http://epaa.asu.edu/epaa/v13n38 (accessed September 22, 2010).

Kulhavy, R.W., W.A. Stock,. and W.A. Kealy. 1993. How geographic maps increase recall of instructional text. *Educational Technology Research & Development* 41, no. 4: 47–62.

Laslo, D. 2004. The St. Louis region, 1950–2000: How we have changed. In *St. Louis metromorphosis: Past trends and future directions*, ed. B. Baybeck and E.T. Jones, 1–23. St. Louis: Missouri Historical Society Press.

Lee, J. 2004. Multiple facets of inequity in racial and ethnic achievement gaps. *Peabody Journal of Education* 79, no. 2: 51–73.

Lipman, P. 2006. "This is America" 2005: The political economy of education reform against the public interest. In *Education research in the public interest: Social justice in action, and policy*, ed. G. Ladson Billings and W.F. Tate, 98–116. New York: Teachers College Press.

Luce, T. 2003. *Reclaiming the intent: Tax increment finance in the Kansas City and St. Louis metropolitan areas*. Washington, DC: Brookings Institution Center on Urban and Metropolitan Policy.

Margo, R.A. 1990. *Race and schooling in the South, 1880–1950: An economic history*. Chicago: The University of Chicago Press.

McKinley, R., M.E Cline, G. Brides, J. Ford, J. Martinez, J. Bybee-Dziedzie, and P.C. Morales. 2005. *Economic impact study: A study of economic impact of the University of Texas System*. San Antonio: Institute for Economic Development, University of Texas–San Antonio.

McKinnon, J. 2001. *The Black population: 2000* (Census 2000 Brief, C2KBR/01-5). Washington, DC: U.S. Department of Commerce.

Miller, L.S. 1995. *An American imperative: Accelerating minority educational advancement*. New Haven, CT: Yale University Press.

Morris, J.E., and C.R. Monroe. 2009. Why study the U.S. South? The nexus of race and place in investigating Black student achievement. *Educational Researcher* 38, no. 1: 21–36.

Nisbett, R.E. 1998. Race, genetics, and IQ. In *The Black–White test gap*, ed. C. Jencks and M. Phillips, 86–102. Washington, DC: Brookings Institution Press.

Oakes, J., K. Muir, and R. Joseph. 2000. *Coursetaking and achievement in mathematics and sciences: Inequalities that endure and change*. Madison: University of Wisconsin, WCER, National Institute of Science Education.

Orfield, M. 2002. *American metropolitics: The new suburban reality*. Washington, DC: Brookings Institution Press.

Pattillo, M. 2007. *Black on the block: The politics of race and class in the city*. Chicago: University of Chicago Press.

Payne, C.M. 2008. *So much reform: So little change, the persistence of failure in urban schools*. Cambridge, MA: Harvard Education Press.

Porter, A.C. 2002. Measuring the content of instruction. *Educational Researcher* 31, no. 7: 3–14.

Primus, W. 2006. Improving public policies to increase the income and employment of low-income non-resident fathers. In *Black males left behind*, ed. R.B. Mincy, 211–48. Washington: Urban Institute Press.

Sampson, R.J., S.W. Raudenbush, and F. Earls. 2009. Neighborhoods and violent crime: A multilevel study of collective efficacy. In *Urban health: Readings in the social, built, and physical environments of U.S. cities*, ed. H.P. Hynes and R. Lopez, 79–97. Sudbury: Jones and Bartlett.

Sanders, M.G., and W.J. Jordan. 2000. Student-teacher relations and academic achievement in high school. In *Schooling students placed at risk: Research, policy, and practice in the education of poor and minority adolescents*, ed. M.G. Sanders, 65–82. Mahwah, NJ: Lawrence Erlbaum Associates.

Schwartz, D.L., and J. Heiser. 2006. Spatial representations and imagery in learning. In *The Cambridge handbook of the learning sciences*, ed. R.K. Sawyer, 283–98. Cambridge: Cambridge University Press.

Shapiro, T.M. 2004. *The hidden cost of being African American: How wealth perpetuates inequality*. Oxford: Oxford University Press.

Slaughter, J.B. 2009. African American males in engineering: Past, present, and a future of opportunity. In *Black American males in higher education: Research, programs and academe*, ed. H.T. Frierson, J.H. Wyche and W. Pearson, 193–208. UK: Emerald Group.

Spencer, M.B., S. Fegley, and D. Dupree. 2006. Investigating and linking social conditions of minority children and adolescents with emotional well-being. *Ethnicity and Disease* 16. S3-67–S3-70.

Stewart, E.B., E.A. Stewart, and R.L. Simons. 2007. The effect of neighborhood context on the college aspirations of African American adolescents. *American Educational Research Journal* 44, no. 4: 896–919.

Stone, C.N. 1993. Urban regimes and the capacity to govern: A political economy approach. *Journal of Urban Affairs* 15, no. 1: 1–28.

Stone, C.N., J.R. Henig, B.D. Jones, and C. Pierannunzi. 2001. *Building civic capacity: The politics of reforming urban schools*. Lawrence: University of Kansas Press.

Tate, W.F. 2006. Do the math: Cognitive demand makes a difference. *Research Points: Linking Research to Education Policy* 4, no. 2: 2–4. http://aera.net/publications/?id=314 (accessed September 22, 2010).

Tate, W.F. 2008. "Geography of opportunity": Poverty, place, and educational outcomes. *Educational Researcher* 37: 397–411.

Tate, W.F. 2009. African-American males and the logic of a geospatial higher education Project. In *Black American males in higher education: Research, programs, and academe*, ed. H.T. Frierson, J.H. Wyche and W. Pearson, 21–35. Bingley, UK: Emerald Group.

Tatum, B.D. 2007. *Can we talk about race? And other conversations in an era of school resegregation*. Boston: Beacon Press.

Thomas, D.E., and H. Stevenson. 2009. Gender risks and education: The particular classroom challenges for urban low-income African American boys. In *Review of research in education*, ed. V.L. Gadsden, J.E. Davis and A.J. Artiles, 160–80. Washington, DC: American Educational Research Association.

Turner, S.E., and J. Bound. 2003. Closing the gap or widening the divide: The effects of the G.I. Bill and World War II on the educational outcomes of Black Americans. *Journal of Economic History* 62: 145–77.

Wang, F. 2006. *Quantitative methods and applications in GIS*. New York: Taylor & Francis.

Wells, A.S., and R.L. Crain. 1997. *Stepping over the color line: African-American students in white suburban schools*. New Haven, CT: Yale University Press.

Wheeler, C.H. 2006. *Neighborhood characteristics matter: When businesses look for a location*. St. Louis, MO: Federal Reserve Bank of St. Louis.

Williams, D.R., and C. Collins. 2001. Racial residential segregation: A fundamental cause of racial disparities in health. *Public Health Reports* 116, no. 5: 404–16.

Wilson, W.J. 1998. The role of the environment in Black–White test score gap. In *The Black – White test gap*, ed. C. Jencks and M. Phillips, 501–10. Washington, DC: Brookings Institution Press.

# Sociocultural knowledge and visual re(-)presentations of Black masculinity and community: reading *The Wire* for critical multicultural teacher education

Keffrelyn D. Brown and Amelia Kraehe

*Department of Curriculum and Instruction, The University of Texas at Austin, Austin, USA*

> In this article we consider the implications of using popular visual media as a pedagogic tool for helping teachers acquire critical sociocultural knowledge to work more effectively with students of color, particularly Black males. Drawing from a textual analysis (McKee 2001, 2003; Rose 2001) conducted in the critical visual studies tradition (Barthes 1977; Hall 1993, 1997) and longstanding discourses on Blackness, Black masculinity and critical visual studies, we explore how the critically acclaimed HBO series, *The Wire*, positions Black males in the local and larger social milieu. While offering a more complex rendering of the Black male, *The Wire* simultaneously presents a myopic representation of the Black man and his place in the larger Black community. This inquiry highlights the pedagogic limitations of using *The Wire*, or any other visual media that reinscribes deficit-oriented knowledge that critical multicultural teacher education seeks to challenge about Blackness and Black people.

It is no secret that teacher education faces a tremendous challenge: helping future teachers acquire the skills, knowledge and dispositions necessary to teach all students effectively. In the case of Black male students, the impetus to cultivate effective teachers is of vital concern considering the disproportionate outcomes they face across K-12 education.[1] In relation to their peers, Black male students experience higher levels of placement in special education services, in and out-of-school suspension and school expulsion rates, school drop out, and lower levels of academic achievement as measured by standardized tests (Brown in press; Fultz and Brown 2008). Preparing teachers from all racial backgrounds to work effectively with Black male students is of special concern but particularly for those who are White and who come from middle-class backgrounds. This is because the vast majority of practicing teachers, and those preparing to become teachers, are White, middle class and often recognize themselves as having limited substantive knowledge about and experiences with groups of color (Gay 2000).

In this paper, we consider the implications of using popular visual media – specifically situated around representations of Black masculinity – as a pedagogic tool for helping teachers acquire critical sociocultural knowledge to work more effectively with students of color, particularly Black males. By sociocultural knowledge, we refer to the knowledge related to the social, cultural, political and economic histories and conditions that shape individuals, communities and the broader social reality (Brown and Kraehe 2010). Drawing from a textual analysis (McKee 2001, 2003; Rose 2001) conducted in the critical visual studies tradition (Barthes 1977; Hall 1993, 1997) and longstanding discourses on Blackness, Black masculinity and critical visual studies, we explore how *The Wire*, a critically acclaimed HBO drama created by David Simon and Ed Burns in 2002, positions Black males in the local and larger social milieu. This examination moves from the perspective that visual media and popular culture play an important role in the construction of social knowledge (Mitchell 2002) and thus, can operate as an education tool (Pauly 2003; Tisdell and Thompson 2007), specifically in the preparation of teachers (Trier 2007).

### Re(-)presenting the black male: Why popular constructions of black masculinity matter

Across the twentieth century education discourses have targeted Black males as a special population in need of rescue and protection (Davis 2003; Noguera 2003; Polite and Davis 1999). Whether positioned as socially deviant or as victims of inequitable, adverse social conditions, these discourses help sustain a normalized, fixed image of what it means to be Black and male in the US and abroad. In the context of schools, these discourses frame how school officials read and choose to act on behalf of the Black male. For example, in an examination of how Black boys get labeled and tracked as having behavior problems in school, Ann Arnett Ferguson (2001) argues that school officials read and make decisions about Black male students based on cultural images about Black maleness found in larger social discourse. This discourse frames Black males as either criminals or as a victimized endangered species. It is for these reasons that representations of Black masculinity matter, particularly in the context of education and K-12 schooling.

Concerns with representations of Black masculinity (and Blackness in a larger sense), however, are not novel or germane only to schools. Looking backwards in time to the late nineteenth/early twentieth century one recognizes how the hopes and dreams of an oppressed US Black nation existed alongside concerted efforts to 'uplift' the race (Cooper 1930; Du Bois 1903 [1994]); Washington 1901 [2000]). The racial uplift project focused on acquiring an education, often centered around literacy (Perry, Steele, and Hilliard 2004), with a larger goal in mind: countering popular dominant racist opinion that Black people, specifically men, were intellectually and socially less capable than their White counterparts. While contentious debate ensued around what such an education should consist of and how it might look (i.e. Booker T. Washington v. W.E.B. Du Bois – see Marable and Mullings 2000), across the twentieth century Black thinkers and activists fashioned in societal discourse, a Black masculine identity, albeit often sexist,[2] that illustrated the Black community[3] was as capable as any other people in the body politic.

Literary scholar Henry Louis Gates (1988) notes that the turn of the twentieth century, Frederick Douglass, a US Black writer and orator, was often characterized as 'the representative colored man of the United States.' Gates illustrates how this use of the term 'representation' extends beyond a common understanding that refers to a particular image or likeness that reflects key attributes found in the larger group in which the image exists. Given that Douglass authored several autobiographies and wrote and delivered hundreds of speeches and essays he 'could not be mistaken for the mean, the mode, or the median of the Afro-American community of the nineteenth century' (Gates 1988, 129). Gates illuminates how this particular notion of representation spoke to the image of the Black male that Douglass wanted to 're-present'. This undertaking sought to challenge the dominant, racist popular view that Blackness was inferior and deficient.[4] Gates (1988, 129) states:

> Douglass, then, was the most representative colored man both because he represented black people most eloquently and elegantly, and because he was the race's great opportunity to re-present itself in the court of racist public opinion. Black Americans sought to re-present their public selves in order to reconstruct their public, reproducible images.

Tropes of representation and re-presentation have played a key role in Black American political discourse about the Black community. Collectively these re(-)presentational efforts play out in multiple venues, often print sources: including literature and school textbooks (Banks 2004) but is perhaps most evident in concerns with how the Black body, particularly the masculine, is picked up and represented in visual media.

Targeting visual media for its representations of Black maleness is not a haphazard undertaking when considering Gates's keen insight about the reproducible nature of representations. As early as the turn of the twentieth century with the release of the film, *The Birth of a Nation*, Black activists challenged how visual media depicted blackness (Rhodes 1993). What gets represented in visual cultural spaces is easily picked up and reproduced in and outside of the media space so it is strategic to target analyses of visual media because it touches the lives of many. Yet in spite of attempts to simultaneously critique and fashion re(-)presentations of Black masculinity that travel in the visual world, the prevailing image of Black masculinity generally fails to trouble stereotypical perspectives about what it means to be a Black male.

In a national and global social context where Blackness continues to signify all that is positioned as aberrant, abnormal and strange asking whether contemporary visual representations of Black masculinity matter remains a relevant, reasonable inquiry. This is especially important to education and schooling where social discourse fashions Black male bodies as occupying a space of presumed risky 'otherness'. The media and art worlds routinely fetishize Black men's bodies (Mercer 1996) in ways that alternately display him as an object of (hyper)sexual longing – some, *thing* (rather than *someone*) that is dangerous yet, desired. In desiring the Black man, one need not like him, or what he signifies. All that is required is illuminating him in ways that make him larger than life, imbued with a sense of abnormal wonderment. He stands out precisely because he does and must exist, outside of the boundaries of normality (Morrison 1992).

How visual culture represents the Black male speaks to the way dominant, socially mainstream discourses construct and imagine him. When these constructions travel globally they frame how one makes sense of what it means to be a Black male. These frames discursively and materially fasten a narrative of Black masculinity that informs social responses to him (e.g. policy; media representations) and opportunities made available to him in society and in school (Ferguson 2001). Through such a lens, the Black male is viewed as different, strange, dangerous and rendered devoid of humanity (Jackson 2006).

## Complicating black male re(-)presentations: looking at *The Wire*

In 2002, the US cable network, HBO, premiered its original series *The Wire*. The weekly, hour long drama presented a gripping portrayal of life in urban Baltimore.

The show, which continued for five seasons, centered on the Baltimore police department and its efforts to curb drug trafficking. Each of the show's five seasons targeted a different social institution that played a role in sustaining the socioeconomic problems facing urban Baltimore (e.g. drug trade, labor unions, political arena, schools, media). While the creators did not seek to produce more positive characterizations of Black males, the series did set out to move beyond the traditional, Hollywood bad–good binary (Golden 1994; hooks 1995) by presenting a more nuanced, thickly textured narrative of urban life than normally found in popular media (Simon 2009).

The academic world has embraced *The Wire*, positioning it as a visual media tool that adeptly represents the complexity of social life in an urban context. Since 2008, scholarly conferences devoted to the topic have taken place in both the US and in England, along with courses on the series cropping up at prestigious private and public universities across the US including Harvard, University of California at Berkeley, Duke, and Middlebury (Bennett 2010). These courses explore the pedagogic merit of using *The Wire* to examine how issues of poverty, class, bureaucracy and economic change impact the social fabric of life in urban America. This is not surprising given that one of the show's creators, David Simon, acknowledges that the sociological text, *When Work Disappears*, written by Harvard sociologist, William Julius Wilson, was the inspiration for season two of the show (Bennett 2010; Simon 2009). Education scholars and social scientists, including William Julius Wilson, who use and/or teach courses devoted to the series, argue that the show helps students make connections between complex theoretical knowledge in ways that related academic work struggles (Chaddha and Wilson 2010; Trier 2007).

**Reading the visual: methods and methodology**

This paper presents the findings from a textual analysis, done in the critical visual cultural tradition (Hall 1997; McKee 2001, 2003; Rose 2001) of representations of the Black masculine found in *The Wire*. We formed our interpretations from the interplay of *The Wire's* diverse visual and verbal 'texts' (Rose 2001). We explored how among the many different representations of Black maleness found in the series (e.g. drug dealer, street thief, white collar professional, blue collar worker, prisoner/ex-convict, drug user, neighborhood child/youth; city/political official, community activist and business owner) three specific characterizations play out. We focused on the street thief, a White collar professional and an 'at-risk' urban youth because we thought these personas could easily fall into the 'good–bad motif often found in media portrayals and in political concerns around Black community and responsibility. We wanted to illustrate how *The Wire* troubles this one-dimensional reading of the Black masculine and its implication on larger discourses about Black community.

There is no consensus on how to analyze and interpret visual text (McKee 2001, 2003; Hall 1997; Rose 2001). From the critical standpoint of visual culture studies, meanings are not fixed within a televisual text; instead, *The Wire*'s representations of Black masculinity are comprised of contradictory images, ideologies and meanings (Sturken and Cartwright 2001). In reading *The Wire*, we employed Hall's (1993) reworking of Barthes's (1977) distinction between connotative and denotative meanings. Denotation, which refers to the literal meaning encoded in a text, hypothetically presumes a direct correspondence between the text and a single, universally agreed upon meaning. Such an assumption of widespread definitive consensus over meaning is problematic, making denotation a theoretical category with little relationship to the ways individuals make sense of texts. According to Hall, connotation better reflects the discursive openness that characterizes the actual practices of diverse viewing audiences. Popular visual texts connote a range of meanings as viewers draw from their personal/cultural prior knowledge, experiences, memories, and feelings as points of congruence or disjuncture with the text's images. At the same time, meanings are not arbitrary. They exist within a sociopolitical hierarchy that places ideological limitations on potential commonsense, legitimate readings.

To decipher connotative encoded meanings of Black male representations in *The Wire*, we utilized two of Hall's (1993) analytic modes. First, by taking a 'dominant-hegemonic position' (Hall 1993, 515), we identified the preferred message and intended ideas. Then, by also adopting a 'negotiated position' (516), we dialogically engaged *The Wire*'s intended reading with alternative, oppositional meanings that emerge outside the logic of the dominant-hegemonic position. In doing so, we were able to highlight the tensions between competing discourses within the *The Wire* as they articulated with historically situated understandings of Black masculinity.

Noting that cultural studies theorists hold ambivalence to embracing a methodology that seeks to define reality and produce objective knowledge, McKee (2001, 2003) acknowledges this epistemic positioning has lead to a lack of definition of what constitutes textual analysis, and a discussion around the limits textual methodologies have on the construction of relevant knowledge. McKee (2001, 2003) describes the different instantiations of textual methodology and the epistemic conditions that frame engagement with this form of scholarship. Eschewing concerns that such an approach is too unwieldy (i.e. contextual) to lack scientific rigor, and hence, importance, McKee argues that textual analysis does not seek to find or measure the 'correct' interpretation of text analyzed, but rather, undertakes the process of signification, or meaning-producing activities that 'breaks down the various elements of a text and labels them' (McKee 2001, 148). The process of meaning-making associated with media textual analysis occurs with a wide expanse of media text, depends heavily on context in which an examined text is embedded (e.g., the entire piece of text examined; the genre of the text; the public context in which the text is circulated), and does not ensure that two researchers looking at the same text will walk away with the same analysis. Fundamentally, this instantiation of textual analysis seeks to understand how texts actually produce meaning when they are circulated in popular media.

In analyzing the representations of Black men portrayed in *The Wire*, we followed a loose working protocol for critically making meaning of visual text (Hall 1997; McKee 2001, 2003; Rose 2001). We watched all of the episodes of the show (n=60), focusing on how one might come to make meaning of the Black masculine in light of the show's characterization. Our interpretative process occurred in relation to multiple, related textual analyses we engaged in around the show. We state at the onset that our interest in doing a textual analysis of the show occurred because of our mutual excitement about the series. The first author watched the show on HBO from its inception in 2002 to its ending in 2008. The second author was interested in viewing the series after learning of the first author's perspective that the show presented a more sociologically complex picture of urban Black life than normally found on television dramas. This endorsement of the show led the second author to watch the entire series.

After the second author watched the series, we wanted to use the show in a sociocultural foundations course that the first author developed and that the second author served first as a graduate student volunteer, and later as a section instructor. We planned to incorporate clips of the show's fourth season (focus on urban schooling) to illustrate key theoretical issues we wanted to illuminate about sociocultural knowledge, schooling and teaching. Given the deeply contextual nature of the show, we realized that students would have to watch more than just a few clips from season four in order to make sense of the ideas we hoped the show would illuminate. We individually watched the entire series again, noting how key theoretical constructs from the course (e.g. meritocracy; structural, historical, institutional factors that frame social opportunity and mobility structures) operated in the show and set up the season four focus on urban schooling. We kept descriptive notes on the characters' movement across the seasons, paying particular attention to denoted and connoted messages about characters' images and their ability or inability to advance socially in society. One of the emerging (but not surprising) themes that emerged was how Black male characters represented in the show. We often discussed how the show presented Black males as collectively embodying complicated and complex personas. Recognizing the challenges Black males encounter in school (and societal) settings, we decided to analyze representations of Black masculinity found in the show. While we were still interested in using the show to illustrate how key issues of meritocracy and opportunity operate structurally in society – a key element of the show, according to its creator David Simon (Simon 2009) – we also wanted to see if and how the show troubled normalized, stereotypical discourses about the Black male often expressed by students in our classes. We thought this was an important focus area given the likelihood that our students would one day have the responsibility for teaching Black males in their K-12 classrooms.

To help us make sense of the representations of Black masculinity we observed in the show we drew from longstanding stereotypical tropes (Jackson 2006; Reddick 1944) and counter-tropes used to characterize Black people (Ladson Billings 2005; Levin 1977; Roberts 1990). When discussing how the show characterized Black males, we noticed how these images aligned both with stereotypical, racist tropes of Black masculinity and those counter-tropes located in a communal-based Black folkloric tradition. What distinguishes these two types of representations is their location – i.e. the former emerged in the context of a dominant, racist White imaginary and the latter, out of artistic expressions found in the Black American community – and the purposes for which each of these existed.

Since as far back as the mid-twentieth century, scholars have identified a set of common stereotypical, racist tropes used to depict Black Americans in media (Jackson 2006; Reddick 1944). Jackson (2006) acknowledges the deeply entrenched nature of these tropes, citing 19 outlined by Lawrence Reddick in 1944. In this paper, we focus on six of these historic tropes: the devoted servant, the sexual superman, the petty thief, the unhappy non-white, the social delinquent and the mental inferior. The *devoted servant* represents the hard-working Black person who is devoted and loyal to serving White people and their interests, while posing no threat to, nor seeking to challenge, the existing status quo. This stereotype is akin to the notion of a 'sell-out' or an 'Uncle Tom'. The *sexual superman* is a Black man who is depicted as a sexual object, while the *petty thief* engages in small time criminal activity. The *unhappy non-White* is the Black person who is perpetually unhappy, but remains powerless to alter her/his condition. The *social delinquent* engages in socially unacceptable behavior, including criminal activity. She/he is seen as deviant and outside of social respectability. Finally, the *mental inferior* is positioned as ignorant and intellectually deficient in relation to Whites. What makes the Black male characters complicated in *The Wire*, however, is the way they simultaneously embody both these traditional stereotypes, as well as counter-tropes found in the Black American folkloric tradition (Ladson Billings 2005; Roberts 1990).

Counter-tropes emerged and existed alongside stereotypical representations of Black Americans across the twentieth century. We argue that counter-tropes served as a counter-narrative (to dominant, White and generally racist imaginings) and a symbol of freedom from oppressive and repressive social conditions. We noted two specific counter-tropes from the Black American folkloric tradition that operated alongside the dominant, stereotypical representations found in the characters we analyzed in *The Wire*, including: The trickster and the bad man. The trickster comes out of the tradition of African trickster tales in which a seemingly safe and sometimes weak animal dupes his more powerful opponent through stealth, cleverness and cunning. The bad man invokes the strong hero who is an outlaw. This character is outwardly strong and feared by both his friends and adversaries. In the following section we illustrate how several key Black male characters in *The Wire* draw from both stereotypical and counter-narrative tropes to help fashion a richly complicated, yet in the end, myopic representation of the Black man and his place in the larger Black community.

## *Daniels, the socially mobile trickster*

A key figure featured in all five seasons of *The Wire* is the Lieutenant Cedric Daniels, a police officer with a secretive and imperfect past within the police department. He is chosen by the Deputy Commissioner Burrell, a high ranking Black man second only to the Commissioner of Police, to lead an investigation into the operations of drug kingpin Avon Barksdale. Burrell is begrudgingly carrying out the orders that have been issued him at the behest of a White judge who has political motives for pushing the case forward. Described by his White commanding officer Major Rawls as a case about 'project nigger' murders that 'don't mean shit to anybody' (Season 1, Episode 1), the investigation is assigned to Daniels specifically because he is perceived by his superiors to be a docile and complaisant company man who will do as they ask without question.

In the context of the show, Daniels' characterization as the 'devoted servant,' a common historical stereotype of Blacks found in Hollywood films (Reddick 1944), is made more complicated by the multiracial make-up of the police department and its members' shared loyalties to the chain of command. Following suit, Daniels echoes the wishes of his superiors in his first meeting with his new team of detectives. Without knowing the full extent of the murder case, Daniels makes clear, 'This case is not going to sprawl' into something more than one or two low-profile arrests (Season 1, Episode 1). He is positioned as the non-threatening lackey, as he relays directives to a rogue detective assigned to him: 'Chain of command, detective. That's how we do things down on this end of the hall' (Season 1, Episode 1).

Although Daniels has sworn to protect and serve the people of his hometown of Baltimore, his personal career ambitions outweigh any solidarity he might have toward the predominantly Black residents of Baltimore's impoverished urban core who have long been terrorized and exploited by drug traffickers and at times the police. This, too, is consistent with popular film representations of servile Blacks contentedly carrying out the wishes of Whites. When one of the White detectives under Daniels' command, who happens to be related to a police major, assaults a Black teenage boy in a housing project, an infuriated Daniels dutifully coaches the detective on the story he should tell the police internal investigation bureau about what happened in order to evade punishment: 'Go practice. You fuck the bullshit up when you talk to internal, I can't fix it. You're on your own' (Season 1, Episode 2).

On the other hand, Daniels can be read as a trickster in the African American tradition, much like 'John the slave driver' (Roberts 1990). This more complex perspective of Daniels as a mid-level manager within the police force emerges as the series progresses. He strategically goes along with the chain of command while surreptitiously advancing a different agenda. By all appearances, Daniels' servile guise – at home and at work – stands him in good stead. As he increases his rank and power within the police department, he also uses his position within the criminal justice system to indirectly protect and improve the Black community by building concrete cases against some of the corrosive criminal elements ravaging Baltimore.

Daniels experiences moments of internal conflict, what Lester, a seasoned Black detective, recognizes as 'wrestling with the angels' (Season 1, Episode 9). After the prior police brutality incident perpetrated against a Black youth by one of his officers, a tormented Daniels talks about his options with his Black wife, Marla. She assesses Daniels' predicament, saying 'You should have hung them.' Daniels responds, 'I hang them, I hang myself. I'm the man in charge, remember? Besides you don't give your people up to IID. You don't do that.' By 'your people' Daniels is referring to his fellow police officers. Marla challenges him with, 'Even if they put a 14-year-old kid into critical care?' Daniels looks at her quietly. She changes focus from the injured boy's civil rights and well-being to the larger picture of Daniels' career:

> The department puts you in a case that it doesn't want. You're given people that are useless or untrustworthy. [...] You push too hard and then the shit hits the fan, you'll be blamed for it. [...] If you don't push hard enough and there are no arrests, you'll be blamed for that, too. [...] The game is rigged. But you cannot lose if you do not play. (Season 1, Episode 2)

Far from simply following orders, we see here that Daniels must maneuver carefully. Lester highlights the moral dilemma that defines Daniels' career: 'You have to ask yourself how you want to live your day-to-day' (Season 2, Episode 7). In true trickster fashion, Daniels negotiates his precarious position in the fraternal police order while doing as much as he can to help those under his leadership and the broader community. Only the trickster is successful in achieving these frequently contradictory goals while continuing to prove himself (or herself) to be indispensable to the system.

Daniels' wife Marla, and to some degree Daniels himself, believes that rising through the ranks within the department will help them grasp the American dream of success through individual upward mobility. Although promotions bring him certain liberties, Daniels also fits the archetypal 'unhappy non-white' (Reddick 1944) who lacks fulfillment in his role at work. In Daniels' case, he is also unhappy in his marriage to Marla. The interactions between the two are void of romantic passion, making them appear more like business partners than lovers. With short-cropped hair and few smiles, Marla is portrayed as a strong and dignified but also controlling Black woman. In scenes with her, Daniels carries himself stoically. His impassive manner with Marla stands as an explanation for the breakdown of his marriage and sets the stage for a sympathetic viewing of his subsequent interactions with his mistress, Rhonda.

Daniels' affair with Rhonda, a White district attorney he works with, commences just as he lands a promotion and is assigned to lead a major crimes unit. He tells Rhonda, that, although he respects and cares about Marla, he was not able to fully be a man when he was in a relationship with her:

She lived through me for a lot of years. Telling herself I was tracked for deputy commissioner at worst and past the police department, who knows ... I guess she wanted more out of me. And after a lot of years and a lot of plans, it turns out I have a better head for police work than I do for climbing the ladder. She hung in there hoping my career would turn into some kind of a big deal, and I probably let her believe it just to keep peace. (Episode 6, Season 3)

As Daniels achieves intimacy with Rhonda, she comes to signify his growing happiness and manhood beyond that which was attainable as Marla's husband and a traditional family man.

*The Wire* plays off white fears of Black masculinity in its overlapping depictions of Daniels' clandestine involvement with Rhonda and his office politics in the police department. He is characterized by higher ranking white (and sometimes Black) police officers as cunning and not to be trusted. The white male officers, in particular, hold the view that Daniels is merely an affirmative action hire politically necessary for appeasing Baltimore's Black 'natives.' Daniels seems to be aware of how this group of influential lawmen view him when he explains to Rhonda that, for his career and Marla's, 'right now I'm more help showing up at some chicken dinner in my wedding ring and dress blues than being the not-yet-divorced husband with the White woman on his arm' (Season 3, Episode 6). From the perspective of the White men and by his own admission, Daniels embodies the threat posed to White men by Black masculinity.

White fear of, and fascination with, Black male sexuality is visually reinforced for the audience when Daniels' body is routinely covered in little more than boxer shorts, usually in scenes with Rhonda. Their professional work dynamic is also sexualized, leaving spectators with a heightened awareness of his adultery. In one instance, during a conversation regarding a criminal case, Rhonda flirtatiously alludes to Daniels' genitals when she remarks, 'Nice suit by the way. [...] I see you dress left' (Season 3, Episode 4). The camerawork further eroticizes the Black male image by gratuitously sweeping across Daniels' entire nude body during sexual intercourse between him and Rhonda. Framed from immediately overhead, the gaze displays Daniels' dark, bare form pulsating on top of Rhonda and calls special attention to his tightening buttocks as he climaxes. Only small portions of Rhonda's face are visible. Mostly we see her pale thighs splayed on either side of his muscular posterior. By contrast, Daniels is never shown in bed with Marla, who is depicted as asexual. Dressing her in clothes that fully cover from her neck to her ankles helps to position Marla as an overbearing, antiseptic killjoy. The re-emergence of this 'sexual superman' (Reddick 1944) stereotype of the Black male can be traced historically to White fear and aggression toward Black manhood openly avowed during reconstruction (Roberts 1990) through the era of Jim Crow. The premise of such trepidation is that Black males with too much freedom will overstep racial boundaries of behavior by defiling White women.

In its portrayal of Daniels, an exemplary Black man according to dominant notions of economic security and career-based achievements, he is free to successfully pursue his own career path only outside the context of the Black family. With Marla, Daniels is left impotent at home and in the workplace. He is unable to sustain an intimate connection with his wife, a Black woman who has pushed him out of their marital bed with her demands. Marla, in the end, is blamed for demanding too much and, consequently, emasculating Daniels. When Marla makes a move to reconstitute their marriage, Daniels deflects her affections, and in doing so he is cut off metonymically from the Black community. His relationship with Rhonda intensifies, and they appear in public restaurants together and behaving affectionately among their colleagues. The show justifies Daniels' symbolic break from the Black community, as one White detective remarks upon seeing him in Rhonda's arms, 'They make a nice couple anyway' (Season 4, Episode 11).

## *Omar, the bad man*

Friend to neither the law nor the drug trade, Omar Little is the central villain in *The Wire*. Omar robs drug dealers for a living and, despite several bounties placed on his head, manages to defy capture for most of the show's five seasons. Omar is characterized as an amplified version of the 'petty thief' trope (Reddick 1944) in his neighborhood of west Baltimore. A tripartite menace with a large gun, he is a constant threat to the livelihood of drug dealers, evades the legal system, and defies the heteronormative family culture that structures this Black community. Notwithstanding his flagrant criminality, Omar acts in accordance with his own interests while adhering to a self-determined code of ethics that permits him to target drug dealers and bars him from injuring innocent 'taxpayers' who are not in the drug game.

Omar is visually marked by a scar running down the center of his face. He lurks in the shadowy, hidden places among the row houses and alleyways of west Baltimore. Though rarely seen in public, he always seems to know the goings on in the neighborhood. Over successive episodes, this mystical, omniscient quality of the 'bad man' of African American folklore (Roberts 1990) is layered with a keen intellect and stealth. The show uses this character to work against the assumptions found in negative media portrayals of Blacks as 'mentally inferior' (Reddick 1944). Omar is a highly effective robber due to his patient surveillance techniques, strategic analyses, and calculated risk-taking rather than wild hunches, luck or supernatural intervention. He identifies himself as 'just a nigga with a plan – that's all' (Season 1, Episode 5). There are a number of scenes that juxtapose Omar's mental acuity with commonsense understandings of Black criminality, as when he is frequently engrossed in reading poetry and other texts during stakeouts and a short stint in prison, recalls details from Greek mythology for the benefit of a police officer working a crossword puzzle, and outwits and delegitimizes a 'shark' attorney who tries to discredit his testimony by vilifying him in a court of law.

Omar is a formidable sight as he makes grand entrances, often whistling a nursery rhyme as he hunts down drug dealers. Brazenly walking the streets and alleys dressed in a cape-like trench coat with an enormous shotgun hanging across his chest, Omar also dons costumes and disguises to set traps and gain entry to heavily guarded drug houses. He intimidates young drug runners and robs corner boys and drug dealers of their cash and highly lucrative drug stashes. A force unto himself, he is a legendary figure in the neighborhood and throughout the underground Baltimore drug trade. Children of all ages run down the street when they spot Omar coming and yell his name in awe but also as a warning to others. Omar's enemies, many of them vicious and unscrupulous, talk about him as invincible and needing to 'be got,' but they also work hard to avoid encounters with him.

Omar negotiates a space between evil and good by exacting punishment on the drug dealers within his own Black community in a manner reminiscent of the Black folk hero bad man, Stackolee, and Robin Hood from European popular culture. He does not, however, share his spoils with the poor and downtrodden in his community like Robin Hood. Instead, Omar is described by one character as 'feeding off the violence and the despair of the drug trade … stealing from those who are themselves stealing the lifeblood from our city ... [and] a parasite who leaches off the culture of drugs' (Season 2, Episode 7). There is arguably a ripple effect from the violence Omar perpetrates. Bunk, a Black detective from the same neighborhood as Omar, takes him to task for his role in several murders and the harm he brings to the community:

> As rough as that neighborhood could be, we had us a community. Nobody – no victim – who didn't matter. And now all we got is bodies and predatory motherfuckers like you! And out where that girl fell, I saw kids acting like Omar. Calling you by name, glorifying your ass! Makes me sick, motherfucker, how far we done fell! (Season 3, Episode 6)

Even with the ensuing escalation of violence by children, many of whom exalt Omar, this 'bad man' seems to position himself as serving a key function in keeping the heavy-handed henchmen and corner boys from proliferating unabated in a city with little political will to address deeply entrenched poverty and corruption.

*The Wire's* critical success trades on the mainstream currency of Omar's violent masculinity while it troubles the familiar villain role by highlighting his gay identity. This added twist is significant in terms of its inscription on the Black male body. Like Daniels, Omar's sexualized body is put on display in several scenes in which he romps and lounges in the bedroom with 'his boy.' At one point, he walks across the bedroom without any clothes, as the viewer is invited to watch every turn of his body. Moments later he emerges wearing an uncharacteristically flamboyant turquoise satin robe and matching pajama bottoms.

Maligned by his enemies as a 'cocksucker' and a 'faggot,' Omar's sexuality represents a challenge to hegemonic Black masculinity, particularly in relation to larger social discourses of Black community and citizenship (Russell 2008). Omar has earned a reputation for unapologetic violence, but this does not diminish the stigma of being perceived as sexually deviant in relation to Black maleness as defined through a normative, heterosexual family structure. The feeling of violation that comes with being robbed at gunpoint is exacerbated among Omar's victims precisely because he falls outside of the limits of the normalized Black manhood.

The show takes care in showing that Omar grew up in the neighborhood he now victimizes and even attended the local school. He is racially and culturally connected to the Black community. Nonetheless, as a sexual outsider, he is severed from full participation. Omar is perceived as less than human and someone to be feared. This sentiment is epitomized in the first season when Omar's partner is tortured and his body mutilated and left out as a public spectacle in retaliation for the theft of a drug dealer's stash of drugs and money. More than a revenge killing, the disfigurement of the young man is a sadistic disciplining in response to Omar's sexual transgressions.

### Namond – *not tricky enough, not bad enough*

*The Wire's* fourth season spotlights the metamorphoses of four Black male teens as they complete their final year at Tilghman Middle School, a microcosm of Baltimore's failed school system and the nation's counterproductive testing-oriented school reforms. Namond Bryce, one of the boys featured, lives at home with his Black mother, where, because of their connection to high ranking members of the drug trade, he enjoys more material comforts than most other neighborhood kids. He sports Timberland boots, the latest NBA and NFL jerseys, and conspicuously large earrings and other 'bling' while his friends get by with donated clothes and food stamps. All his life Namond has been told he will proudly follow in his father's footsteps as a drug 'soldier.' Now, as Namond comes of age, the stakes of the drug game rapidly escalate, and his street credentials are tested.

The show introduces Namond on the front stoop of a run-down city building. Cars drive by slowly and Namond rests several yards from the corner where his boss, Bodie, sells off a package of dope. Namond's ambivalence toward his future as a 'soldier' is illustrated when his friends Michael and Randy find him reclining against the step deeply engrossed in a magazine instead of what is happening on the street:

| | |
|---|---|
| Michael: | This corner is dead man. You still workin'? |
| Randy: | Yeah, cause we gonna go under the row and catch some fresh birds. |
| Namond: | I don't know. Let me see if I can bounce. Hold up. [He stands up and jogs over to Bodie] Hey, B. |
| Bodie: | Sup? |
| Namond: | I want to know I can leave early 'cause me and the fellas want to go down to [the store] for some back-to-school stuff. |
| Bodie: | What you need back-to-school stuff for? Yo' ass stay suspended. |
| Namond: | Come on, stop playin', B. |
| Bodie: | If it wasn't for social promotion, yo' ass would still be in pre-k, motherfucka. Probably daycare out this bitch. [Sigh] Fuck it. [Looks at his right-hand man] Ay, yo man. Pay this late-to-work, early-to-play nigga out for five hours, yo. [Turns back to Namond who is smiling.] Yo, you owe me extra time tomorrow, though. [Namond's facial expression quickly goes from joy to disappointment.] (Season 4, Episode 1) |

After Namond takes the payment, he walks back toward his friends. Bodie continues to complain, saying, 'Young'uns don't got a scrap of work ethic nowaday, man. If it wasn't for his pops, I wouldn't even bother' (Season 4, Episode 1). This encounter in which Namond thinks he can outfox Bodie foreshadows future scenes in which he turns out not to be tricky enough.

Namond is positioned as the stereotypical 'social delinquent' (Reddick 1944) who schemes in various ways. Focused on gaining the admiration of his three friends, Randy, Michael and Dukie, with his nice clothes and his long hair pulled back into a ponytail, Namond wears the mask of a trickster. He talks about 'standin' tall' like a man, that is, like a drug 'soldier,' and he mirrors this image of manhood by bullying and humiliating his meek friend, Dukie, for the benefit of onlookers.

Unlike other kids, Namond is able to take advantage of the legacy of his father Wee-bey, a notorious drug soldier currently serving time in prison. In school and on the corner, Namond enjoys the high profile that comes with being Wee-bey's son. He uses his wits, sharp tongue, and his father's reputation to pass as 'hard' until he is pushed to the point of violence. In situations where the rules of the corner demand that Namond put physical force behind his words, he avoids and sometimes flees from confrontation. For a while, he is able to impress others with his 'player' performance and delude himself with the quick money he makes 'slingin'' dope on the corners. As he and his three friends mature over the school year, things change for them. Street life is increasingly hostile and unforgiving with the rise of a new drug lord. In this setting, Namond finds that looking like a drug soldier is not enough to maintain credibility, and his verbosity is no longer an asset, as it exposes the 'real' Namond.

Underlying the depiction of Namond is a belief that children are innocent and pure until they face a critical moment when they could either be corrupted or saved from the brink of evil. Namond experiences a crisis in which his future is uncertain. His pivotal juncture is analogous to storylines of White male popular culture heroes, including Peter Parker in *Spiderman*, Luke Skywalker in *Star Wars*, and the more recent creation Harry Potter, in the series by the same name, who come to a fork in the road and must decide whether to follow the path of good or evil. Unlike his three friends whose lives stand in contrast to his good fortune, Namond is positioned as the lucky one in the group who is able to escape from his community.

Freedom from poverty and the drug game into which Namond was born comes only after he declares he is not like his father and disavows his mother, who has pushed Namond onto the corner. 'I can't go home,' Namond cries. 'She [his mother] expect me to be my father, but I ain't him. I mean the way he is and shit. It ain't in me' (Season 4, Episode 12). As a broken young man, Namond is depicted as powerless before he is delivered from his family and community by Bunny Colvin, a retired Black policeman turned teacher. Bunny negotiates guardianship with Namond's father. Namond not only leaves his mother's home, but he severs all ties to his former neighborhood and family.

Finally we see Namond thriving in a middle class home where his loquaciousness, which had been a liability in school and on the streets, now enables him to flourish on the debate team of his new school. In a closing scene, Namond is quietly writing on the front porch one morning when Doughnut, a friend from the old neighborhood, drives up in a stolen car. They silently nod to each other from a cautious distance, and Namond smiles to himself. This image of Namond and his friend suggests that Black males are perpetually at risk of a life of poverty, drugs, addiction, murder, theft, and victimhood, and thus they must literally be cut off and rescued from their families and communities if they are to become successful Black men. The message is that there is no place in the urban community for Namond to thrive. Fundamentally, outside of a complete and irreversible disconnection from his community, no hope for success exists for this (or any other promising) Black male youth.

## Discussion of findings and implications

*The Wire* presents a complicated Black masculinity that defies easy categorization: i.e. moral/amoral, intelligent/streetwise, wise/foolish, successful/unsuccessful. Simultaneously, Black manhood is situated in the context of larger political and socioeconomic factors, rather than only psychological influences that frame how Black males move in and across social worlds. Recognizing longstanding concerns around re(-) presentation in Black political discourse, how, then, does one make sense of the Black masculine represented in *The Wire*? It is clear from the treatment of the three characters presented previously that the dominant-hegemonic reading of the show is that the Black male can and does perform in different ways. Black males do not fall into a one-dimensional, stereotypical image of Black maleness. However, when negotiating connoted meanings, one recognizes how traditional tropes continue to operate in the show's characterizations. Tropes of fear/subservience, sexual prowess, social deviancy and 'at-riskness' play out in the three males examined in this paper. These stereotypes, however, exist alongside counter-tropes that make more complex the messages embodied in the traditionally racialized characterizations identified previously. While the outward, surface level image of the Black males aligned with typical media stereotypes about Black masculinity, underneath this veneer one finds complicated personas that subvert traditional readings and understandings about the Black man. Janus-faced, these Black males, positioned alternately as sexual studs, fearful and subservient to Whites, and as social deviants/miscreants simultaneously operate as strategic, intelligent tricksters that seek individual freedom and humanity by transcending the narrow social boxes in which they seemingly sit.

Though *The Wire* presents a complex set of images of the Black male that renders him more realistic to life – human, thoughtfully complicated, struggling against social forces that seek to confine and define his being – these images simultaneously situate him as an 'other' in that he fundamentally operates outside the confines of the Black community. Whether characterized as unable to connect with and socially achieve in partnership with a Black woman, or as an abnormal, sexual deviant, or finally, as a youth that can only find success when taken out of his familial and community context, blackness is stripped of its historical-political context and collective responsibility. In this way the community that literally and metaphorically surrounds, nurtures and sustains the Black male withers away, either by necessity (i.e. Daniels needs to move up the corporate ladder and Namond into a new social environment, both away from their respective emasculating Black wife/Black mother) or by default (i.e. the Black neighborhood's fear and partial 'othering' of Omar because he is gay[5]). These re(-)presentations, then, fall short of fashioning a Black male persona that is human, complex *and* politically aware of/concerned with his place in the larger Black community. Instead, *The Wire's* Black male exists precariously in and between two worlds that he alternately desires and repels, supports yet neglects.

We argue that while *The Wire* retreats from a simplistic characterization of urban life and Blackness that is one-dimensional and traditionally stereotypic, the show successfully commingles familiar stereotypes and counter-tropes of Black urban life in a photographic 'reality code' (McCarthy 1998, 95) common to television news and entertainment (e.g. *Cops*; *The Squad: Prison Police*; and *Lockup*). This commingling further naturalizes what appears to be a more 'authentic rendering' of the Black male than the one encountered in traditional, one-dimensional stereotypical visual representations. Yet it is this complex imagining of the Black masculine and his place in the larger Black community that presents a special challenge to teacher educators seeking to use *The Wire* to help students rethink traditional constructions of the urban Black male. Providing future teachers with the sociocultural knowledge and experiences needed to recognize, cultivate and mine out the sociocultural consciousness, beauty, intellectual capability and resources of Black students – particularly males – and the families and community they come from is of singular importance to working effectively with African American students (Gay 2000; Howard 2001; Ladson Billings 2009). Armed without this sociocultural knowledge and orientation to teaching, a teacher might easily view Black males, their families and larger community as deficient, deprived and lacking of cultural resources (Brown 2010). This perspective at best, positions the Black male student as troubled, in need of rescue by a benevolent other (outside of his community), or at worst, demonizes him as incapable of learning or succeeding altogether. In either instance, the Black male remains perpetually 'at-risk' – a threat to the larger dominant White society and to his own fragile, deficient Black community. Instead of recognizing those places where beauty, sociculutral consciousness and resiliency reside in the Black urban community – components vital to a culturally relevant/responsive approach to teaching for African American students – viewers of *The Wire* encounter an urban Black community that is disconnected, doomed, marginalized and deprived.

Thus, we offer that when using *The Wire* (or any other visual media) an instructor must acknowledge not only the content material identified as relevant for the specific inquiry, but also the related content and associations, often referred to as hidden curriculum (Apple 2004) that viewers may inadvertently pick up as well. We want to make clear that we do not dismiss the pedagogical value of using *The Wire*. The show is complicated, complex and theoretically rich and as such, offers a visual pallet that is ripe for discussion, analysis and critique (Bennett 2010; Chaddha and Wilson 2010; Trier 2007). We do, however, move from the position that consumption of this particular visual (or any) medium must be thoughtfully and critically orchestrated. Instructors must take care not to present the work in decontextualized ways, an approach that is often necessary when showing film media clips because of time constraints. Instructors must also identify the kinds of background sociocultural knowledge students need in order to make sense of the images shown. Engaging in this kind of intentional pedagogy is necessary in all teaching situations, but takes on added impetus in the context of trying to teach complex ideas from a critical multicultural teacher education perspective (Brown and Kraehe 2010). Without doing so, students viewing this work may draw from partial, inaccurate and deficit-oriented sociocultural knowledge that circulates within dominant social discourse and televisual simulations that critical multicultural teacher education seeks to challenge.

## Notes

1. In this paper we use the terms Black and African American interchangeably.
2. We recognize the masculinist project of conflating discourses of race uplift and the Black community with the masculine. This conflation bespeaks historic and contemporary discourse (both lay and scholarly) that assumes the sociopolitical and economic uplift of the Black community occurs in relation to the sociopolitical and economic advancement of Black males (e.g. see Carby 2000; Gaines 1993; Ross 2004; Shin and Judson 1998; Summers 2004). Implicit in this discourse is the assumption that Black men serve as the defacto leaders and face of the Black race.
3. Scholars have troubled the notion of a unified, linear 'Black community' by illustrating the historically contingent, discursive, and contentious practices that shape the contours of Black political thought (Dawson 2001; Glaude 2000; Brown 2009). This, however, does not negate the shared (albeit contested) communally-shared symbolic and material relationship that is recognized as the Black community by African Americans and those of African descent in the US.
4. Since the middle ages Western European thought has linked together discourses of deficiency and Blackness and Black people. While drawing from different epistemic and ontological discursive rules, these perspectives fundamentally positioned Black people as innately and later culturally deprived and inferior to those of Western European descent (Jordan 1974; Wynter 2005)
5. In an interview with National Public Radio, Michael K. Williams, the actor who played Omar in *The Wire* discusses the tensions he experienced when trying to sensitively play a gay Black male character. On playing Omar, Williams notes the care he took in trying to present a gay Black male character that was not 'over the top' with his sexuality. He hints at the longstanding contentious relationship between homosexuality and the Black community, when stating that he wanted 'the character to be taken seriously by his peers and his [Black] community.' At the same time, he did not want to offend the gay community either. Interestingly, Williams later points out that it was not uncommon for fans to approach him and express their love for Omar's 'bad man' persona, while simultaneously disparaging and distancing themselves from Omar's sexuality (National Public Radio, personal interview, January 22, 2008).

## References

Apple, M.W. 2004. *Ideology and curriculum*, 3rd ed. New York: Routledge.

Banks, J.A. 2004. Multicultural education: Historical development, dimensions, and practice. In *Handbook of research in multicultural education*, 2nd ed., ed. J A. Banks and C.A. McGee, 50–65. San Francisco: Jossey-Bass.

Barthes, R. 1977. *Image, music, text*. New York: Hill & Wang.

Bennett, D. 2010. This will be on the midterm. You feel me? Why so many colleges are teaching *The Wire*. http:// www.slate.com/id/2245788/ (accessed December 7, 2010).

*Birth of a nation*. Directed by D.W. Griffith, USA. David W. Griffith Corp., 1915.

Brown, A.L. 2009. 'O brotha where art thou?' Examining the ideological discourses of African American male teachers working with African American male students. *Race Ethnicity & Education* 12, no. 4: 473–93.

Brown, A.L. In press. 'Same old stories': Examining historical and educational discourses about black males, 1930s to the present. *Teachers College Record* 113, no. 9.

Brown, K.D. 2010. Is this what we want them to say? Examining the tensions in what pre-service teachers say about risk and academic achievement. *Teaching and Teacher Education* 26, no. 4: 1077–87.

Brown, K.D., and A. Kraehe. 2010. The complexities of teaching the complex: Examining how future educators construct understandings of sociocultural knowledge and schooling. *Educational Studies* 46, no. 1: 91–115.

Carby, H.V. 2000. *Race men*. Cambridge, MA: Harvard University Press.

Cooper, A.J. 1930. On education. In *The voice of Anna Julia Cooper*, ed. C. Lemert and E. Bahn, 248–58. New York: Rowman & Littlefield.

Chaddha, A., and W.J. Wilson. 2010. Why we're teaching 'The Wire' at Harvard. Washington Post. http://www.washingtonpost.com/wp-dyn/content/article/2010/09/10/AR201009 1002676.html?referrer=emailarticle (accessed September 17, 2010).

Du Bois, W.E.B. 1903 [1994]. *The souls of black folk*. New York: Dover.

Davis, J.E. 2003. Early schooling and academic achievement of African American males. *Urban Education* 38, no. 5: 515–37.

Dawson, M.C. 2001. *Black visions: The roots of contemporary African-American political ideologies*. Chicago: University of Chicago.

Ferguson, A.A. 2001. *Bad boys: Public schools in the making of black masculinity*. Ann Arbor: University of Michigan.

Fultz, M., and A.L. Brown. 2008. Historical perspectives on African American males as subjects of education policy. *American Behavioral Science* 51, no. 7: 854–71.

Gaines, K. 1993. Assimilationist minstrelsy as racial uplift ideology: James D. Corrothers's literary quest for black leadership. *American Quarterly* 45, no. 3: 341–69.

Gates, H.L. 1988. The trope of a new Negro and the reconstruction of the image of the black. *Representations* 24: 129–55.

Gay, G. 2000. *Culturally responsive teaching: Theory, research and practice*. New York: Teachers College Press.

Glaude, E. 2000. *Exodus!: Religion, race, and nation in early nineteenth-century black America*. Chicago: University of Chicago.

Golden, T. 1994. My brother. In *Black male: Representations of masculinity in contemporary American Art*, ed. T. Golden, 19–43. New York: Whitney Museum of American Art/ Harry N. Abrams, Inc.

Hall, S. 1993. Encoding, decoding. In *The cultural studies reader*, ed. S. During, 508–17. London; New York: Routledge.

Hall, S. 1997. Introduction. In *Representation: Cultural representations and signifying practices*, ed. S. Hall, 1–11. London and Thousand Oaks: Sage Publications.

hooks, b. 1995. *Art on my mind: Visual politics*. New York: The New Press.

Howard, T. 2001. Telling their side of the story: African American students' perceptions of culturally relevant teaching. *Urban Review* 33, no. 2: 131–49.

Jackson, R.L. 2006. *Scripting the black masculine body: Identity, discourse, and racial politics in popular media*. Albany: State University of New York.

Jordan, W. 1974. *The white man's burden: Historical origins of racism in the U.S.* New York: Oxford.

Ladson-Billings, G. 2005. *Beyond the big house: African American educators on teacher education*. New York: Teachers College Record.

Ladson Billings, G. 2009. *The dreamkeepers: Successful teachers of African American children*, 2nd ed. San Francisco: Jossey-Bass.

Levin, L.W. 1977. *Black culture and black consciousness: Afro-American folk thought from slavery to freedom.* Oxford: Oxford University Press.
Marable, M., and L. Mullings. ed. 2000. *Let nobody turn us around: Voices of resistance, reform and renewal.* Lanham, MD: Rowman & Littlefield.
McCarthy, C. 1998. *The uses of culture: Education and the limits of ethnic affiliation.* New York: Routledge.
McKee, A. 2001. A beginner's guide to textual analysis. *Metro Magazine* 127/128: 138–49.
McKee, A. 2003. *Textual analysis: A beginner's guide.* London: Sage.
Mercer, K. 1996. Just looking for trouble: Robert Mapplethorpe and fantasies of race. In *Black British cultural studies: A reader*, ed. H.A. Baker, Jr., M. Diawara, R.H. Lindeborg, 278–92. Chicago: The University of Chicago.
Mitchell, W.J.T. 2002. Showing seeing: A critique of visual culture. *Journal of Visual Culture* 1, no. 2: 165–81.
Morrison, T. 1992. *Playing in the dark: Whiteness and the literary imagination.* New York: Vintage.
National Public Radio. Personal interview, January 22, 2008. Michael K. Williams: He's only playing tough. http://www.npr.org/templates/story/story.php?storyId=18299087&sc=emaf (accessed September 17, 2010).
Noguera, P. 2003. The trouble with Black boys: The role and influence of environmental and cultural factors on the academic performance of African American males. *Urban Education* 38, no. 4: 431–59.
Pauly, N. 2003. Interpreting visual culture as cultural narratives in teacher education. *Studies in Art Education* 44, no. 3: 264–84.
Perry, T., C. Steele, and A. Hilliard. 2004. *Young, gifted and black: Promoting high achievement among African American students.* Boston: Beacon.
Polite, V., and J.E. Davis. 1999. *African American males in school and society: Policy and practice for effective education.* New York: Teachers College Press.
Reddick, L.D. 1944. Educational programs for the improvement of race relations: Motion pictures radio, the press, and libraries. *The Journal of Negro Education* 13, no. 3: 367–89.
Rhodes, J. 1993. The visibility of race and media history. *Critical Studies in Mass Communication* 10, no. 2: 184–91.
Roberts, J.W. 1990. *From trickster to badman: The black folk hero in slavery and freedom.* Philadelphia: University of Pennsylvania Press.
Rose, G. 2001. *Visual methodologies.* Thousand Oaks: Sage Publications.
Ross, M.B. 2004. *Manning the race: Reforming black men in the Jim Crow era.* New York: New York University Press.
Russell, T. 2008. The color of discipline: Civil rights and black sexuality. *American Quarterly* 60, no. 1: 101–28.
Shin, A., and B. Judson. 1998. Beneath the black aesthetic: James Baldwin's primer of black American masculinity. *African American Review* 32, no. 2: 247–61.
Simon, D. 2009. Transcript: David Simon on why he created *The Wire*. http://entertainment.timesonline.co.uk/tol/arts_and_entertainment/books/article6872920.ece (accessed December 14, 2009).
Sturken, M., and L. Cartwright. 2001. *Practices of looking: An introduction to visual culture.* New York: Oxford University Press.
Summers, M. 2004. *Manliness and its discontents: The black middle class and the transformation of black masculinity, 1900–1930.* Chapel Hill: University of North Carolina.
Tisdell, E., and P. Thompson. 2007. 'Seeing from a different angle': The role of pop culture in teaching for diversity and critical media literacy in adult education. *International Journal of Lifelong Education* 26, no. 6: 651–73.
Trier, J. 2007. Teaching theory through popular culture text. *Teaching Education* 18, no. 2: 151–65.
Washington, B.T. 1901 [2000]. *Up from slavery.* New York: Signet Classics.
Wilson, W.J. 1996. *When work disappears: The world of the new urban poor.* New York: Alfred A. Knopf.
Wynter, S. 2005. On how we mistook the map for the territory, and re-imprisoned ourselves in our unbearable wrongness of being, of Désêtre. In *Not only the master's tools: African American studies in theory and practice*, ed. L. Gordon and J.A. Gordon, 107–69. Boulder, CO: Paradigm Publishers.

# Living the dream or awakening from the nightmare: race and athletic identity

Louis Harrison Jr.[a], Gary Sailes[b], Willy K. Rotich[c] and Albert Y. Bimper Jr.[a]

[a]Department of Curriculum and Instruction, The University of Texas at Austin, Austin, USA; [b]School of Health, Physical Education, and Recreation, Indiana University, Bloomington, Indiana, USA; [c]Department of Physical Education, St. Bonaventure University, St. Bonaventure, New York, USA

> Education is often viewed as the door that leads out of poverty for many students of color. But for many African American boys and young men, the dream of becoming a professional athlete is a door that appears to be wide open. Considering the over-representation of African American athletes in revenue-producing sports in colleges, universities and at the professional ranks, it is no surprise that many African American male youth develop aspirations for, and identify with the athletic role. These aspirations may become even more focused and intense if they ascend to the level of division I college athletes. The identification with the athlete role is likely to intensify as they get closer to the goal of professional sport. Most individuals occupy multiple identities or roles in life such as sibling, student, spouse, employee, athlete, etc. Identity salience and strength depends on the importance of that role. Athletic identity has been defined as the degree to which an individual identifies with the athletic role. Few studies have examined the impact and influences of race on athletic role identification. This study explores the relationship between race and athletic identity. Division I-A African American and Caucasian American football student–athletes' responses to the Athletic Identity Measurement Scale were analyzed (Brewer, Raalte, and Linder 1993). Results indicated that African American football student–athletes have a stronger athletic identity compared to their Caucasian American counterparts. Differences in specific items on the scale indicated that African American student–athletes were more internally focused on their sport, felt that others perceive them only as athletes, and see sport as the focal point in their lives. Differences in these items and implications of these results suggest that there is a potential impact on academic achievement and the student–athlete's aspirations.

Several studies indicate that many African American students' primary aspiration is to become a professional athlete (Harrison, Lee, and Belcher 1999; Lee 1983). African American athletes occupy some of the most recognized, admired and respected spaces in society, thus, having large numbers of African American youth identify with high profile athletes may be somewhat expected. While conventional wisdom indicates that for students of color, education is the door to economic opportunity, many African American males have bought into the idea that sport, not education, provides the most viable means of attaining success. In fact, studies indicate that African American males have higher aspirations and expectations for becoming professional athletes than their Caucasian counterparts (Harrison, Lee, and Belcher 1999; Lee 1983). It is thought that athletic aspirations may negatively influence academic ambition and achievement as young African American males may view athletic careers as more easily attainable. This is likely due to the increase in media exposure of revenue-producing collegiate sport where African American over-representation is evident. This is also bolstered by the pervasive belief that African Americans are better suited or naturally gifted for athletic endeavors (Harrison 1999; Hodge et al. 2008). The persistent beliefs of African Americans' athletic superiority has been espoused in past writings (e.g. Entine 2000), that appear to lend legitimacy to the beliefs that African Americans are superior athletically. Thus, a career in professional sport is viewed as more attainable than a career in a professional field accessed through education. Though the stereotyping of African Americans as natural athletes has been viewed as an external influence for their over-representation in particular sports (Harrison 2001), self-stereotyping may be an even more powerful factor in this phenomenon (Oakes, Haslam, and Turner 1994). Thus the study of racial influences in sport participation and performance levels remains an unsettled issue.

**Racial influences in sport**

The study of racial influences in sport as determined by biological or genetic means, has a historically inauspicious and questionable reputation (Wiggins 1997). In the United States, as well as other countries, visual assignment of individuals to a specific racial designation can often be inaccurate. Genetically speaking, the boundary lines drawn between the different races have been profoundly blurred which make it difficult to assign race as a simple determinant of successful athletic performance. Recently, terms such as biracial or multiracial have been accepted as demographic indicators that give, at best, vague clues as to the racial lineage of an individual. The study of the genetic and biological basis for race has been termed fruitless and composed of incongruous categories that defy logic and are inherently inconsistent (Dole 1995).

Race as a social construct, rather than a biological factor, reveals a common sociopolitical history. For example, being labeled an African American has less to do with shared bio-genetic information and more to do with shared psychosocial and political experiences (Cunningham 2007; Eitzen and Sage 2003; LaVeist 1996). Unlike genetic or biological constructs of race, social conceptions of race are based on the social significance of the physical similarities or differences ascribed to racial groups that are most often not genetically based (Coakley 2004). Most often individuals in the USA with mixed racial heritage that include African ancestry are often categorized as Black or African American. Prominent examples include President Barak Obama, golfer Tiger Woods, baseball player Derek Jeter and basketball player Jason Kidd.

Historically, African American over-representation in particular sports has been examined genetically, anthropometrically, physiologically, and sociologically (Miller 1998; Wiggins 1997). The profusion of proposed theories and examination of the idea of African American athletic superiority is a testimony to the complexity of this phenomenon. Works such as Entine's (2000) *Taboo*, tend to reinforce the idea of biological determinism and cloud the empirical realities of how potent psychosocial influences and historical and institutional racism manipulate patterns of identity, sport access and choices for African American athletes. Furthermore, the relatively small differences in genetically or physiologically determined factors do not account for the large evident and obvious over-representation of African Americans in particular sports like football and basketball (Hunter 1998). For example, while African Americans comprise about 13% of the US population, in college football approximately 45% and in professional football about 67% of its players are African American. Basketball's African American population displays an even more drastic disparity with about 59% in college and 75% in the professional ranks (Lapchick 2007). These glaring over-representations often lead to the development of overly simplistic explanations for the observed differences.

Though the volume of research on these issues has somewhat waned in recent years, the perception of genetically determined superiority of African American athletes still persists. Recent research affirms the persistence and pervasiveness of these beliefs (Hodge et al. 2008; Sheldon, Epstein, and Petty 2007). Through the years, speculation, hypotheses and theories regarding the 'natural' physical abilities of African American athletes have forged the thinking of entire populations (Hoberman 1997). These ostensibly scientific theories and hypotheses have worked to form the origin of today's African American athlete stereotype. Recently, Sheldon and others (2007) illustrated this protracted viewpoint and suggested that adherence to a genetic explanation of racial differences in athletic performance was related to racial prejudice and negative stereotyping of the intellectual abilities of African American athletes.

Though a significant volume of historical research has been dedicated to explaining the over-representation of African Americans in particular sports (e.g. Entine 2000; Harrison 2001; Harrison, Harrison, and Moore 2002; Harrison, Azzarito, and Burden 2004; Hunter 1998; Miller 1998; Wiggins 1997), the volume and diversity of perspectives indicate that a unidimensional theoretical viewpoint will not likely account for all of the obvious disparities in sport performance and participation levels between African American and Caucasian American athletes. The notion of differences in levels of athletic identity among these two groups adds still another dimension to this complex issue.

## Athletic identity

For young people, particularly African American youth, sport participation and developing sport skills is a significant aspect of life and is a critical factor in the development of social acceptability and prestige (Harrison 2001; Harrison, Harrison, and Moore 2002). This is especially important during adolescence when parental and family influence gives way to peer group association and approval which often develop around sport (Payne and Isaacs 2005). This is particularly true in African American boys who often utilize sport performance as a mechanism to exhibit masculinity (Majors 1990). Harrison and his colleagues (2002) make a compelling argument for the relationship between racial identity development and athletic identity development. Using the Cross model of racial identity development (Cross 1995), the authors argue for corresponding development of racialized contexts for viewing engagement in, and valuing of sport participation. Brown and others (2003) utilizes a racial identity centrality theoretical construct to explain the ambivalent attitudes of athletes toward the perception of racial discrimination. Harrison and colleagues further suggests that the very racial identity influences that prompt the development of sport skills and athletic identity may also shield the elite African American athlete from discrimination and thus promote the perception of a post-racial society.

For many African American male student athletes, the development of a racial identity and an athletic identity may evolve along parallel pathways (Brown et al. 2003; Harrison, Harrison, and Moore 2002). Though many may view this propensity toward sport simply as choices made by African American youth, Noguera (2003) points out that both cultural and structural influences are at play. Those that cheer on game day and sneer on Monday are just as culpable as those that play the game.

To realize one's aspiration to participate in sport at the elite level requires long hours of intense and dedicated preparation, practice and commitment. In today's athletic world, to rise to the level of a college or professional athlete requires considerable talent coupled with the participant's ardent level of commitment to their sport. This commitment often calls the athlete to forsake many other interests that may occupy significant quantities of time including academic endeavors. A college athlete's schedule is highly intolerant of conflicts with practice and competition schedules. It requires that the athlete make important choices as to where he or she will dedicate time, effort, and resources. Interests that are in conflict with the athletic role are often sacrificed or put on hold until athletic interests are placated (Brewer, Raalte, and Linder 1993). While college athletes' studies are scheduled and attended to for the maintenance of academic eligibility, it often pales in comparison to the time and effort expended on athletic pursuits. Most college athletes have a daily schedule that would challenge even the best time managers. The National Collegiate Athletic Association (NCAA) attempted to limit the time devoted to athletic activities to provide sufficient time for academics. The NCAA mandates that participation in athletic activities be limited to four hours per day, 20 hours per week, with one day off per week from all athletic activities (NCAA 2006, 236).

Most athletes, and those familiar with student athletes' daily schedule snicker at this somewhat feeble attempt by the NCAA to provide adequate time for academics and limit overbearing athletic responsibilities. Most college athletes' schedule affirms that this rule is superficial and inconsequential at best. This 20 hours per week rule is simply circumvented by using of 'non-mandatory practice sessions' (NCAA 2006, 272) supervised by strength and conditioning coaches. Although these sessions are 'non-mandatory,' there are likely significant consequences of missing them, particularly for an athlete vying for playing time or a possible starting position. Eitzen (2003, 112) concurs that NCAA officials have attempted to limit growing time demands by coaches, but has been unsuccessful.

An ardent level of commitment is an important and necessary prerequisite for participation at the level of the elite athlete. The importance one assigns to their role as an athlete is critical to rise to the upper echelons of athletic competition. Most athletes spend many years preparing for their athletic roles. Few athletes rise to elite levels of competition after only a few years of participation. In fact, by the time elite athletes reach the collegiate level, most have participated in their respective sport for the majority of their lives. For elite level athletes, there are few other activities in life that figure as prominently as sport. Subsequently, for most elite athletes, the time and effort dedicated to sport comprises a significant portion, or the majority of their social and personal identity.

The degree to which the athlete identifies with, or views themselves in the role of an athlete, has been termed 'Athletic Identity' (Brewer, Raalte, and Linder 1993). Recent research suggests that developing a potent athletic identity has performance advantages. An athlete with a pronounced athletic identity will likely sacrifice extraneous external activities to narrow their focus to on athletic development and competition. Increased levels of athletic identity have been found to be related to superior athletic performance, confident psychological consequences during training, and enhanced body image (Horton and Mack 2000).

Unfortunately, disadvantages to elevated athletic identity have also been reported. Negative consequences such as increased social isolation and decreased social activity (Horton and Mack 2000), negative psychological responses, and severe identity depression (Brewer, Raalte, and Linder 1993) have been reported. Higher levels of athletic identity are correlated with experiencing serious difficulties when disengaging from high levels of sport participation, especially when it was due to injury (Brewer, Raalte, and Linder 1993). With the intense focus on athletic pursuits, athletes often sacrificed other sources of identity and often neglected other sources of self-fulfillment (Webb et al. 1998).

Harrison and others (2002) provide a conceptual analysis of the relationship of the development of athletic identity and racial identity. While athletic identity has been examined theoretically and empirically, no known studies have empirically explored athletic identity's relationship with, and influence of race. The purpose of this study is to explore the relationship between race and athletic identity by determining if differences in athletic identity exist by race. A secondary purpose was to closely examine the specific items on the instrument used, the Athletic Identity Measurement Scale (Brewer, Raalte, and Linder 1993), for differences by race to determine if specific areas of difference exist and examine these issues.

## Method

The participants were 109 NCAA Division I football student–athletes from a large predominantly Caucasian American southeastern American university. The institution has a proud football tradition and a record of success. Appropriate IRB approval was secured before surveying the athletes. The participants were members and former members of the university's football team. While the sample was not random the researchers attempted to survey all available players. Both African American and Caucasian American players were recruited to secure surveys. The athletes' self-identified racial categorization was 67 African Americans and 42 Caucasian Americans. The Athletic Identity Measurement Scale (AIMS) (Brewer, Raalte, and Linder 1993) was administered and the responses were totaled to determine degree of athletic identity. The AIMS was developed to provide a measure of the degree to which an athlete identifies with their role as an athlete. The AIMS has been widely utilized in sport identity research. This instrument underwent rigorous validation and reliability analysis during its development for university populations. Reliability of the AIMS for this population was acceptable (Cronbach's $\alpha = .77$). Data were analyzed via analysis of variance (race by Athletic Identity score).

## Results

The results indicated that African American football student–athletes had a higher athletic identity scores than Caucasian American football student–athletes ($F(1, 104) = 6.156$, $p=0.015$, see Table 1). Follow up analyses revealed significant differences on individual AIMS items #5 ($p=.042$; I spend more time thinking about sport than anything else), #7 ($p=.020$; Other people see me mainly as an athlete), and #9 ($p=.015$; Sport is the only important thing in my life) (see Tables 2 and 3). African American football student–athletes had significantly higher scores than their Caucasian American counterparts on these three items. Two other items approached significance including items #3 (p=.056; Most of my friends are athletes), and #6 (p=.051; I need to participate in sport to feel good about myself). While not demonstrating statistical significance,

Table 1. Analysis of variance for athletic identity total score.

| Source | df | Mean Square | F | p |
|---|---|---|---|---|
| Between Groups | 1 | 7.901 | 6.156 | 0.015 |
| Within Groups | 104 | 133.495 | 1.284 | |
| Total | 105 | 141.396 | | |

Table 2. Means and standard deviations for AIMS items.

| Item # | Race | Mean | Std. Deviation |
|---|---|---|---|
| | Af. Am (N=64) | | Ca. Am. (N=41) |
| 1 | Af. Am. | 4.52 | 0.734 |
| | Ca. Am. | 4.49 | 0.597 |
| | Total | 4.50 | 0.681 |
| 2 | Af. Am. | 4.30 | 0.885 |
| | Ca. Am. | 4.29 | 0.716 |
| | Total | 4.30 | 0.820 |
| 3 | Af. Am. | 4.25 | 0.816 |
| | Ca. Am. | 3.90 | 0.889 |
| | Total | 4.11 | 0.858 |
| 4 | Af. Am. | 3.11 | 1.114 |
| | Ca. Am. | 2.68 | 1.128 |
| | Total | 2.94 | 1.134 |
| 5 | Af. Am. | 3.16 | 1.224 |
| | Ca. Am. | 2.66 | 0.965 |
| | Total | 2.96 | 1.151 |
| 6 | Af. Am. | 2.98 | 1.339 |
| | Ca. Am. | 2.49 | 1.052 |
| | Total | 2.79 | 1.253 |
| 7 | Af. Am. | 3.97 | 1.023 |
| | Ca. Am. | 3.44 | 1.026 |
| | Total | 3.76 | 1.052 |
| 8 | Af. Am. | 3.63 | 1.047 |
| | Ca. Am. | 3.93 | 0.818 |
| | Total | 3.74 | 0.971 |
| 9 | Af. Am. | 2.30 | 1.256 |
| | Ca. Am. | 1.73 | 0.923 |
| | Total | 2.08 | 1.166 |
| 10. | Af. Am. | 3.73 | 1.172 |
| | Ca. Am. | 3.44 | 1.074 |
| | Total | 3.62 | 1.138 |

Table 3. Analysis of variance for athletic identity items.

| Source | | df | Mean Square | F | p |
|---|---|---|---|---|---|
| Item 1 | Between Groups | 1 | 0.000 | 0.000 | 0.983 |
| | Within Groups | 105 | 0.483 | | |
| Item 2 | Between Groups | 1 | 0.010 | 0.015 | 0.903 |
| | Within Groups | 105 | 0.682 | | |
| Item 3 | Between Groups | 1 | 2.668 | 3.726 | 0.056 |
| | Within Groups | 105 | 0.716 | | |
| Item 4 | Between Groups | 1 | 3.903 | 3.116 | 0.080 |
| | Within Groups | 105 | 1.252 | | |
| Item 5 | Between Groups | 1 | 5.414 | 4.234 | 0.042* |
| | Within Groups | 105 | 1.279 | | |
| Item 6 | Between Groups | 1 | 5.873 | 3.898 | 0.051 |
| | Within Groups | 105 | 1.507 | | |
| Item 7 | Between Groups | 1 | 5.954 | 5.546 | 0.020* |
| | Within Groups | 105 | 1.074 | | |
| Item 8 | Between Groups | 1 | 2.204 | 2.389 | 0.125 |
| | Within Groups | 104 | 0.922 | | |
| Item 9 | Between Groups | 1 | 7.901 | 6.156 | 0.015* |
| | Within Groups | 104 | 1.284 | | |
| Item 10 | Between Groups | 1 | 1.683 | 1.299 | 0.257 |
| | Within Groups | 105 | 1.296 | | |

Note: *Indicates statistical significance (p≤.05).

the difference in raw scores (means) between the two groups on were large enough to warrant notice and consideration (see Tables 2 and 3).

## Discussion

The results of this study point to an additional factor that may be important to the debate regarding the influence of race on athletic performance and participation. To observe individuals on the same team, with many of the same coaches, under similar influences, yet displaying significant differences in athletic identity by race demonstrates the potent influence of race in athletic contexts. Because athletic identity has been suggested as an important factor in athletic performance (Horton and Mack 2000), racial differences in athletic identity should be considered as a potent influence in participation patterns and performance.

## Being confined to the dream

It is also important to note the specific items on the AIMS that displayed differences by race. Item 5 (I spend more time thinking about sport than anything else) suggests that these African American football student–athletes had a more ardent internal focus on their sport than their Caucasian American counterparts. The increasing complexity of sport, especially American football, requires significant concentration and focus to recognize and react appropriately in game situations. Though item 5 does not ask specifically what aspect of the sport consumed the athlete's thoughts, Driskell and others (1994) suggest that mental practice for motor skills significantly enhances performance. Spending more time thinking about sport and possibly mentally rehearsing in preparation for athletic competition can be advantageous.

Though the African American athletes' athletic identity may be of value at game time, it may serve as a handicap in the academic environment where pervasive stereotypes still persist (Baucom and Lantz 2001; Engstrom, Sedlacek, and McEwen 1995; Engstrom and Sedlacek 1991; Hodge et al. 2008). To truly understand this concept, further research on the thought processes of athletes is necessary.

The African American athletes in this study also indicated that they were perceived by others, essentially, as athletes. Item 7 (Other people see me mainly as an athlete) likely has strong racial connotations as the context was a predominantly Caucasian American university. Though approximately 50% of Division I football players are African American, the vast majority of African American athletes compete at predominantly Caucasian American colleges and universities (Eitzen 2003, 20). Simons and others (2007) referred to the double stigma of being African American and an athlete, in that unlike many Caucasian American athletes, an African American on a predominantly Caucasian American campus is somewhat conspicuous. Add to that an unusually large body and/or muscular frame often required for playing football makes the identity of African American student athletes difficult to conceal.

Additionally, responses to Item 7 acknowledges the likelihood of others' negatively stereotyping African American athletes essentially in an athletic role driving what has been termed as stereotype threat. Stereotype threats exist when one is fearful of being negatively judged by others because of prevailing stereotypes of one's group affiliation (Stone et al. 1999). Steele and Aronson (1995) define it as being at risk of confirming, as self-characteristic, a negative stereotype about one's group. Although, being viewed as an athlete is not necessarily detrimental, there is a negative connotation attached to being perceived mainly as an athlete as it fails to acknowledge other coexisting identities and magnifies prevailing stereotypical views. Thus, an athlete affected by stereotype threat is well aware of the negative academic stereotypes held by others and more apt to perform below their actual capabilities (Steele 1997).

Several authors indicated that many university faculty held unfavorable attitudes toward student athletes (Baucom and Lantz 2001; Engstrom, Sedlacek, and McEwen 1995; Perlmutter 2003). Recent research affirmed that over half the athletes surveyed encountered negative remarks from faculty that portrayed them as 'dumb jocks' (Simons et al. 2007). Sociologist Harry Edwards argues that the African American 'dumb jock' is systematically and socially created (Edwards 1984). Factors contributing to this construction are the double negative labels African American athletes face as the dumb athlete distortion and the unintelligent African American stereotype. This double negative influence potentially results in stereotype threat effects and self-fulfilling prophecies (Eitzen 2006).

Additionally, fellow students often harbor negative perceptions of student athletes' (Engstrom and Sedlacek 1991; Sailes 1993; Simons et al. 2007). These negative viewpoints are often magnified when the athlete is African American. Engstrom and Sedlacek (1991) indicated a heightened degree of students' suspicion of athletes obtaining As, suggesting that non-athlete peers perceive that student–athletes were incapable of academic excellence. When both faculty and fellow students viewed a student–athlete 'mainly as an athlete', it was likely to cause appreciable damage to the athlete's self-esteem and academic identity.

**Being conformed to the dream**

Finally, AIMS item 9 (Sport is the only important thing in my life), reveals the most prominent difference between African American and Caucasian American athletes among all AIMS items. Though it was the most modest score for all the items, it displayed more discrepancy by race than any item within the instrument. This may indicate that sport, in this case football, is valued significantly more by African American athletes than their Caucasian American counterparts. Despite the modest scores for both groups of athletes in item 9, the extent of the variance in this item is a cause for concern among African American athletes. Lally and Kerr (2005) provide recent evidence that strong athletic identity deters the career preparation of collegiate athletes. These authors add that when the athletes in their study began to develop mature career aspirations in the fourth and fifth years, it was at a time when they also realized that they lacked the required academic qualifications to achieve them. None of the athletes in Lally and Kerr's study were described as football student–athletes and their study was conducted in a Canadian university, a context that is less plausible than the US football environment. Thus, it is likely that the lack of career preparation would be exaggerated in African American athletes. The prospect of entering professional football and the sizeable salaries professional athletes may attain provide ample fuel for the development and sustaining of a persistent athletic identity.

Murphy and others (1996) suggest that stronger athletic identity is related to identity foreclosure which is defined as making a commitment to identity role without exploring other role possibilities. This is likely intensified by the demands of collegiate athletics and the isolation of the athletic environment which limit the exploratory opportunities of college athletes. This narrow focus by African American athletes will likely be reinforced by coaches and sport administrators whose jobs are based on winning. When this is exacerbated by the influence of pervasive stereotypical conceptions of African American athletes (Harrison 2001) and the likelihood of self-stereotyping (Biernat, Vescio, and Green 1996), it is understandable why African American athletes say 'sport is the only important thing in my life.' Past findings, that significantly more African American youth see themselves as professional athletes than their Caucasian counterparts, provide evidence that this narrow focus on sport begins and develops long before the college years (Harrison 1999; Lee 1983).

**Being awakened from the dream**

Educators and academic advisors can benefit from implications of this study. Those that work with athletes on a daily basis off the field play a key role in their development. Allowing and encouraging explorations of other identities is salient to the development of student–athletes' self-concepts. African American student–athletes must occupy multiple roles as an African American, athlete, and student. Thus, it remains important to ensure that African American athletes – in this case, football players – don't foreclose their identity overshadowing other pertinent aspects and possibilities in their identity development.

It is also incumbent to disperse the responsibility for the development of African American athletes' identity. Coaches, academic advisors, faculty and fellow students should be educated on the impact they have on the identity development of African American athletes. It is imperative that efforts are made by all to recognize and destroy prevailing stereotypes and embrace the African American as a human being first. Further steps should be taken to develop alternative identities that these athletes may assume when playing days are over. It is important to diminish the vast difference in the accolades athletes receive for their athletic endeavors and those received from academic pursuits. This is an indictment on all who passionately cheer in stadiums on Saturdays then sneer in classrooms at these same athletes Monday through Friday.

## Conclusions

This study is not without limitations. The limited geographical focus represents the athletic identity of a specific group of football student–athletes at one university. The relatively small sample size may also be of concern when one considers the number of athletes involved in collegiate football programs. Additionally, this study was confined to males in the context of American football and may not generalize to other sports and to female athletes. Albeit, these findings beg for more extensive study.

Limitations withstanding, this study presents more potential evidence from the psychosocial perspective for the race/sport debate. Careful study of athletic identity has the potential to provide yet another compelling perspective of these often debated issues. Moreover, the results of this investigation cannot be ignored. Significant differences were found on several variables in a comparison of same-sport African American and Causian American athletes.

Those in educational contexts are well aware of the athletic identity development of many young African American males. Far too often sport is framed as the red carpet pathway out of poverty and obscurity and into fame and fortune. While a few do achieve their dreams, the vast majority are rudely awakened at a point where they have forgone their opportunity secure a valid and valuable education. Far too many young African American males sacrifice massive amounts of time, effort and pain in pursuit of an athletic career without making a single dollar from their efforts. Professional sport is one of the few careers that requires one to volunteer their services for a significant portion of one's life, including virtually all of one's adolescence, for an astronomically small chance of ever achieving gainful employment on the field. Additionally, it develops skills that are largely of no use in other occupations. Not many fortune 500 companies are seeking employees with running, blocking and tackling skills. Though transferable skills such as leadership, communication, and team building skills are claimed, they are not the focus of many for many football programs and seldom traits ascribed to African American athletes. No doubt, further study is warranted to investigate the impact of athletic identity and stimulate continuing dialogue about the race based cultural differences between African American and Caucasian American athletes participating in college athletics.

## References

Baucom, C., and C.D. Lantz. 2001. Faculty attitudes toward male Division II student athletes. *Journal of Sport Behavior* 24: 265–76.

Biernat, M., T.K. Vescio, and M.L. Green. 1996. Selective self-stereotyping. *Journal of Personality and Social Psychology* 71: 1194–209.

Brewer, B.W., J.L.V. Raalte, and D. Linder. 1993. Athletic identity: Hercules' muscles or achilles heel? *International Journal of Sport Psychology* 24: 237–54.

Brown, T.N., J.S. Jackson, K.T. Brown, R.M. Sellers, S. Keiper, and W.J. Manue. 2003. "There's no race on the playing field": Perceptions of racial discrimination among white and black athletes. *Journal of Sport and Social Issues* 27: 162–83.

Coakley, J.J. 2004. *Sport in society: Issues and controversies.* Boston: McGraw-Hill.

Cross, W.E. 1995. The psychology of Nigrescence: Revising the Cross model. In *Handbook of multicultural counseling,* ed. J.G. Ponterotto, J.M. Casas, L.A. Suzuki and C.M. Alexander, 93–122. Thousand Oaks, CA: Sage.

Cunningham, G.B. 2007. *Diversity in sport organizations.* Scottsdale: Holcomb Hathaway.

Dole, A.A. 1995. Why not drop race as a term? *American Psychologist* 54: 40.

Driskell, J.E., C. Copper, and A. Moran. 1994. Does mental practice enhance performance? *Journal of Applied Psychology* 79: 481–92.

Edwards, H. 1984. The black dumb jock: An American sports tragedy. *College Board Review* 131: 8–13.

Eitzen, D.S. 2003. *Fair and foul: Beyond the myths and paradoxes of sport.* New York: Rowman & Littlefield Publishers Inc.

Eitzen, D.S. 2006. *Fair and foul: Beyond the myths and paradoxes of sport.* 3rd ed. New York: Rowman & Littlefield Publishers Inc.

Eitzen, D.S., and G.H. Sage. 2003. *Sociology of North American sport.* New York: McGraw Hill.

Engstrom, C.M., and W.E. Sedlacek. 1991. A study of prejudice toward university student-athletes. *Journal of Counseling & Development* 70: 189–93.

Engstrom, C.M., W.E. Sedlacek, and M.K. McEwen. 1995. Faculty attitudes toward male revenue and non-revenue student-athletes. *Journal of College Student Development* 36: 217–27.

Entine, J. 2000. *Taboo: Why black athletes dominate sports, and why we are afraid to talk about it.* New York: Public Affairs.

Harrison, L., Jr. 1999. Racial attitudes in sport: A survey of race-sport competence beliefs. *Shades of diversity: Issues and strategies,* A Monograph Series, 2. Reston, VA: American Alliance for Health Physical Education, Recreation and Dance.

Harrison, L., Jr., Lee, A., and D. Belcher. 1999. Self-schemata for specific sports and physical activities: The influence of race and gender. *Journal of Sport and Social Issues* 23: 287–302.

Harrison, L., Jr. 2001. Understanding the influence of stereotypes: Implications for the African American in sport and physical activity. *Quest* 53: 97–114.

Harrison, L., Jr., C.K. Harrison, and L. Moore. 2002. African American racial identity and sport. *Sport Education and Society* 7: 121–33.

Harrison, L., Jr., L. Azzarito, and J. Burden Jr. 2004. Perceptions of athletic superiority: A view from the other side. *Race Ethnicity, and Education* 7: 149–66.

Hoberman, J. 1997. *Darwin's athletes: How sport has damaged black America and preserved the myth of race.* New York: Houghton Mifflin.

Hodge, S.R., F.M. Kozub, A.D. Dixson, J.L. Moore III., and K. Kambon. 2008. A comparison of high school students' stereotypic beliefs about intelligence and athleticism. *Educational Foundations* 22, no. 1–2: 99–119.

Horton, R.S., and D.E. Mack. 2000. Athletic identity in marathon runners: Functional focus or dysfunctional commitment? *Journal of Sport Behavior* 23: 101–19.

Hunter, D.W. 1998 Race and athletic performance: A physiological review. In *African Americans in sport,* ed. G.A. Sailes, 85–101. New Brunswick, NJ: Transaction.

Lally, P.S., and G.A. Kerr. 2005. The career planning, athletic identity, and student role identity of intercollegiate student athletes. *Research Quarterly for Exercise and Sport* 76: 275–85.

Lapchick, R.E. 2007. 2004 racial and gender report card. The Institute for Diversity and Ethics in Sport: DeVos Sport Business Management Program, University of Central Florida.

LaVeist, T.A. 1996. Why we should continue to study race…but do a better job: An essay on race, racism and health. *Ethnicity and disease* 6: 21–9.

Lee, C.C. 1983. An investigation of the athletic career expectations of high school athletes. *The Personnel and Guidance Journal* 61: 544–47.

Majors, R. 1990. Cool pose: Black masculinity and sports. In *Sport, men, and the gender order: Critical feminist perspectives,* ed. M.A. Messner and D.F. Sabo, 109–14 Champaign, IL: Human Kinetics.

Miller, P.B. 1998. The anatomy of scientific racism: Racialist responses to black athletic achievement. *Journal of Sport History* 25: 119–51.

Murphy, G.M., A.J. Petitpas, and B.W. Brewer. 1996. Identity foreclosure, athletic identity and career maturity in intercollegiate athletes. *The Sport Psychologist* 10: 239–46.

NCAA. 2006, July. National Collegiate Athletic Association 2006–07 Division I Manual. Indianapolis: NCAA

Noguera, P.A. 2003. The trouble with black boys: The role and influence of environmental and cultural factors in the academic performance of African American males. *Urban Education* 38: 431–59.

Oakes, P.J., S.A. Haslam, and J.C. Turner. 1994. *Stereotyping and social reality.* Cambridge: Blackwell.

Payne, V.J.G., and L.D. Isaacs. 2005. Human motor development: A lifespan approach. Boston: McGraw-Hill.

Perlmutter, D. 2003. Black athletes and white professors: A twilight zone of uncertainty. *Chronicle of Higher Education* 50, no. 7: B7.

Sailes, G.A. 1993. An investigation of campus typecasts: The myth of black athletic superiority and the dumb jock stereotype. *Sport Sociology Journal* 10: 88–97.

Sheldon, J.P., T.E. Jayaratne, and E.M. Petty. 2007. White Americans' genetic explanations for a perceived race difference in athleticism: The relation to prejudice toward and stereotyping of Blacks. *Athletic Insight: The Online Journal of Sport Psychology* 9: 31–56. http://www.athleticinsight.com/Vol9Iss3/RacePDF.pdf (accessed March 20, 2010).

Simons, H., C. Bosworth, S. Fujita, and M. Jensen. 2007. The athlete stigma in higher education. *College Student Journal* 41, no. 2: 251–73.

Steele, C.M., and J. Aronson. 1995. Stereotype threat and the intellectual test performance of African Americans. *Journal of Personality and Social Psychology* 69: 797–811.

Steele, C.M. 1997. A threat in the air: How stereotypes shape intellectual identity and performance. *American Psychologist* 52: 613–29.

Stone, J., C.I. Lynch, M. Sjomeling, and J.M. Darley. 1999. Stereotype threat effects on black and white athletic performance. *Journal of Personality and Social Psychology* 77: 1213–27.

Webb, W.M., S.A. Nasco, S. Riley, and B. Headrick. 1998. Athletic identity and reactions to retirement from sports. *Journal of Sport Behavior* 21: 338–62.

Wiggins, D.K. 1997. "Great speed but little stamina": The historical debate over black athletic superiority. In *The new American sport history: Recent approaches and perspectives*, ed. S.W. Pope, 312–38. Urbana: University of Illinois Press.

# Appendix

## Athletic Identity Measurement Scale (AIMS)

**Instructions:** This questionnaire is designed to measure people's attitudes about athletic issues. There are no right or wrong answers. **Different people have different viewpoints**. So, try to be as honest as you can. Beside each statement, circle the number that best describes how you feel. Use the scale below to respond to each statement.

| 1 | 2 | 3 | 4 | 5 |
|---|---|---|---|---|
| Strongly disagree | Disagree | Uncertain | Agree | Strongly agree |

| | | | | | |
|---|---|---|---|---|---|
| 1 | 2 | 3 | 4 | 5 | 1. I consider myself an athlete. |
| 1 | 2 | 3 | 4 | 5 | 2. I have many goals related to sport. |
| 1 | 2 | 3 | 4 | 5 | 3. Most of my friends are athletes. |
| 1 | 2 | 3 | 4 | 5 | 4. Sport is the most important part of my life. |
| 1 | 2 | 3 | 4 | 5 | 5. I spend more time thinking about sport than anything else. |
| 1 | 2 | 3 | 4 | 5 | 6. I need to participate in sport to feel good about myself. |
| 1 | 2 | 3 | 4 | 5 | 7. Other people see me mainly as an athlete. |
| 1 | 2 | 3 | 4 | 5 | 8. I feel bad about myself when I do poorly in sport. |
| 1 | 2 | 3 | 4 | 5 | 9. Sport is the only important thing in my life. |
| 1 | 2 | 3 | 4 | 5 | 10. I would be very depressed if I were injured and could not compete in sport. |

# Research concerns, cautions and considerations on Black males in a 'post-racial' society

Tyrone C. Howard and Terry Flennaugh

*Graduate School of Education & Information Studies, University of California, Los Angeles, USA*

> Black males continue to be one of the most academically marginalized groups of students in US schools, and undoubtedly the role of race and racism has largely influenced these experiences. The paradox of the underperformance of Black males has been the election of President Obama in 2008. The Obama election has led some to question whether or not race and racism continue to be pertinent factors in how racially diverse groups experience life in the United States. This article takes an examination of research on Black males in what some are attempting to label the United States' first 'post-racial' era. In this article, the authors take exception to the term 'post-racial' and any suggestion that the United States is beyond race, and that race no longer matters in US life, law, policy, and life experiences. The article calls for researchers to be mindful of important cautions, concerns, and considerations as they engage in scholarly inquiry on Black males.

The 2008 election of President Barack Obama initiated a growing amount of discussion about the United States entering its first ever 'post-racial' era. Some see the purported 'post-racial' era as the beginning of a new and progressive time in United States life, law, and politics, where race is no longer relevant; an era where America's history of racial strife and discrimination could be considered issues of the past, with little to no contemporary meaning as to how an increasingly racially diverse society experiences life in the twenty-first century (Pierre and Jeter 2009). The election of an African American man, who ran for president as a race-neutral candidate signaled a major paradigm shift about how the United States deals, or chooses not to deal, with the explosive issue that is race (Howard 2010). Though race has played out in a multitude of ways with different groups over the United States' history, arguably the group that has been most vilified by racial animosity, angst and hatred has been Black men (Polite and Davis 1999). From the inception of slavery and the role that Black men played in that horrific institution, to the thousands of Black men who were brutally lynched during the eighteenth, nineteenth and twentieth centuries (Allen et al. 2000), racial stigmatization has plagued Black men for well over three centuries (Madhubuti 1990). Hence the irony of a Black man becoming the most powerful and influential leader of the free world provides perfect fodder for the call of a post-racial society in America. How could have Obama's election occurred if racial discrimination still exists? Would Obama have been elected if not for the millions of White voters who supported his candidacy? Yet, these are only a few of the questions that could and have been posed by the post-racial advocates. However, what cannot be lost in the discussion of a post-racial society are the dismal realities that still confront many people of color in the United States.

An examination of labor, justice, and education data reveals a grim reality faced by growing numbers of Black males in the United States. According the Bureau of Labor Statistics (2009), the average Black worker earns just over $600 per week, about 80% of what the median White worker earns. The US Department of Justice (2009) reports that Black men are incarcerated at 6.6 times the rate of White men, with almost one in 20 Black men spending some time in jail or prison at some point in their life. Approximately 37% of all male inmates in 2008 were Black, down 41% from 2000, despite the fact that Black males only make up 7% of the nation's population. Young Black males are more likely to be suspended or expelled from school at a rate higher than any other sub group (Skiba and Peterson 2000; Skiba et al. 2007). Black males also continue to drop out of schools at an alarming rate and attend college at disproportionately lower rates. During the 2005–2006 academic year, 47% of African American males did not receive diplomas with their classmates after four years of high school (Schott Foundation for Public Education 2008). In fact, dropout rates were as high as 80% in some of America's major urban cities such as Detroit, Michigan. Furthermore, the likelihood that Black males will suffer from a multitude of mental health or substance abuse challenges has been well documented (Poussaint and Alexander 2000). For example, from 1980 to 1995, the suicide rate for African American male youth (aged 15–19) increased by 146% and now parallels the levels of White males and is double that of Black women (Gary, Scruggs, and Yarandi 2003; Joe and Kaplan 2001).

This article takes an examination of research on Black males in what some are attempting to label the United States' first 'post-racial era.' We take exception to the term 'post-racial' and any suggestion that we are beyond race, and that race no longer matters in US life, law, policy, and life chances. Cornel West (2009) writes that 'we must not confuse the empty media category of "post-racial" with the reality of America becoming less racist. The former is an empty illusion; the latter is a grand achievement' (240). More specifically, we challenge this notion when it comes to educational research and in the schooling experiences of Black males. In examining the schooling experiences of Black males, we assert that race has always mattered, and continues to matter, even with the election of a Black man as president. We assert that any attempt to dismiss or overlook race as a significant variable in the ways that Black males experience school further marginalizes a group that has experienced numerous forms of racism and exclusion over the past three centuries in the United States (Noguera 2008; Price 2000). Undoubtedly, educational marginalization issues have direct connections to race and gender. Black females face many of the same challenges in schools and society as Black males and these challenges have been well chronicled (Evans-Winters 2005). However, the nexus of race and gender seems to have more detrimental effects for Black males as evidenced by their lower academic outcomes, higher suspension, expulsions, and dropout rates, and significantly declining college admission rates. We contend that issues affecting Black males in schools remain highly racialized and require ongoing examination from equity-minded researchers[1] who are concerned with improving their conditions. The current state of educational affairs for Black males in a 'post-racial' society poses significant risks for them that researchers and practitioners must be aware of as they engage in scholarly inquiry.

The goal of this article is to present research *cautions, concerns and considerations* that should be adhered to for research on, about, or involving Black males. We raise these issues because failure to pay special attention to the manner in which Black males and their experiences are described and analyzed can be grossly misguided if not given deliberate thought and careful consideration. There are three primary charges that we will argue researchers should be mindful of before participating in this work that we will elaborate on in this article: (1) we want to offer a strong caution to those doing work regarding Black males, and who ignore race as a variable in examining their school experiences; (2) we want to address concerns that are potential problems when researchers fail to acknowledge, or to understand the complex historical context of Black males and research in the United States; and (3) we want to put forward considerations for future research on Black males being informed by new paradigms, transformative frameworks and methods, and an overall mode of inquiry concerned with transforming the life experiences of Black males.

## A rationale for a measured approach on research and Black males

The significance of a Black male president cannot be understated. This monumental and historical feat represents a major social hurdle that has been cleared by citizens of the United States, and provides tangible evidence that racial animosity has decreased compared to a generation ago. It also provides convincing evidence that race relations have improved, and that on some level people's angst and fears about Black people in general, and Black men in particular and their intelligence, have been altered by authentic personal experiences and positive cross-racial interactions. Yet, we would be remiss not to acknowledge the various forms of racism that continued in the US leading up to the election of Barack Obama. As Bobo and Charles (2009) point out that Obama's ability to bridge the racial divide were undermined by two troubling trends during the primaries. First, particularly in New Hampshire and several subsequent contests, White voters appeared to tell pollsters one thing about their support for Obama, but then subsequently voted against him on the ballot. Second, Bobo and Charles (2009) note, '...throughout the primary season, especially in its later stages in such states as Ohio, Pennsylvania, Kentucky, and West Virginia, it is clear that a non-trivial number of White voters openly rejected Obama largely on the basis of race' (255). Even during the prolonged healthcare debate, images depicting President Obama as a witch doctor and even Adolf Hitler represent the many veiled and unveiled racist views that remain a part of America's narrative. What cannot be lost amidst the euphoria of the Obama election are the realities still faced by young Black males in the twenty-first century, and a fundamental question that must be asked is 'What has fundamentally changed about the experience of Black males in American society?' Obama himself has cautioned against those who seek to deem him as a messiah who will cure all the country's ills. He has also stated the quality of conditions for the urban poor (where many Black males reside) remain a huge challenge for the country. While we can all be heartened by the fact that Obama has become president, how long can the joyful reality of his presidency compete with the dismal reality that schools and society are still unjust and uncaring spaces for many Black males?

One of the purposes of social science research is to examine society through individuals' relationships in and to various social, political, and cultural contexts. Social science research, at least in theory, should provide a much needed method of inquiry into various challenges faced by populations in the quest for a more harmonious and just nation-state, and to work toward attainment of the goals and aims best suited for the public interest (Tate 2006). To that end, our role as social scientists should be to identify problems that exist, raise important questions about them, identify reliable modes of inquiry into them, and offer plausible interventions for disrupting the problems faced by the larger society. The challenge faced by the social sciences is that issues of race, class and gender add layers of complexity to the arduous situations that increasing members of the society finds itself in. Thus prompting scholars to contend that if research is done for the good of public interest, what public interest are we talking about? And whose interest are we serving? (Grant 2006). Perhaps more than any other nation in the world, the United States has been beset by its inability to deal with a past that has been steeped in racial inequities and discord which has created a different reality for countless numbers of its non-White citizens (Wilson 2009). These racial inequities have manifested themselves in a multitude of areas from economic opportunities, political viability, healthcare disparities, as well as to educational experiences and overall life chances (Omi and Winant 1994). Before we advance to a post-racial society, we need to shed an intense spotlight on the legacy that race has left on United States, and what it means for individuals whose interests have not been well served by racial hierarchies and race-based policies which have been created.

Previous research on Black males has helped to provide useful insights into examining and understanding contributing factors to their educational and social disenfranchisement (Anderson 2008; Gill 1992; Madhubuti 1990; Noguera 2008; Polite 1994; Polite and Davis 1999). What is most obvious in each of these works is the salience of race. Each of these works explicitly identifies the history and complexity of racialized experiences that Black males encounter in US schools and society. We share similar concerns to previous scholars in problematizing the importance of race in the schooling experiences of Black males, and offer cautions about what the failure to recognize race can do, and what it may mean for Black males, as well as other non-White populations. This work is specifically concerned with African American males in PreK-12 schools because of the persistent disenfranchisement that many of them continue to experience. We seek to take a divergent path in this article by making a call for thoughtful research paradigms and alternative theoretical frameworks that can help to identify methods for developing more nurturing schooling environments that cater to African American males in PreK-12 schools. Moreover, we seek paradigms that give more credence to the significance of race and ethnicity and all of their manifestations in education (Lee 2007). Race, in particular has been, and remains under theorized in education (Ladson Billings and Tate 1995), therefore any efforts to move beyond race seek to extract a core variable in explaining why we see disparate educational experiences and outcomes.

The need for carefully conducted, race-based research on Black males is critical, because much of the inquiry on this population has centered on deficit-based, pathological accounts of Black males (Polite 1994). These works in the social and biological sciences have contributed to distorted constructions of Black men, and have led to what Earl Ofari Hutchison (1997) refers to as the 'assassination of the Black male image.' Memories of the Tuskegee experiment and the complete absence of moral and ethical standards provide an important cautionary tale about how Black males[2] have been objectified in the name of science and research. Selden's (1999) work on the Eugenics movement offers yet another cautionary tale of how racial inferiority of Blacks was constructed and 'proven' in the name of scientific inquiry. Washington (2006) chronicles the long, disturbing history of Blacks and illegal medical testing and contends that 'dangerous, involuntary and nontherapeutic experimentation upon African Americans has been practiced widely and documented extensively at least since the eighteenth century' (7), and she pays particular attention to the manner in which Black males were often the primary targets of these efforts, and how in many ways this historical account continues to keep many Black men from voluntarily being involved as participants in scientific research. A plethora of works have documented the long and sordid accounts that have demonized Black males as intellectually inferior, prone to violence, and unworthy of being fit for society, and have used research to justify these outcomes (Gould 1981; Horsman 1981). This article seeks to put forward a framework that will disrupt problematic frameworks and methodologies that appear innocuous on the surface but may still reify distorted accounts of Black males. Recently, a number of works have begun to allow Black males to offer their own accounts of these experiences. These works have been important because they have sought to shift the paradigm on Black males from one that renders them as subjects, to a more nuanced and rigorous one that seeks to have Black males author their own stories and experiences (Dimitriadis 2003; Duncan 2002; Howard 2008; Price 2000).

Considerations of race-based research are not new, and continue to take on a more prevalent place in educational research and theory. Stanfield (1993) has written about the historical reluctance of social scientists to explicitly examine sensitive issues such as race, ethnicity, and discrimination in their work. He called for researchers to be willing to talk about the particular challenges and unique stances that are essential to doing research on racialized populations. Banks (1993) has raised the question about the epistemological stance of researchers as they engage in work with diverse populations, and called for researchers to reflect on, and identify their own positionality, and to examine what this means for their research in a multicultural society. Tillman (2002) called for culturally sensitive research approaches for African Americans which she asserts are critical for understanding the cultural and racial nuances involved in examining the African American experience. She states that 'it is important to consider whether the researcher has the cultural knowledge to accurately interpret and validate the experiences' of a particular group (4). Milner (2007) makes a similar call when he refers to the *seen, unseen,* and *unforeseen* approaches for thinking about race, culture, and equity in research. His research outlines an important framework for researcher racial and cultural positionality that should inform social scientists working with diverse populations. We build on the important work of these scholars who make a call for careful thought about the manner in which race-based research should be conducted. What these researchers remind us is that research is not neutral, it is never apolitical, and that for researchers whose works examine diverse populations, a number of key considerations should be given important thought, and that failure to do so only creates further racial hierarchies. More importantly, these scholars do not suggest that racial or cultural outsiders cannot effectively do quality research on diverse populations, but that it is crucial to be armed with a cultural and racial knowledge base that does not demonize diverse populations, yet recognizes the contextual nature of race, class, culture and gender.

## Black males, race, and post-racial research: the cautions

The cautions that we put forward are centered on the careful nature that individuals should take when dealing with research on Black males. The very nature of the term 'caution' suggests pausing, and giving careful forethought while being attentive to the possible dangers that may lie ahead. We assert that this is vitally important given the historical manner in which Black men have been portrayed, misrepresented, and distorted in the name of research. One of the initial questions concerning researchers interested in Black males is 'who can do this work?' A number of researchers have raised questions about the reliability of members outside of particular groups and the manner in which they can or cannot conduct research with a given population (Banks 1993; Gordon 1997; Scheurich and Young 1997). Our purpose is not to debate the merits of the reliability of insider and outsider perspectives. We maintain that culturally sensitive and humanistic research with, on, or about Black males can be conducted by members of any particular ethnic, racial, or gender group but there should be particular attention given to the historical contexts, political realities, and the complexities that are part of the Black male experience.

Our first note of caution is for researchers to recognize the multifaceted nature of Black male identity. Research on the educational experiences of Black males has to recognize the complexity that is Black male identity within the context of learning institutions. For well over a century, the fields of education and psychology have struggled to adequately address the significant challenges Black males face in constructing identities that function in academic achievement settings. Du Bois (1903) paid particular attention to the internal conflict that Black men faced in a United States that, on one hand promoted individual freedoms, while on the other hand, limited the rights of communities of color. His notion of double-consciousness recognized the psychological and socio-historical realities of American oppression and sought to shed light on the complex ways Black men develop a sense of self in the United States. In the time since then we have seen the manifestation of this conflict in soaring dropout rates, high levels of incarceration, and the deterioration of health in the Black community, particularly among young Black men.

A number of works have documented how the complexity of identity, race, and schooling intersect to shape the experiences of young people (Conchas 2006: Duncan 2002; Nasir, McLaughlin, and Jones 2009). Fordham (1988) sought to explore the process by which African American students achieve academic success. Her findings suggest that in order to succeed academically, African American students must disassociate themselves from African American social and cultural norms. Believing that this process happens consciously or unconsciously, Fordham asserted that these students must leave behind values, beliefs, and customs of their own community in order to embrace the culture of school. Fordham and Ogbu (1986) describe this phenomenon as 'the burden of acting White' which they contend has to do with the prevailing notion that academic success is a White characteristic. The resulting effect is the development of African American oppositional identities in schools. Their work has received a great deal of attention and acceptance in the academic community over the past two decades. However, some scholars have critiqued the usefulness of this work as an explanation for explaining the persistent academic underachievement of Black students (Ainsworth-Darnell and Downey 1998; Ward 1990).

Ward (1990) proposed an alternative explanation for high-achieving African American high school students. Ward found that racial identity, personal commitment, and academic achievement successfully converged during the high school years. Ward reported that students felt good about their race and were personally strengthened by their racial status. She concluded that African American students must reject society's negative assessment of Blackness and construct identities that value African American culture. Ward's findings were later supported by the work of Tyson, Darity, and Castellino (2005) who found that racialized ridiculing of high-achieving Black students was not identified by African American high school students as being a reason for not enrolling in advanced placement courses. Ainsworth-Darnell and Downey (1998) state: '[The oppositional identity] argument is misplaced. If anything, African Americans maintain *more* pro-school values and are *more* likely to esteem their high-achieving peers than are Whites. What African Americans lack, however, are the material conditions that foster the development of skills, habits, and styles rewarded by teachers' (551). Similar findings were discovered by Mickelson (2003) who discovered that Black students had a high regard for education despite their poor performance, hence her contention of the achievement–attitude paradox.

An additional caution we put forward is to recognize the contextual nature of behavior. In other words, much of the work on Black males does center on observed behavior, however, much of this work is done without critical analysis of factors that contribute to such behavior. For example, research that examines the experiences of people living in poverty must be aware that conditions tend to influence the manner in which people interpret and respond to the harsh realities that poverty can bring. Wilson (2009) states that 'distinct cultural frames in the inner city have not only been shaped by race and poverty, but in turn often shapes the response to poverty including … the perpetuation of poverty' (16). This is not to suggest a culture of poverty argument as much as it is meant to seek an explanation for why certain behaviors occur and to investigate the context which influences them. A critique of the behavior of people living in poverty without a critique of the structural, historical, and social forces which creates the circumstances and environments which prompt certain types of behavior is shortsighted, dangerous, and is the type of analysis that reinforces deficit-based thinking and theory. A careful understanding of history is warranted to make authentic meaning of how and why young Black males respond to their home, school, and community environments in the way they do. The work of researchers cannot operate from a frame of reference that further pathologizes young Black males, or renders them as the root cause of their disenfranchisement. Noguera (2008) suggests that 'Black males often adopt behaviors that make them complicit in their own failure' (23). The recognition of the social, economic, and political contexts which shapes these behaviors are rarely included in the analysis of young Black men. One example is the incessant criticism of hip hop and rap music. A more careful, critical, and culturally informed analysis of hip hop culture and music reveals a more complex and creative manner of self-expression for many urban youth. The failure to engage in more comprehensive analysis of behaviors and the factors which influence them contribute to only blaming the victim (Ryan 1976). These frames of reference will only reinforce problematic paradigms about Black males. In line with Noguera's (2008) contention about Black males contributing to their own demise, Wilson (2009) poses the following question to social scientists about race and poverty, 'How much of the framing of racial beliefs at the national level is based on the actual observed cultural traits among the inner-city poor and how much of it is the result of bias media reports and racial stereotypes?' (16) To that end, what researchers need to consider are similar questions about how they have developed their viewpoints of Black males. What experiences have constructed the images? And how authentic are the portrayals?

The third and final caution that we would offer is to pay attention to the intersectionality of race, class, and gender. The intersectionality of race, class, and gender are vital in research concerned with young Black males, because each marker in its own ways profoundly influences their identity construction and meaning making. Black males, like any population of students, possess multiple identities that are profoundly shaped by race, socioeconomic status, and gender in all of their complex manifestations. Patricia Hill Collins (2004) refers to the intersectional paradigm as an analytical framework that explains the interrelationships of political and social systems of race, class, gender, and other social divisions that may capture more accurately the complex realities of oppression and marginalization for non-dominant groups. The social and political arrangements and intersection of these identities play out in unique ways that have critical implications for racial and gender minorities, and in particular for young Black males. Anne Ferguson (2001) writes:

> Sex is a powerful marker of difference as well as race. While the concept of intersecting social categories is a useful analytical device for formulating this convergence, in reality we presume to know each other instantly in a coherent, apparently seamless way. We do not experience individuals as bearers of separate identities as gendered and then raced or vice versa, but both at once. The two are inextricably intertwined and circulate together in the representation of subjects and the experience of subjectivity. (22–3).

A conceptual framework with an explicit examination of the ways that race and racism manifest themselves and their juxtaposition with gender in education may offer new analysis into the underachievement of African American males, and provide new insight and direction for reversing their school achievement.

## The concerns

The primary concern we have is that as a research community we have fallen terribly short in examining the complexities associated with the perennial under performance of Black males in US schools. Some researchers have raised the question as to whether we as a research community really care about the plight of young Black males (Howard 2008), others have suggested that not enough scholarly inquiry has occurred because young Black males have been rendered as being 'beyond love' (Duncan 2002), and some posit that Black males are miners' canaries in our nation's schools (Noguera 2008). One of our pressing concerns is that at a time when race and poverty continues to shape the experiences of countless numbers of young Black males, some are suggesting that we give greater attention to the 'post-racial' society that we are currently experiencing (Metzler 2008). The failure to recognize race can omit a critical variable in understanding the schooling experiences of Black males. A number of scholars have examined the manner in which young Black males disengage from schools and the traditional ways it has been arranged (Ogbu 1987; Fordham and Ogbu 1986). Prudence Carter (2005) outlines a framework of why some Black students succeed, and why some do not. One of her contentions is that many Black students who do not succeed in schools are what she refers to as *noncompliant believers*, or students who exert minimal to no effort to acquiesce to the norms and codes of mainstream schooling. These accounts of norms and codes are directly tied to students' cultural knowledge, which is typically a by-product of race and racial socialization

(Lee 2007). The concern with omitting race and the influence that race may have on Black males has the potential to overlook, devalue, or misunderstand the complex types of cultural knowledge that Black males possess based on their experiences in their homes, neighborhoods and communities. The race–culture connection has been explored in a number of scholars works (Lee 2007; Nasir 2002), and should be thoroughly understood when engaging in this work.

A second pressing concern on research on Black males in a post-racial context is the problematic nature of adopting colorblind context for educational research. Bonilla-Silva (2003) outlines four central frames around the potential dangers of colorblind ideology in the work we do as practitioners and researchers. These four frames, *abstract liberalism, naturalization, cultural racism*, and the *minimization of racism*, each elaborate on the problems with the egalitarian, 'racism is behind us' approach that can become acceptable if the belief that we have entered a post-racial society exists. The mere mention of a colorblind approach to our research poses a set of problematic contradictions. Crenshaw (1997) suggests that a colorblind approach seeks to conceal the power and ugliness of race, but at the same time highlights the very significance of it by claiming that to acknowledge it would lead to troublesome outcomes. We argue that a careful analysis of the school outcomes and experiences of Black males would uncover ugly realities that researchers should be willing to examine in an open, straightforward, and critical manner. Undoubtedly, we believe that the centrality of race is a part of this examination, and colorblind approaches would dismiss such accounts. Gotanda (1991) reiterates the shortcomings with colorblindness, stating that it serves to maintain racial subordination. Thus our concern becomes omitting race negates perhaps the primary part of students' identity that shapes their schooling experiences. Nasir and others (2009) call for 'the need for a nuanced conception of African American racial identity that considers both the strength of the identity and the local meaning of the identity' (107). To better understand this identity race is vital. The call for a colorblind approach frequently seeks to cover the past indignities that have afflicted people of color and Black people in particular. Hence, for many researchers race becomes the paradigmatic paradox, the variable that many least want to engage in, yet it may very well be the variable that offers the most valuable insight into how people see the world around them.

Stinson's (2008) study of Black males and how they negotiate sociocultural discourses around race and mathematics provides a cogent example of how researchers can situate race as a central component of young people's educational experiences. Incorporating a critical postmodern theoretical analysis, Stinson discovered that the highly successful students in his study found their realities to be extremely racialized, despite the fact that each of them was high performing students. Several of the participants talked about the ongoing efforts they had to put forth to combat the stereotypical images of Black males, which characterizes them as genetically inferior and academically incapable. In addition, their stories illustrate the sophisticated steps that they had to take to disarm the fear, and alter the low expectations that many of their teachers had towards them. Studies such as Stinson's underscore how the utility of interrogating race with young Black males has the potential to provide important understanding of how they experience school, how they navigate such structures, ideologies, and practices, and how schooling environments can be racially affirming and culturally supportive. The opening up of Black male discourses about how they experience schools can be illuminating, but researchers must also be prepared for harsh critiques that such approaches can produce. Some Black males may provide stinging indictments of schools and schooling practices, White people, White supremacy, and the ideological frames that support its maintenance. Our most pressing concern about individuals conducting race with Black males is a refusal to acknowledge the pernicious affects that the legacy of racism had, and continues to have, on Black males. Therefore, anything short of such an approach should be carefully rethought and reconsidered.

An additional concern that we have is the gross generalization that can take place when examining Black males. One of the mistakes that can be made is to assume that all Black males are at risk. We want to be clear that not all young Black men are failing in schools (we recognize the disturbing numbers that are), all Black males do not reside in large, urban centers, most Black males are not aggressive, hostile, and prone to violence, despite repeated media and social portrayals of them as being such. Research on Black males should seek to identify high-achieving Black males, or document the experiences of Black males in suburban or rural communities which may provide more insight into the realities of this population. We also argue that not enough work has looked the experiences of biracial Black males, who often have a differing account of how they experience race. The concern should also recognize that race continues to matter for many young Black males, yet others may contend that it is less of a factor in their lives. Giving attention to such viewpoints may prove useful in developing a more nuanced, comprehensive, yet complex characterization of Black males; a characterization that can depict them as thoughtful, caring, sensitive, high-achieving, nurturing sons, siblings, friends, fathers, brothers and uncles.

**The considerations**

There are a number of considerations that we offer as a framework for inquiry on Black males. These considerations are informed by the important work that has been done by scholars over the past three decades (Brown and Davis 2000; Davis 2001, 2003; Duncan 2002; Franklin 1991; Gibbs 1988; Hopkins 1997; Howard 2008; Madhubuti 1990; Noguera 2008; Nasir, McLaughlin, and Jones 2009; Polite and Davis 1999; Polite 1994; Price 2000). This body of work serves as an important starting point on the experience of Black males, racial identity, and the need to rethink existing research, policy and practice in order to create more optimum schooling experiences and life chances for Black males. One of the considerations is to allow Black males to be the author of their own experiences. Black males have been picked, prodded, analyzed, interpreted, spoken to, spoken for, and spoken about for over three centuries. The salience of allowing young Black males to name, describe, analyze, and interpret their experiences cannot be stated enough. bell hooks (2004) says that 'every black male in the United States has been forced at some point in his life to hold back the self he wants to express, to repress and contain for fear of being attacked, slaughtered, destroyed' (xii). Each life has its own unique trajectory, set of experiences, triumphs, tragedies, conflicts and contradictions that represent human beings fighting and striving for self-actualization, who better to report these accounts than the actors who have endured these realities. Allowing young Black males to probe into the intricacies, and ponder the possibilities of hope for school reform and individual uplift can prove to be liberating. Unfortunately, for too long the accounts of Black males have been told by others who are neither Black, nor male, and the veracity of such depictions have contributed to the distorted image of Black men (Young 2008). As the Nigerian proverb goes 'Don't let the lion tell the giraffe's story.' Research which allows Black males to be the authors of their own experiences is not only liberating for the individual, in the name of self-actualization, self-critique, and self-authorship, but can be radically enlightening in the pursuit of social equity. Ayers (2006) writes the purpose of 'social justice research [is] to resist harm and redress grievances, research with the explicit goal of promoting a more balanced, fair, and equitable social order' (88).

A second consideration is to incorporate non-traditional frameworks to be used in research. Narrative theory, for example can offer critical insight into how Black males understand and describe their realities. Coulter and Smith (2009) contend that narrative research 'strives to portray experience, to question common understandings.' (577). Denzin (1992) lauds the value of narrative researcher because it introduces the centrality of emotion that is frequently lacking in traditional research, and Barone (2001) describes narrative research as a framework that 'strives to portray experience, to questions common understandings, to offer a degree of interpretive space' (150). One of the advantages to non-traditional frameworks would be to recognize the ways in which race, language, culture, literacy, lived experiences, and historical context influence the way that knowledge is constructed and maintained over time. Yosso's (2005) framework on cultural capital presents an illuminating framework of the unique, yet diverse ways that communities of color respond to their social environments, and how cultural practices can be interpreted in deficit or transformative ways, and she makes a strong call for the latter. Milner (2007) argues that the use of transformative frameworks 'can be useful to researchers serious about interpreting and representing people and communities of color in ways that honor those communities and in ways that maintain their integrity' (397). What we are suggesting is for researchers to be thoughtful, reflective, non-judgmental, and illuminating in their work on African American males. We make a call for researchers to probe into new territories about their experiences, to seek alternative ways of describing how race, gender, and school intersect for Black males. It is also important to take note of the delicate manner in which identity is constructed, maintained, and transformed over time for Black males. All of these areas are tightly connected to race, and would abruptly disrupt the call for post-racial examinations of schooling experiences. An example of this type of research would be Conchas' (2006) research on race and high-achieving urban youth. His research solicited accounts from Black and Latino students to name the obstacles to their school success, and overwhelmingly Black students talked about the need to confront racial segregation and stereotypes. Employing a cultural–ecological framework to examine the intersection of race and school experiences, Conchas found that students in his study cited intense racial segregation in their school, divisions within racial groups, and variance in institutional support along racial lines as factors that are rarely examined to create more equitable school. Schools in the United States are experiencing unprecedented racial and ethnic diversity, and outcome data of student performance consistently shows the disparate outcomes that fall along racial and class lines.

To further highlight the problems with the call for a post-racial society, consider the manner in which socioeconomic status has played out in this country over time. A number of men, all of whom were White and who came from impoverished conditions, were elected president (e.g. Lincoln, Regan, Clinton). Yet none of their elections resulted in a call for recognition of a 'post-poverty' or 'post-class' era. These calls were not heeded because despite the fact that individuals have overcome the obstacles of poverty it did not negate that widespread poverty continued to afflict millions of people then and now. We ask that similar conditions and acknowledgement be given when it comes to the issue of race. Recognition of race, racism, and all of their manifestations remains essential in the twenty-first century even though race relations have improved over the past century.

An example of one of the more probing and penetrating frameworks that could be helpful for work on Black males would be critical race theory. Critical race theory in education seeks to give much needed attention to the role of race in educational research, scholarship, and practice (Dixson and Rousseau 2006; Ladson Billings 2000; Solórzano and Yosso 2002; Parker et al. 1999). The inclusion of a critical race framework in education is essential when one considers the perennial underachievement of African American, Latino/Latina, Native American, and certain Asian American students in US schools. Educators can ill-afford to subscribe to the notion that mere coincidence explains the perpetual school failure of students of color. At some point, the question must be posed: What's race got to do with it? A similar question can be posed when it comes to the educational disenfranchisement of Black males. What does race have to do with the perennial underachievement and exclusion of Black males? Critical race theory in education is an evolving methodological, conceptual, and theoretical construct that attempts to dismantle racism in education. It provides scholars with unique ways to ask the important question of what racism has to do with inequities in education by centering the discussion on racism. A cogent example of how this type of research is carried out would be the work by Nasir and others (2009), who examined the various meanings of racial identity for African American high school students. By allowing students to offer insight into contemporary identity markers, and the social landscape which shapes their formation, Nasir and others allowed African American students to name, describe, analyze, and critique how complex, fluid, and often contradictory their identities become. More importantly, this work helped to disrupt the static characterizations of race and gender, wherein students offered keen insights into how race intersects with social consciousness, cultural context and history, and academic orientation converge in shaping how they view themselves and the world around them.

The final consideration is that this work is to be done in a manner that is authentically concerned with transforming the schooling experiences and life chances of Black males. Unfortunately many see research on or about Black males as just another publication on curriculum vitae, or studying the 'in' topic of the day. We assert that this work is controversial at heart, and should be transformative in nature because it seeks to humanize a dehumanized population. It works to reconstruct an image that has been terribly distorted over time. We strongly suggest for those who are faint of heart, and unwilling to listen, to think long and hard about the criticisms of school structures, racial ideologies, and historical remnants of race and racism to reconsider if this work is for them. As two Black males who have encountered the terrain that is public education in the United States, we know all too well that this is the road less traveled. Moreover, we contend that this work should not just be reduced to theory, but should become part of a much larger effort and movement to reconstruct how society, and consequently, educator researchers and practitioners see Black males. Robin Kelly (2002) reminds us that 'social movements do not simply produce statistics and narratives of oppression; rather the best ones do what great poetry does: transport us to another place, compel us to relive horrors and, more importantly, enable us to imagine a new society' (9).

To consider the magnitude of the type of research that is needed to produce new knowledge about Black males, we pose a critical question: What is the researchers' response to the extended misery, suffering, and education malpractice that far too many Black males endure in America's schools and society? How will you act? How will we all act? What steps are we as a research community willing to take to end exclusion and injustice? Cornel West (2009) states that 'your life becomes your response. Your response doesn't take the form of a written-down, reasoned-out argument. Your response becomes the quality of your day-to-day behavior. The question doesn't go away. It remains powerful and daunting ... do what you can to help the least among us' (101). We offer these cautions, concerns, and considerations with the hope that they remain ever present in the work that we do with Black males, as well as other racially marginalized populations. The questions remain as poignant as ever about how we construct a knowledge base about how to transform the schooling experiences of the least among us, let us hope that our work becomes a vital component in significantly changing the schooling experiences of racially diverse populations so that the day arrives when we truly are a post-racial America.

## Notes

1. We refer to equity minded researchers as scholars and practitioners whose works are concerned with issues tied to equity, access, and the eradication of discriminatory practices and policies which create inequitable schooling conditions.
2. It should be noted that Black women were also victims of the Tuskegee experiments given that they were sexual partners and wives of many, if not most, of the affected Black men. Hence Black women also suffered from untreated venereal diseases and often cared for the untreated men.

## References

Ainsworth-Darnell, J., and D. Downey. 1998. Assessing the oppositional culture explanation for racial/ethnic differences in school performance. *American Sociological Review* 63: 536–53.

Allen, J., A. Hilton, J. Lewis, and L.F. Litwack. 2000. *Without sanctuary.* Santa Fe, NM: Twin Palms Publishers.

Anderson, E., ed. 2008. *Against the wall: Poor, young, Black, and male.* Philadelphia, PA: University of Pennsylvania Press.

Ayers, W. 2006. Trudge toward freedom: Educational research in the public interest. In *Education research in the public interest: Social justice, action, and policy*, ed. G. Ladson Billings and W.F. Tate, 81–97. New York: Teachers College Press.

Banks, J.A. 1993. The canon debate, knowledge construction, and multicultural education. *Educational Researcher* 22, no. 5: 4–14.

Barone, T. 2001. *Teaching eternity: The enduring outcomes of teaching.* New York: Teachers College Press.

Bobo, L., and C. Charles. 2009. Race in the American mind: From the Moynihan Report to the Obama Candidacy. *The Annals of the American Academy of Political and Social Science* 621: 243–59.

Bonilla-Silva, E. 2003. *Racism without racists: Colorblind racism and the persistence of racial inequality in the United States.* Lanham, MD: Rowman & Littlefield.

Brown, M.C., and J.E. Davis. 2000. *Black sons to mothers: Compliments, critiques, and challenges for cultural workers in education.* New York: Peter Lang.

Bureau of Labor Statistics. 2009. http://www.bls.gov/news.release/wkyeng.t02.htm (accessed November 25, 2009).

Carter, P.L. 2005. *Keepin' it real: School success beyond black and white.* New York: Oxford University Press.

Collins, P.H. 2004. *Black sexual politics: African Americans, gender, and the new racism.* New York: Routledge.

Conchas, G.Q. 2006. *The color of success: Race and high-achieving urban youth.* New York: Teachers College Press.

Coulter, C.A., and M.L. Smith. 2009. The construction zone: Literary elements in narrative research. *Educational Researcher* 38, no. 8: 577–90.

Crenshaw, K.W. 1997. Color-blind dreams and racial nightmares: Reconfiguring racism in the post-civil rights era. In *Birth of a nation'hood,* ed. T. Morrison and C.B. Lacour, 97–168. New York: Pantheon.

Davis, J.E. 2001. Black boys at school: Negotiating masculinities and race. In *Educating our black children: New directions and radical approaches*, ed. R. Majors, 169–82. New York: RoutledgeFalmer.

Davis, J.E. 2003. Early schooling and academic achievement of African American males. *Urban Education* 38, no. 5: 515–37.

Denzin, N. 1992. The many faces of emotionality: Reading persona. In *Investigating subjectivity: Research on lived experience*, ed. C. Ellis and M.G. Flaherty, 17–30. Newbury Park, CA: Sage.

Department of Justice. 2009. www.ojp.usdoj.gov/bjs (accessed November 25, 2009).

Dimitriadis, G. 2003. *Friendships, cliques, and gangs: Young black men coming of age in urban America.* New York: Teachers College Press.

Dixson, A.D., and C.K. Rousseau. 2006. *Critical race theory in education.* New York: Routledge.

Du Bois, W.E.B. 1903. *The souls of black folk.* New York: Penguin Group.

Duncan, G.A. 2002. Beyond love: A critical race theory ethnography of the schooling of adolescent black males. *Equity & Excellence* 35, no. 2: 131–43.

Evans-Winters, V.E. 2005. *Teaching black girls: Resiliency in urban classrooms.* New York: Peter Lang.

Ferguson, A.A. 2001. *Bad boys: Public schools in the making of black masculinity.* Ann Arbor: The University of Michigan Press.

Fordham, S. 1988. Racelessness as a factor in black students' school success: Pragmatic strategy or pyrrhic victory? *Harvard Educational Review* 58, no. 1: 54–84.

Fordham, S. 1996. *Blacked out: Dilemmas of race, identity, and success at Capital High.* Chicago: The University of Chicago Press.

Fordham, S., and J. Ogbu. 1986. Black students school success: Coping with the "burden of acting white." *Urban Review* 18: 176–206.

Franklin, C. 1991. The men's movement and the survival of African American men in the 90s. *Changing Men* 21: 20–21.

Gary, F.A., F.C. Scruggs, and H.N. Yarandi. 2003. Suicide among African Americans: Reflections and a call to action. *Issues in Mental Health Nursing* 24: 353–75.

Gibbs, J. 1988. *Young, black, and male in America.* New York: Auburn House.

Gill, W. 1992. Helping African American males: The cure. *The Negro Educational Review,* 63, 31–6.

Gordon, E. 1997. African American males and the second reconstruction. In *Proceedings of the Kenneth B. Clarke Colloquium Series,* Vol. 2. New York: IRADC, City University of New York.

Gotanda, N. 1991. A critique of "our constitution is color-blind". *Stanford Law Review* 44: 1–68.

Gould, S.J. 1981. *The mismeasure of man.* New York: W.W. Norton.

Grant, C.A. 2006. Multiculturalism, race, and the public interest: Hanging on to great-great-granddaddy's legacy. In *Education research in the public interest: Social justice, action, and policy*, ed. G. Ladson Billings and W.F. Tate, 158–72. New York: Teachers College Press.

hooks, b. 2004. *We real cool: Black men and masculinity.* New York: Routledge.

Hopkins, R. 1997. *Educating black males: Critical lesson in schooling, community, and power.* New York: State University of New York Press.

Horsman, R. 1981. *Race and manifest destiny: The origins of American racial Anglo-Saxonism.* Cambridge, MA: Harvard University Press.

Howard, T.C. 2008. Who really cares? The disenfranchisement of African American males in PreK-12 schools: A critical race theory perspective. *Teachers College Record* 110, no. 5: 954–85.

Howard, T.C. 2010. *Why race and culture matter in schools: Closing the achievement gap in America's classrooms.* New York: Teachers College Press.

Hutchison, E.O. 1997. *The assassination of the black male image.* New York: Touchstone.

Joe, S., and M. Kaplan. 2001. Suicide among African American men. *Suicide & Life Threatening Behavior* 31: 106–21.

Kelly, R.D.G. 2002. *Freedom dreams: The Black radical imagination.* Boston: Beacon Press.

Ladson Billings, G. 2000. Racialized discourses and ethnic epistemologies. In *Handbook of qualitative research*, 2nd ed., ed. N. Denzin and Y. Lincoln, 257–77. Thousand Oaks, CA: Sage.

Ladson Billings, G., and W.F. Tate. 1995. Toward a critical race theory of education. *Teachers College Record* 97, no. 1: 47–68.

Lee, C.D. 2007. *Culture, literacy, and learning: Taking blooming in the midst of the whirlwind.* New York: Teachers College Press.

Madhubuti, H. 1990. *Black men: Obsolete, single, dangerous?* Chicago: Third World Press.

Metzler, C.J. 2008. *The construction and rearticulation of race in a post racial America.* Bloomington, IN: Authorhouse.

Mickelson, R. 2003. When are the racial disparities in education the result of racial discrimination? A social science perspective. *Teachers College Record* 105, no. 6: 1052–85.

Milner, H.R. 2007. Race, culture, and researcher positionality: Working through dangers seen, unseen, and unforeseen. *Educational Researcher* 36, no. 7: 388–400.

Noguera, P.A. 2008. *The trouble with black boys…and other reflections on race, equity, and the future of public education.* San Francisco: Jossey-Bass.

Nasir, N. 2002. Identity, goals, and learning: Mathematics in cultural practice. *Mathematical Thinking and Learning* 4, nos. 2–3: 213–47.

Nasir, N., M. McLaughlin, and A. Jones. 2009. What does it mean to be African American? Constructions of race and academic identity in an urban public high school. *American Educational Research Journal* 46, no. 1: 73–114.

Ogbu, J. 1987. Opportunity structure, cultural boundaries, and literacy. In *Language, literacy, and culture: Issues of society and schooling*, ed. J. Langer, 123–45. Norwood: Ablex Press.

Omi, M., and H. Winant. 1994. *Racial formation in the United States: From the 1960s to the 1990s.* New York: Routledge.

Parker, L., D. Deyhle, and D. Villenas. 1999. *Race is…race isn't: Critical race theory and qualitative studies in education.* Boulder, CO: Westview.

Pierre, R.E., and J. Jeter. 2009. *A day late and a dollar short: High hopes and deferred dreams in Obama's "Post-Racial" America.* Hoboken, NJ: Wiley & Sons.

Polite, V. 1994. The method in the madness: African American males, avoidance, schooling, and chaos theory. *Journal of Negro Education* 60, no. 30: 345–59.

Polite, V., and J. Davis. 1999. *African American males in school and society. Practices and policies for effective education.* New York: Teachers College Press.

Poussaint, A.F., and A. Alexander. 2000. *Lay my burden down: Suicide and the mental health crisis among African Americans.* Boston: Beacon Press.

Price, J. 2000. *Against the odds: The meaning of school and relationships in the lives of six African American men.* Westport, CT: Ablex Publishing.

Ryan, W. 1976. *Blaming the victim.* New York: Vintage.

Scheurich, J.J., and M.D. Young. 1997. Coloring epistemologies: Are our research epistemologies racially biased? *Educational Researcher* 26, no. 4: 4–16.

Schott Foundation for Public Education. 2008. Given half a chance: The Schott 50 state report on public education and black males. Cambridge, MA: The Schott Foundation for Public Education. http://www.schottfoundation.org (accessed September 1, 2009).

Selden, S. 1999. *Inheriting shame: The story of eugenics and racism in America.* New York: Teachers College Press.

Solórzano, D., and T. Yosso. 2002. Critical race methodology: Counterstorytelling as an analytical framework for educational research. *Qualitative Inquiry* 8, no. 1: 23–44.

Skiba, R.J., and R.L. Peterson. 2000. School discipline: From zero tolerance to early response. *Exceptional Children* 66: 335–47.

Skiba, R.J., S. Robert, R.S. Michael, A.C. Nardo, and Reece L. Peterson. 2007. The color of discipline: Sources of racial and gender disproportionality in school punishment. *The Urban Review* 34, no. 4: 317–42.

Stanfield, J. 1993. *A history of race relations research: First-generation recollections.* Newbury Park, CA: Sage Publishers.

Stinson, D.W. 2008. Negotiating sociocultural discourses: The counterstorytelling of academically (and mathematically) successful African American male students. *American Educational Research Journal* 45, no. 4: 975–1010.

Tate, W.F. 2006. In the public interest. In *Education research in the public interest: Social justice, action, and policy,* ed. G. Ladson Billings and W.F. Tate, 247–60. New York: Teachers College Press.

Tillman, L.C. 2002. Culturally sensitive research approaches. *Educational Research* 31, no 9: 3–12.

Tyson, K., W. Darity, and D. Castellino. 2005. It's not "a black thing": Understanding the burden of acting white and other dilemmas of high achievement. *American Sociological Review* 70: 582–605.

Ward, J. 1990. Racial identity formation and transformation. In *Making connections: The relational worlds and adolescent girls at Emma Willard School,* ed. C. Gilligan, N. Lyons and T. Hanmer, 215–32. Cambridge, MA: Harvard University Press.

Washington, H.A. 2006. *Medical apartheid: The dark history of medical experimentation on Black Americans from colonial times to the present.* New York: Random House.

West, C. 2009. *Brother West. Living and loving out loud. A memoir.* New York: Smiley Books.

Wilson, W.J. 2009. *More than just race: Being black and poor in the inner city.* New York: Norton.

Young, A. 2008. White ethnographers and the ethnography of African American men: Then and now. In *White logics, white methods,* ed. E. Bonilla-Silva and T. Zuberi, 179–202. Lanham, MD: Rowman & Littlefield.

Yosso, T.J. 2005. Whose culture has capital? A critical race theory discussion of community cultural wealth. *Race Ethnicity and Education* 8, no. 1: 69–91.

# New possibilities: (re)engaging Black male youth within community-based educational spaces

Bianca J. Baldridge[a], Marc Lamont Hill[b] and James Earl Davis[c]

[a]Sociology and Education, Teachers College, Columbia University, New York, NY, USA;
[b]Anthropology and Education, Teachers College, Columbia University, New York, NY, USA;
[c]Education, Leadership, and Policy Studies, Temple University, Philadelphia, PA, USA

>   Despite the assertion that due to an Obama presidency America has become a post-racial society, Black males still face a unique social crisis. In this article, we hold that both race and gender continue to work in tandem to produce a certain set of social outcomes for young Black men in America despite this assertion. The educational, economic, and social mobility of young Black men is often limited due to structural constraints that are exacerbated by the intersectional dynamism of race, gender, and social class. As young Black men continue to experience social hardships, they are being pushed further and further away from traditional school contexts. Drawing from qualitative interviews with 24 young Black male participants from EmpowerYouth, a national community-based organization, this study highlights the importance of alternative sites of education and youth development for Black male youth. Findings from this study indicate that flexibility, applied educational and work experience, and positive healthy adult–youth relationships provided by EmpowerYouth, granted solace for young Black males who traversed through difficult circumstances within traditional school contexts. Our findings speak to the need to create new and relevant educational models that address the unique and complex circumstances of young Black men in America. Ultimately, as young Black males are often considered to be social burdens, this study shows how successful community-based programs like EmpowerYouth reframe young Black males as a valued segment of society that deserve support, care, and educational sites that are able to respond to their distinct academic and social needs.

Since the historic election of Barack Obama, post-racial rhetoric has consumed national discourse in ways that reflect a deep social irony. As small numbers of African Americans reach new levels of economic, social, and educational success, the broader racial cohort continues to linger at the bottom of nearly all indices of social prosperity and mobility. For young Black males (and, increasingly, Black women), this contrast is particularly sharp, as they continue to be over-represented in prisons and under-represented in the nation's workforce and colleges. Further, as neoliberal approaches to educational policy continue to normalize privatization, standardization, and the deskilling of teachers and students (Giroux 2003), schools are becoming increasingly inflexible, often denying second or third chances for students who need them (Davis 2006). While considerable research has examined some of these structural issues (Ferguson 2000; Noguera 1996), there remains a dearth of research that examines how young Black men make sense of their schooling experiences, as well as their transition out of traditional schools and into alternative community programs and schools. Additionally, insufficient attention has been paid to the role of community support spaces that facilitate opportunities for young Black men that are not often available in traditional school contexts.

To address these lacunae, this article explores the role of community-based organizations that support young Black males in their academic achievement, as well as their personal development and civic engagement. Drawing from qualitative interviews with young Black male participants of EmpowerYouth, a national community-based program for low-income students who have dropped out or been forced out of traditional schools, we examine how young Black males make sense of their traditional schooling experiences and their negotiation of alternative educational contexts. Specifically, this article spotlights some of the key obstacles, many of which emerge at the intersection of race, class and gender, that contribute to the premature departure of Black males from traditional school contexts.

The article also examines how the form and structure of the EmpowerYouth program served as a more functional alternative to traditional schooling contexts. In particular, the young Black men in the study found that EmpowerYouth provided them with more stable and productive relationships with teachers and peers, more authentic learning experiences, and opportunities to imagine and nurture new conceptions of manhood. Such findings underscore the significance of community-based youth organizations and other alternative educational spaces as viable and valuable sites of possibility for improving the educational experiences of Black males.

## Intersectional approaches to studying Black males

As we argue throughout this article, Black males face a unique social crisis. Such a claim demands a close examination of the respective roles played by race and gender in constituting the conditions faced by young Black men. Rather than assuming an 'either–or' stance, in which we choose between race and gender as the primary determinant of social outcomes, we follow the lead of critical race and gender scholars by focusing on the intersections of race and gender. By adopting an intersectional analysis, we are able to understand how the social constructs of race and gender mutually construct and reinforce one another (Collins 1998). Research on intersectionality has focused on the ways that race, class, gender, and nation interact in compounding ways, particularly those who are subjugated to marginal positions based on their social identities (Collins 1998; McCall 2005).

The most influential body of work on gender–race intersectionality has emerged from Black feminist and multicultural feminist studies. Black feminist scholarship has shown how separate theories of race and gender do not fully capture the complex nature of human experiences as simultaneous and linked identities (Browne and Misra 2003; Glenn 1999; hooks 1989). An example of this linkage is the dominant stereotype of Black males as hypersexual and violent Black man, who was conceived as a threat to society, and most especially to White women (Brown and Misra 2003; Davis 1981). This fear was not merely abstract, as it served as a primary justification for lynching and other acts of civic terror against all Black Americans, but especially Black males (Davis 1981). Other examples can be found within the labor market.

Empirical studies have shown that Black males were regularly described by employers as 'lazy,' 'belligerent,' or 'dangerous' and therefore sometimes less likely to be hired for jobs (Kirschenman and Neckerman 1991). In these instances, both the racist narratives and their material consequences were not reducible to racial or gendered explanations, but an outgrowth of both. As Browne and Misra (2003) argue, 'there are social constructions of gender that are racialized and social constructions of race that are gendered to create a particular experience' (490). It is from this position that we examine the experiences of young Black men, who are both out-of-school and out-of-work, as simultaneously 'racialized' and 'gendered' subjects.

**Young Black males in 'post-racial' America**

Since the 2008 presidential election, the term 'post-racial' – the idea that race is no longer an influential factor in social life – has taken on new life within American public discourse. As race scholars have argued, post-racial rhetoric has been a tool of the political Right used to maintain the status quo of the American power structure (Marable 2000). By framing colorblindness and 'colormutenes' as social ideals (Crenshaw et al. 1995; Pollock 2004), an ideology also adopted by liberal race theorists (Williams 1997), any form of 'race-talk' is viewed as socially regressive and per se racist. From this post-racial posture, we obscure the role of race as the persistent predicate for various forms of social inequality (Teasley and Ikard 2009).

While critics and powerbrokers attempt to capitalize on the current post-racial zeitgeist, Black Americans still struggle for economic equality and social mobility. African Americans and Latino/as make up less than 5% of the wealth in the US and they constitute at least 25% of the population. The median net worth of Black families is slightly greater than $20,000, compared to Whites at slightly over $140,000 (Teasley and Ikard 2010). Moreover, the small wealth gains made by African Americans in recent years have nearly vanished in light of the economic downturn of the late 2000s. Prior to the economic downtown, however, Black men were already in depression-level economic distress with regard to income, wealth, and employment opportunities (Cawthorne 2009).

Post-racial rhetoric is particularly troublesome when addressing Black male youth, whose lives remain plagued by the effects of racism. While federal and local policy decry community underdevelopment and school failure, few acknowledge the unique social, political, and economic conditions that low-income Black males experience on a day-to-day basis (Ginwright, Noguera, and Cammarota 2005). Young Black males continue to be a vulnerable population, lingering at the bottom of every marker of social prosperity, as well as the top of nearly every marker of social misery (Noguera 2008). Recent statistics have shown that Black males have the highest rates of incarceration with one out of three men aged 20–34 incarcerated; they also have the highest rates of arrests, violent attacks, and homicides (Pew Charitable Trusts 2008). These conditions are further intensified by poverty, as young Black men who reside in both urban and rural contexts with high levels of concentrated poverty are more likely to receive poor social services, low quality healthcare, housing, and education, as well as limited opportunity for economic and social mobility. Scholarship on poverty has shown that the impact of high levels of concentrated poverty on Black males creates a multiplying effect that spills over into other social institutions that are vital to the livelihood of communities and the healthy development of youth (Gabarino 1999). One of the key examples of this effect is the educational sphere, where the circumstances of Black males are particularly precarious.

**Black males in educational contexts**

The climate of public education for Black males in challenging social and economic contexts is a formidable one. Despite comprising only 6% of the nation's population, Black males account for nearly one-third of all student dropouts (Aud, Fox, and KewelRamani 2010). According to census data, 42% of Black males will have failed an entire grade level at least once by the time they reach high school. Only 18% of Black males are enrolled in college and less than half of Black students who obtain a college degree are male (Aud, Fox and KewelRamani 2010). Class privilege fails to shield Black males disparate educational outcomes, as middle class Black males still fall behind in grade point averages and standardized test scores compared to White students (Noguera 2008).

Studies show that Black males are routinely targeted in schools and viewed as dangers to the school environment (Ginwright 2009; Males 1999; Noguera 1996). This narrative is rooted in a broader majoritarian narrative that frames Black males as civic threats that warrant containment and policing (Anderson, 2009; Barker 1988). As a consequence of this narrative, Black male students are often treated as criminals within school contexts (Ferguson 2000; Giroux 2009) and more likely to be expelled, suspended, or removed from classroom instruction than other racial and ethnic groups for the same behaviors (Gregory, Skiba, and Noguera 2010; Greene and Winters 2006; Holzman 2004). These severe punishments are a result of zero tolerance policies – another outgrowth of the current hegemony of neo-liberal approaches to education policy (Bourdieu and Wacquant 2001) – which are ostensibly colorblind but disproportionally impact Black males (Johnson and Howard 2009). Another outgrowth of this discipline gap is that Black male students are routinely mislabeled as having severe mental and behavioral challenges, resulting in their over-representation in special education programs (Noguera 1996, 2003).

Educational researchers have offered a range of explanations for the educational plight of Black males. Historical approaches demonstrate the impact of intergenerational patterns of institutional racism on the life outcomes of Black males (e.g. Leary 2005; Young 2004). Scholars have also linked the obstacles facing young Black men to current structural inequality and stratification processes across racial, class, and gender lines that manifest within public schools. Specifically, these scholars have demonstrated how limited social and economic opportunities within neighborhoods coupled with poorly funded and under-resourced schools further cripple the educational and social outcomes for Black students (Ferguson 2000; Wilson 1996). A subset of these scholars has focused on the reproduction of inequality and social stratification through school-based processes like ability grouping and tracking, both of which increase segregation and underperformance within school classrooms (Oakes 1985).

The educational performance of Black males is also undermined by their engagement with the everyday processes of traditional schooling contexts. As Davis (2006) demonstrates, the concerns and perspectives of Black men are often unfairly ignored or dismissed by teachers and school-level administrators. Studies also demonstrate that Black males are more likely to have negative interactions with school officials and receive unfair treatment by teachers and security officers than their peers from other racial/ethnic groups, as well as their Black female counterparts (Ginwright 2004;

Kunjufu 1990; Noguera 1996; Woodland et al. 2009). Black male students are routinely deprived of forms of curriculum and pedagogy that respond to their social realities and experiences (Davis 2006; Hill 2009; Jordan and Cooper 2003; Lynn 2006). Considerable research has also shown that expectations of Black students held by teachers, significantly shapes academic achievement (Kellow and Jones 2008; Lewis and Kim 2008; Noguera 1996; Oates 2003). In addition to draconian discipline policies, Black males are also forced to navigate institutions in which teachers and administrators have low expectations for their achievement (Ferguson 2000).

As Fine (1991) argues, this confluence of low expectations, negative interactions, draconian discipline policies, and inadequate educational resources effectively undermines the educational possibilities of Black male youth. Such an argument is critical, as it points to the ways that young Black males not only underperform or abandon formal education, but are also systematically forced out of traditional schooling contexts. It is from this position that many education workers have looked to alternative education programs as a means by which to improve the educational chances of Black male youth. One of the most intriguing sites for this type of work has been community-based youth organizations.

## The importance of community-based organizations for young Black males

During the 1960s, education policies stemming from the New Deal and the Great Society played a significant role in establishing opportunities for low-income youth and young adults to gain employment (Kantor and Lowe 1995). Many of these opportunities came in the form of employment programs that provided marginalized youth of color with chances to make money while continuing their education. In the late 1970s and early 1980s, many urban centers were devastated by unprecedented rates of unemployment, substance abuse, and crime. Following this period, the non-profit sector increased; mentoring programs, employment programs, and after-school academic enrichment programs began to surface in poor urban contexts throughout the country in places such as, New York, Oakland, and Los Angeles (Ginwright 2009). By the early 1990s, the Carnegie Council on Adolescent Development's Task Force on Youth Development and Community Programs began to provide national attention to the growing importance of community-based work for youth (McLaughlin, Irby, and Langman 1994). The task force highlighted the salience of the networks that community-based organizations provided for young people. As a result of the task force, many organizations received widespread recognition and funding to support their endeavors. Specifically, organizations such as Boys & Girls Clubs of America were highlighted as successful examples of programs that receive national attention and federal funding to carry out their missions (McLaughlin, Irby, and Langman 1994).

A growing body of research has explored the significance of community-based youth organizations (CBYOs) in the educational lives of Black males (Fashola 2003; Ginwright 2009; Hirsch 2005; Woodland 2008; Woodland et al. 2009). Considerable diversity exists among CBYOs with regard to mission, structure, method of service delivery (Eccles and Appleton-Gootman 2002). CBYOs are regularly situated both within and outside of traditional school buildings; they operate before, during, and after the traditional school day (Eccles and Appleton-Gootman 2002). While some programs focus on the strengths, talents, and gifts of youth, others focus on 'fixing' youth by addressing their shortcomings and deficits (Damon 2004).

Despite considerable variation among CBYOs, they are marked by several key features. While often situated within the same social, political, and economic contexts as traditional schools, CBYOs are typically not held to the same type of bureaucratic constraints that schools are forced to negotiate (Eccles and Appleton-Gootman 2002). Consequently, they are able to function with greater curricular and programmatic flexibility. In addition, most CBYOs have less hierarchical structures, enabling them to engage in more democratic forms of interaction with program workers and students. CBYOs often provide services to youth such as academic tutoring, recreational activities, college preparation, racial and ethnic awareness, gender-specific programming, leadership development, and civic engagement (Eccles and Appleton-Gootman 2002; McLaughlin 2000). As a result, CBYOs are in a critical position to increase the level of support available to overburdened schools and address the unique needs of vulnerable populations.

Empirical research suggests that CBYOs provide favorable experiences and outcomes for the youth they serve. Studies suggest that young people who are engaged in community-based programs are more likely to have high levels of social trust (Mahoney et al. 2005; McLaughlin 2000). Studies also suggest that CBYOs facilitate the development of social capital for young people and a deeper understanding of the social context in which they live and learn (Ginwright 2007, 2009; Kirshner 2004; Teachman, Paasch, and Carver 1996). Case studies of particular CBYOs highlight how such spaces enable youth to explore and develop their social identities, more effectively navigate their schools and communities, and function as safe spaces that encourage social critique and activism (Ginwright 2007, 2009; McLaughlin, Irby, and Langman 1994). In addition, studies suggest that CBYOs support students' academic achievement, also help build meaningful relationships between peers and adults, develop resistance skills against risky behaviors, and develop youth capacities and transferable skill sets (Lakin and Mahoney 2006; Miller 2003; Roth and Brooks-Gunn 2003). As Davis (2006) argues, CBYOs provide crucial 'second chances' for youth, a disproportionate number of whom are Black male, that have dropped out or been forced out of traditional schools. Given the social dangers attached to Black male drop outs – for example, Black males without high school diplomas are more likely to live in economic distress and poverty and four times more like to be arrested (Bowman 2002; Fine 1991; Nembhard 2005) – CBYOs serve as a crucial safety net for Black male youth.

While the current literature makes a compelling argument for the value of CBYOs, there remains a lacuna of research that examines how young Black males make sense of their engagement within these types of programs (Woodland et al. 2009). In particular, there is a dearth of scholarship that highlights the experiences of Black male youth before, during, and after their involvement with CBYO programs. It is within this space that we situate this study, which explores the experiences of young Black men aged 18 to 25, the majority of who dropped out of high school. In the same vein as Young (2004) and Howard (2008), we position the voices of young Black men as the central focus of this article as they critically assess their experiences in traditional schooling environments and the EmpowerYouth program.

## Methods and study description

The site for this study is the EmpowerYouth (pseudonym) program, a federally funded non-profit youth leadership and community development program. The program, which serves more than 10,000 annually, focuses low-income youth in both urban and rural environments. Like many of the CBYOs detailed in the literature, Empower Youth prides itself on providing opportunities for youth in need, to change not only their lives, but also their communities. EmpowerYouth offers job training, as well as education and life skills assistance to out-of-school youth. As a youth community development program, the organization addresses major issues facing low-income neighborhoods, such as housing, employment, crime prevention, education, and leadership development. Young people, aged 16–24, take courses at EmpowerYouth sites to work toward their GEDs or high school diplomas, learn job skills and serve their communities by building affordable housing. Started in the late 1970s in the Northeastern United States, the EmpowerYouth philosophy is driven by belief in 'rebuilding' the lives of out-of-work and out-of-school youth as a means of expanding their educational, social, and economic possibilities.

EmpowerYouth serves as a rich site of inquiry, as its structural, ideological, and programmatic features are reflective of the CBYOs most commonly discussed in the research literature. There are nearly 300 EmpowerYouth sites throughout the country, including most major US cities. The curriculum of EmpowerYouth is centered on providing students with a mixture of job experience through renovating an actual home in the participants' community, classroom work leading to a high school diploma or an equivalent (if needed), and community service. Additionally, every student participant has the opportunity to receive personal counseling and assistance in developing a personal growth plan. EmpowerYouth students alternate their time each week between a construction site where they build housing for those who are homeless or on a low-income and at the program's alternative school to work towards their high school diploma or GED. Classes are set up with only a few students to ensure that teachers provide individualized instruction and attention to students. Another unique feature of the program is that EmpowerYouth participants are included in the decision making of the organization, through an elected policy committee. Through this opportunity, students are encouraged to learn valuable skills that help them become ethical community leaders.

## Methods and procedures

The data for this study emerges from 24 close case studies with young Black men, aged 18 to 30, who graduated from the EmpowerYouth program. These interviews were part of a larger study of former EmpowerYouth participants at various sites throughout the country. The participants were selected to provide a purposive sample of different types of students who had completed the program at each site. The selection of interview participants was carried out through a database of all graduates for the program generated by local staff. In addition to the names and addresses of graduates, the database included information on students' graduation date, gender, race/ethnicity, age, marital status, current occupational/schooling status and whether they had children. Based on the proportional representation of these characteristics at each site, we tried to identify potential interviewees who reflected these demographics. For instance, if 50% of the list of graduates were African American males, half of the interview group selected represented this racial and gender group. Thus at each site we interviewed a sample of students that were reflective of the graduates from that site. In addition, we deliberately included two graduates at each site who were neither currently employed or in school. From this sample, we produced 57 interviewees, 24 of whom are the African American males who are included in this study.

Although the 24 participants come from various cities around the country, many of them had similar upbringings and personal challenges. Specifically, many of the participants were raised in single-parent households and encountered difficult obstacles within their neighborhoods, including the lure of street culture and the temptation to sell drugs in order to make money for their own needs or to support their families. The majority of participants' families struggled financially. Several of the young men in the study at one point in time were arrested for offenses like petty theft and drug possession. Some of the young men arrived at EmpowerYouth as a last chance opportunity to do something positive with their lives, while others were held back so many times in traditional schools that dropping out of school and attending a non-traditional program like EmpowerYouth to obtain their GED proved to be the most practical option.

Interviews with EmpowerYouth graduates were conducted as part of seven site visits in Los Angeles, Philadelphia, Boston, Madison, St. Louis, Bloomington and York. Each participant was interviewed once for approximately 90–120 minutes. All interviews were audio taped and transcribed with participants' permission, resulting in 1600 pages of data. Analytic memos were kept throughout the data collection period to effectively preserve the content of assertions made at various stages and to gain what Glaser (1978) calls 'theoretical sensitivity.' As expected, the majority of analysis took place at the end of the data collection stage. After reading through the collected data, interview transcripts were coded and categorized to facilitate the development of analytic concepts and themes.

### 'Smart enough to drop out'

Participants found their traditional schooling experiences to be highly problematic and ultimately unbearable. The common theme that emerged from participant interviews was that students overwhelmingly had negative schooling experiences that were further complicated by their social and economic conditions. As a result of these experiences, students believed that leaving school was not only convenient, but their best available option. The stories of Casey, Myles, and Darnell serve as representative cases of this phenomenon, which was articulated by nearly all interviewees.

An example of this pattern comes from Casey, a 22-year-old youth from St. Louis, Missouri, who dropped out of school in the tenth grade before joining the Empower Youth program. Casey had been dismissed from the school in his own county, which forced him to attend a school that did not include any of the peers from his community. This led to a sense of social isolation that was not addressed or even acknowledged by the school:

> I was in a school all by myself. I didn't know anybody and it's hard to make friends because everyone is so cliquish. I'm not saying that the school could've fixed that but they could've at least talked to me about it. Like how they don't think that being by yourself in school doesn't make a difference?

In addition to social problems, Casey found little value in his learning experiences. He explained, 'I mean, you don't learn nothing. You learn nothing. I mean, they pass you if you show up to class … There's no real point in going.' As such, school attendance quickly became a perfunctory rather than an intrinsically valuable or rewarding practice.

Like other participants, Casey had a difficult upbringing and moved around a lot, staying with extended relatives from time to time. He soon became uninterested in school and began 'running the streets all the time at night' while doing odd jobs to help support himself and his family. After working several low-wage jobs, Casey decided that he wanted to obtain his GED in order to increase his chances in the job market. He was attracted to the EmpowerYouth program, because he could take courses to work towards his GED and simultaneously earn money by doing the work provided by the program.

Myles, a 21-year-old former participant from St. Louis, was 17 when he dropped out of school. Despite his desire to succeed in school, Myles found that his school environment 'was [an] obstacle' to educational success. Specifically, Myles pointed to peer social relations and lack of teacher support as powerful impediments to learning. According to Myles, by the time he got to the sixth grade, school became a 'fashion show,' in which social status and mobility were largely determined by the price and variety of clothing and jewelry that students wore. Due to his family's financial difficulties, Myles was forced to wear the same 'broke gear' (inexpensive clothing) every day, subjecting him to intense teasing from his peers. Myles often responded to his feelings of shame and embarrassment by getting into physical altercations with students or, more often, by skipping school altogether, both of which led to increased levels of punishment from the school. Although Myles says that he attempted to explain his circumstances to school authorities, his concerns and complaints were dismissed or altogether ignored. As a result of his poor attendance and lack of engagement, Myles's grades suffered and he was expelled and forced to transfer to another school.

Myles was eager to transfer because he was worried about being accepted by his peers and he also wanted to be in a school where teachers would offer rigorous and engaged instruction. By the time he was finally able to transfer, the new school wanted him to repeat all four years of high school in order to graduate. Myles explains:

> I want somebody to teach me and at the same time, I want somebody, I need somebody to be hard on me. So it's, like, I'm trying to go to a different school. But soon as a I get there, I was like they want me to do four years over, and I'm like ... 17 going on 18? I added that up. Shit I'm not going to be out of high school 'til I'm 20 [laughs]. I'm like, I'm not doing this. So I just dropped out. And I cried the day when I dropped out. I couldn't get into another school. I just, I cried.

Myles's comment speaks to the dilemma that many EmpowerYouth described in their interviews. Despite their desire to (re)commit themselves to educational success, schools did little to encourage them to stay. Instead, the schools forced them to stay in traditional programs as an older student, which presented them with significant social and financial problems.

Darnell, a participant from Boston shared similar perspectives about his school experience. He explained how difficult it was to attend school without having clean clothes and being forced to wear the same clothes multiple days in a row. Like Myles, Darnell and many of his peers often chose to skip school rather than deal with the social consequences of their economic circumstances. These consequences, he explained, were exacerbated by his school's teachers and administrators, whom he described as largely ineffective and indifferent. He explains:

> [I]t's a few teachers that really push you to, they, they know your potential and stuff like that. But there was a few that just lay back, like the students ...

Darnell further explains that:

> all you had to do was show up, you know what I'm saying?

Rather than just 'show up,' Darnell elected to drop out entirely and pursue full time employment.

When asked to describe his exit from high school, Casey responded by saying that he 'was smart enough to drop out!' Casey's remark speaks of his belief that his schooling context was incompatible with both academic and social success and, therefore, not worth engagement. Such comments were typical, as students regularly challenged the majoritarian narrative of education as a universal agent of social mobility by linking their decision to drop out to their recognition of the dysfunctional and counterproductive nature of schooling in their individual lives. Additionally, their stated reasons for dropping out also challenge dominant narratives of Black male anti-intellectualism, social indifference, and outright nihilism, as their respective decisions for leaving school were linked to a desire for more authentic and rigorous educational environments.

This is not to suggest that the participants' analyses of their schooling environment was fully accurate, nor that their decision to drop was prudent. Rather, their comments demonstrate the ways in which traditional school contexts are complicit in the exodus of Black male students by not responding to the values, concerns, and lived realities that they face. Furthermore, they foreshadow the critical role played by teachers in the EmpowerYouth program.

### *'Not like regular teachers'*

As the research literature has shown, healthy youth–adult relationships are crucial for positive youth development (Lakin and Mahoney 2006). Participants in Empower Youth indicated that teachers in the program were 'not like regular teachers' and, as a result, many sought to build meaningful relationships with them. Myles shared that EmpowerYouth instructors were closer to him than his teachers in traditional schools and actually saw and believed in his potential. He also pointed to the various ways that EmpowerYouth teachers regularly engaged students in ways that were radically different than their experiences in traditional schools. For example, teachers in EmpowerYouth devoted the first five minutes of every class meeting to facilitating conversations with students about their personal lives, job experiences, and other topics that were of significance to them. In addition to creating closer bonds between specific teachers and students, such dialogues reflected EmpowerYouth's institutional commitment to valuing the in-school and out-of-school lives of its students. The examples of Kareem, James, and Larry serve as telling cases of this phenomenon.

Kareem, a participant from Philadelphia dropped out of school after completing the tenth grade, provides another example of this sentiment. When asked what he thought could be improved about his school experience, Kareem explained, 'the one-on-one wasn't really as good as it could be.' In contrast, during his time in the EmpowerYouth program, Kareem finally felt like he was able to build strong relationships with teachers, whom he and other participants described as 'more real.' He explains:

> The teachers, that's one thing about it. The teachers was good, man. They, they sit down with you, they want to know about your personal life and everything. They just, they was cool. The teachers was cool, man.

Kareem also explained that many instructors, in addition to taking active interest in students' lives, play the role of 'father figure' to the students in the program. Such characterizations of EmpowerYouth staff members speak not only to the positive nature of their relationships, but also highlight the particular types of relationships that Black male students found valuable. Specifically, participants consistently stated that they valued the prevalence of male teachers who took demonstrated interest in students' out-of-school lives, provided positive examples as role models, and also offered appropriate and consistent forms of discipline. Given the frequency of absentee or non-custodial fathers among research participants, as well as within the broader African American community (Randolph 1995; Wade 1994), the role of EmpowerYouth staff as 'father figure' was particularly critical in positively responding to the lived realities of Black male students.

Although James graduated from high school, he shared that he was 'not as motivated as [he] should have been' to continue onto college. He began hanging out with the 'wrong crowd' and briefly sold marijuana. Eventually, he grew tired of the low wages and high dangers of selling drugs and decided to 'do more with his life,' prompting him to enter the EmpowerYouth program. The positive student–teacher relationships in EmpowerYouth were significant to James's experience. In particular, he explains:

> Harry was the best, man. He, it's like [pause] Harry would take an issue, look at it from all the sides, yeah. He would bring you in there, teach you how to do the same thing, look at all the sides, and let you do it...without the, trying to condemn 'em from making mistakes. See, making mistakes, that's okay. That's what Harry's philosophy was. And every time I made a mistake, Harry let me make that mistake, Harry let me make that mistake, and I was okay. I learned from it. To this day, you know, I think about, wow, I probably messed up more houses than I actually built at EmpowerYouth.

James's relationship with Harry, which was similar to many of the teacher–student relationships described by EmpowerYouth students, is a model of the healthy adult–youth relationships described by youth development scholars (Meltzer et al. 2006; Roth and Brooks-Gunn 2003). EmpowerYouth teachers were regularly described as patient, committed to students' potential for success, and eager to build positive relationships with them. Additionally, as James explained, EmpowerYouth teachers viewed mistakes as opportunities for mentoring, growth, and development rather than punishment. Such an approach stood in sharp contrast to their traditional schooling experiences, which, as described above, were marked by impersonal, rigid, and largely punitive responses to student 'mistakes.'

Larry, a participant from a Los Angeles EmpowerYouth site, dropped out of high school in his senior year. Like many of the other participants, Larry found considerable value in the program's ability to foster strong relationships between students and teachers. In addition to the aforementioned reasons, Larry cited the program's practice of hiring former students as a key factor in its success. By hiring former program members, he explained, students were guaranteed to have teachers who are close to them in both age and experience:

> It's really important that they hire people that used to be in the program because they are more like us. Like, they're younger and been through a lot of the same stuff as we did ... I mean, especially ... when they dealing with new students. Like when they come in, they got a problem, like, 'Oh, so-and-so ... That's somebody who can relate to them'.

In addition, Larry and other students pointed to the existence of former students as concrete evidence that they could also be successful in the program.

### *'From boyhood to manhood'*

Participants spoke candidly and consistently about the significance of the Empower Youth program on their lives and careers. Specifically, many of the young men claimed that EmpowerYouth programming gave them opportunities and skills that better prepared them for their transition into adulthood. For them, the program not only provided opportunities to earn money, but also served as a space for reimagining their roles as citizens, leaders, and workers. For the participants, this transition was routinely described as the process of becoming 'real men.' While definitions of 'manhood' varied slightly among participants, each reflected a broader and more positive conception of male adulthood that they attributed to their involvement with the EmpowerYouth program.

According to Kareem, the EmpowerYouth program exposed him and his peers to a wider range of possibilities for Black manhood. He explains:

> It's given me a whole lot of opportunities, helped me see, helped me be able to get in touch with a whole lot of different places about myself and stuff like that. It helped me grow up ... It just helped me grow up. And, be a man.

For Kareem, the community service projects were a critical site for this process of self-discovery and 'grow[ing] up.' In addition to helping him recognize new skills and interests, the projects were the first space in which he realized that he could use his talents to serve and enhance his community. Like other participants, this experience allowed Kareem to reject and challenge hegemonic narratives of Black male youth as civic threats and social burdens (Giroux 1996). In doing so, he was able to embrace more redemptive conceptions of Black manhood that enhanced the 'generational identity' (Hill 2009) of himself and his peers.

Participants also talked about EmpowerYouth as a space that allowed them to develop as leaders and mentors. James, for example, explained that his service experiences as a tutor for young children provided a 'stepping-stone' for his current career as a youth worker as well as a strong transition into manhood. He explains:

> I never really thought I liked children until I started tutoring children at EmpowerYouth. I really thought I didn't like them because I never associated with them [laughs]. And, um, that propelled me to another dimension far as um connections and career. To this day I love children, so wow, it was the best thing that ever happened to me, you know?

He later added:

> [The experience] also helped me to make that change from boyhood to manhood. I became a man not just a worker.

For James, the difference between 'man' and 'worker' hinged upon the positive impact of his chosen career on the lives of others. While workers were capable of just 'taking a check,' he linked manhood to a vision of service and commitment that was nurtured through the life skills training that EmpowerYouth offered. In particular, he cited the relationship building and conflict management segments of the program as the spaces that reinforced this idea.

Participants also talked about EmpowerYouth's focus on applied projects as a crucial part of the transition into manhood. They routinely pointed to the impact of job site training and other 'real world' educational opportunities in helping them understand the rigors and demands of employment. Alex notes:

> [Y]ou actually did work, you know ... they actually put you out on a job site and showed you what the world was gonna be about and stuff like that ... And here it's like a job, you know, I mean, we're there to do work and, you know, and work, and school here, too, you know, um, a lot was different. But you know, but out there it wasn't, it wasn't all about the job. It was about learning ... And they showed me that if, even if I do learn and do school things, there's still money in it ...

For Alex and others, the ability to function in the 'real world,' specifically in the workplace, was a critical part of becoming a man. He and others cited punctuality, focus, and hard work as necessary values, both for work and manhood that they learned through EmpowerYouth. They also credited EmpowerYouth with prioritizing real-world experience without dismissing the importance of classroom learning. While it is unclear that this message was fully embraced by participants – in conversations, they regularly prioritized 'real' (i.e. job site) learning over classroom learning – they nonetheless valued the program's emphasis on multiple sites of learning.

## Conclusion

In this article, we aimed to prioritize the voices of young Black men who made the transition from traditional schools to EmpowerYouth, as well as understand how they made sense of their experiences within these contexts. Through their stories, we are better able to understand the complex social, cultural, and economic forces that obstruct their pathways to educational success. Such insights not only serve as powerful rejoinders to the current post-racial discourse, but also prompt us to locate innovative solutions to the current educational crisis of Black males.

Programs like EmpowerYouth provide a necessary alternative for Black males and other youth who are rendered vulnerable because of their social position and educational experiences. By offering programmatic flexibility, applied educational experiences, and more healthy adult–youth relationships, community-based (and other alternative) youth programs are better prepared to respond to the unique dilemmas faced by twenty-first century Black male youth. In addition to helping to 'repair' the educational experiences of Black male youth, such programs can also serve a prophylactic function, providing some of the necessary support to prevent undesirable outcomes such as disaffection, underperformance, and drop outs.

While this article has highlighted the value of alternative sites of education, its findings are also instructive to educational practitioners, administrators, and policy makers within traditional schooling contexts. By examining the structure, practices, and mission of programs like EmpowerYouth, we find valuable models for school reform. More broadly, our findings speak to the need to develop educational models that respond to the unique circumstances of Black males in America, which include structural, historical, and cultural explanations. From this position we are better able to provide strategies and approaches that meet the complex educational needs of Black male youth.

Finally, this article illustrates the importance of reframing young Black males within schooling and larger societal contexts. While contemporary educational and social policy often frame Black male youth as social burdens and civic threats, successful programs like EmpowerYouth are informed by a vision of Black male youth as worthwhile sites of investment, support, and care. By re-imagining Black male youth in these terms at the level of policy, pedagogy, curriculum, and mentoring, we create new sites of possibility for improving the educational crisis faced by Black males.

## References

Anderson, E. 2009. *Against the wall: Poor, young, black, and male. The city in the 21st century*. Pennsylvania: University of Pennsylvania Press.

Aud, S., M. Fox., and A. KewalRamani. 2010. *Status and trends in the education of racial and ethnic groups*. (NCES 2010-015). U.S. Department of Education, National Center for Education Statistics. Washington, DC: U.S. Government Printing Office.

Barker, G. 1988. Non-violent males in violent settings: An exploratory qualitative study of prosocial low-income adolescent males in two Chicago (USA) neighborhoods. *Childhood* 5: 437–61.

Bourdieu, P., and L. Wacquant. 2001. Neoliberal newspeak: Notes on the new planetary vulgate. *Radical Philosophy* 108: 1–6.

Bowman, D.H. 2002. Delinquent youths. *Education Week*. Washington.

Browne, I., and J. Misra. 2003. The intersection of gender and race in the labor market. *Annual Review of Sociology* 29: 487–513.

Cawthorne, A. 2009. Weathering the storm: Black men in the recession. Special policy report. Center for American Progress. www.americanprogress.org.

Collins, P.H. 1998. Intersection of race, class, gender, and nation: Some implications for Black family studies. *Journal of Comparative Family Studies* 29.

Crenshaw, K., N. Gotanda, and G. Peller. 1995. *Critical race theory: The key writings that formed the movement*. New York: The New Press.

Damon, W. 2004. What is positive youth development? *The Annals of the American Academy of Political and Social Science* 591: 13–24.

Davis, A. 1981. *Women, race, and class*. New York. Vintage Books.

Davis, J.E. 2006. Research at the margins: Dropping out of high school and mobility among African American males. *International Journal of Qualitative Studies in Education* 19: 289–304.

Eccles, J., and J. Appleton-Gootman, eds. 2002. *Community programs to promote youth development*. Washington, DC: The National Academic Press.

Fashola, O.S. 2003. Developing the talents of African-American male students during nonschool hours. *Urban Education* 38: 398–430.

Ferguson, A.A. 2000. *Bad boys: Public schools and the making of black masculinity*. Ann Arbor: University of Michigan Press.

Fine, M. 1991. *Framing dropouts: Notes on the politics of an urban public high school*. Albany: State University of New York Press.

Gabarino, J. 1999. *Lost boys: Why our sons turn to violence and how to save them*. New York: Free Press

Ginwright, S. 2004. *Black in school: Afrocentric reform, urban youth, and the promise of hip hop culture*. New York: Teachers College Press.

Ginwright, S. 2007. Black youth activism and the role of critical social capital in black community organizations. *American Behavioral Scientist* 51, no. 3: 403–18

Ginwright, S. 2009. *Black youth rising: Activism and radical healing in urban America*. New York: Teachers College Press.

Ginwright, S., P. Noguera, and J. Cammarota. 2005. Youth, social justice, and community: Towards a theory of urban youth policy. *Social Justice* 32, no. 3: 59–68.

Giroux, H.A. 1996. *Fugitive cultures: Race, violence, and youth*. New York: Routledge.

Giroux, H.A. 2003. *The abandoned generation: Democracy beyond the culture of fear*. New York: St. MacMillian Press.

Giroux, H.A. 2009. *Youth in a suspect society: Democracy or disposability?* New York: Palgrave MacMillan.

Glaser, B. 1978. *Theoretical sensitivity: Advances in the methodology of grounded theory.* Mill Valley, CA: Sociology Press.

Glenn, E.N. 1999. The social construction and institutionalization of gender and race: An integrative framework. In *Revisioning gender*, ed. M. Ferree, J. Lorber, B. Hess, 3–43. Thousand Oaks, CA: Sage.

Greene, J.P., and M.A. Winters. 2006. *Leaving boys behind: Public high school graduate rates.* Center for Civic Innovation at the Manhattan Institute. www.manhattaninstitute.org/pdf/er_48.pdf (accessed August 15, 2010).

Gregory, A., R. Skiba, and P. Noguera. 2010. The achievement gap and the discipline gap: Two sides of the same coin? *Educational Researcher* 39, no. 1.

Hill, M.L. 2009. *Beats, rhymes and classroom life: Hip hop pedagogy and the politics of identity.* New York: Teachers College Press.

Hirsch, B.J. 2005. *A place to call home: After school programs for urban youth.* Washington, DC: American Psychological Association.

Holzman, M. 2004. *Public education and black male students: A state report card. Schott educational index.* Cambridge, MA: The Schott Foundation for Public Education.

hooks, b. 1989. *Talking back: Thinking feminist, thinking Black.* Cambridge, MA: South End Press.

Howard, T.C. 2008. "Who really cares?" The disenfranchisement of African American males in preK-12 schools: A critical race theory perspective. *Teachers College Record* 110, no. 5: 954–85.

Johnson, E., and T.C. Howard. 2009. Issues of difference contributing to US education inequality. *Inequality in education. CERC Studies in Comparative Education* 24, no. 1: 444–60.

Jordan, W.J., and R. Cooper. 2003. High school reform and black male students: Limits and possibilities of policy and practice. *Urban Education* 38, no. 2: 196–216.

Kantor, H., and R. Lowe. 1995. Class, race, and the emergence of federal education policy: From the New Deal to the Great Society. *Educational Researcher* 24, no. 3: 4–21.

Kellow, J.T., and B.D. Jones. 2008. The effects of stereotypes on the achievement gap: Re-examining the academic performance of African American high school student. *Journal of Black Psychology* 34, no. 1: 94–120.

Kirschenman, J., and K. Neckerman. 1991. 'We'd love to hire them, but …' The meaning of race for employers. In *The urban underclass,* ed. C. Jencks and P.E. Peterson, 203–34. Washington, DC: Brookings Institution.

Kirshner, B. 2004. Democracy now: Activism and learning in urban youth organizations. Unpublished doctoral dissertation, Stanford University.

Kunjufu, J. 1990. *Countering the conspiracy to destroy black boys.* Chicago: African American Images.

Lakin, R., and A. Mahoney. 2006. Empowering youth to change their world: Key components of community service program to promote positive development. *Journal of School Psychology* 44: 513–31.

Leary, J. 2005. *Post traumatic slave syndrome: America's legacy of enduring injury and healing.* Portland, OR: Uptone.

Lewis, J.L., and E. Kim. 2008. A desire to learn: African American children's positive attitudes toward learning within school cultures of low expectations. *Teachers College Record* 110, no. 6: 1304–29.

Lynn, M. 2006. Race, culture, and the education of African Americans. *Educational Theory* 56, no. 1: 107–19.

Mahoney, J., R. Larson, J. Eccles, and H. Lord. 2005. *Organized activities as developmental contexts for children and adolescents.* New York: Routledge.

Males, M. 1999. *Framing youth: Ten myths about the next generation.* Monroe, ME: Common Courage Press.

Marable, M. 2000. *How capitalism underdeveloped black America: Problems in race, Political economy, and society.* Boston: South End.

McCall, L. 2005. The complexity of intersectionality. *Signs: The Journal of Women in Culture and Society* 30, no. 5: 1771–800.

McLaughlin, M. 2000. *Community counts: How youth organizations matter for youth development.* Washington, DC: Public Education Network.

McLaughlin, M.W., M. Irby, and J. Langman. 1994. *Urban sanctuaries: Neighborhood organizations in the lives and futures of inner-city youth.* San Francisco: Jossey-Bass.

Meltzer, I., J. Fitzgibbon, P. Leahy, and K. Petsko. 2006. A youth development program: Lasting impact. *Clinical Pediatrics* 45, no. 7: 655–60.

Miller, B.M. 2003. *Critical hours: After school programs and educational success.* Quincy, MA: Nellie Mae Foundation.

Nembhard, G.J. 2005. On the road to democratic economic participation: Educating African American Youth in the postindustrial global economy. In *Black education: A transformative research and action agenda for the new century*, ed. J. King, 225–40. Mahwah, NJ: Lawrence Erlbaum.

Noguera, P. 1996. Responding to the crisis confronting California's Black male youth without furthering marginalization. *The Journal of Negro Education* 65, no. 2: 219–36.

Noguera, P. 2003. The trouble with black boys: The role and influence of environmental and cultural factors on the academic performance of African American males. *Urban Education* 38, no. 4: 431–59.

Noguera, P. 2008. *The trouble with black boys: And other reflections on race, equity, and the future of public education.* San Francisco: Jossey-Bass.

Oakes, J. 1985. *Keeping track: How schools structure inequality.* New Haven: Yale

Oates, G.L.S.C. 2003. Teacher-student racial congruence, teacher perception, and test performance. *Social Science Quarterly* 84, no. 3: 508–25.

Pew Charitable Trusts. 2008. *One in 100: Behind bars in America 2008.* Washington, DC: Pew Charitable Trusts. www.pewcenteronthestates.org.

Pollock, M. 2004. *Colormute: Race talk dilemmas in an American school.* Princeton, NJ: Princeton University Press.

Randolph, S. 1995. African American children in single-mother families. In *African American single mothers: Understanding their lives and families*, ed. B.J. Dickerson, 117–45. Thousand Oaks, CA: Sage.

Roth, J.L., and J. Brooks-Gunn. 2003. What exactly is a youth development program? Answers from research and practice. *Applied Developmental Science* 2: 94–111.

Teachman, J., K. Paasch, and K. Carver. 1996. Social capital and dropping out of school early. *Journal of the Marriage and the Family* 48, no. 3: 773–83.

Teasley, M., and D. Ikard. 2009. Barack Obama and the politics of race: The myth of postracism in America. *Journal of Black Studies* 40: 411–23.

Wade, J.C. 1994. African American fathers and sons: Social, historical, and psychological considerations. *Families in Society: The Journal of Contemporary Human Services* 75: 561–70.

Williams, P. 1997. *Seeing a color-blind future: The paradox of race.* New York: The Noonday Press.

Wilson, W.J. 1996. *When work disappears: The world of the new urban poor.* New York: Random House.

Woodland, M. 2008. Whatcha doin' after school? A review of the literature on the influence of after school programs on young Black males. *Urban Education* 43: 537–60.

Woodland, M., J. Martin, L. Hill, and F. Worrell. 2009. The most blessed room in the city: The influence of a youth development program on three young black males. *The Journal of Negro Education* 78, no. 3: 233–45.

Young, A. 2004. *The minds of marginalized black men: Making sense of mobility, opportunity and future life chances.* Princeton, NJ: Princeton University Press.

# Index

academic literature: AAmales 23–5
African American athletes 91–100
African American Rites of Passage programs 25
African American students' historical knowledge 36–7, 41–3
American Council of Education 7
American education: global political economy 28–9
Anderson, C.A.: and Tate, W.F. 56
Anderson, M.G.: and Harry, B. 55
Angelou, M. 46
apathy and disrespect 23
Aronson, J.: and Steele, C.M. 98
Ashmore, H.S. 39
Association for Black Foundation Executives 22
Association for the Study of Negro Life and History 45
athletic identity 94
Athletic Identity Measurement Scale (AIMS) 95; means and standard deviations 96; questionnaire 103
athletic identity and race study 91–100; AIMS items 96; identity items analysis 97; participants racial identity 95; racial identity development 93, 95; total score variance 96
Ayers, W. 115

Baldridge, B.J.: Hill, M.L. and Davis, J.E. 4, 121–34
Baldwin, J.: *Nobody Knows My Name* 40–1, 46
Banks, J.A. 109
Barnes, T.H. 45
Barone, T. 115
Barthe, R. 76
Becker, C. 46
*Being a Black Man* (Merida) 23
Belbenoit, R.: *Dry Guillotine* 33
Bell, D. 42
Bembry, R. 41

Bennett, W.L.: and Edelman, M. 17
Bimper, A.Y. 3, 91–100
biotechnology: Metro St. Louis 58, 60–8
*The Birth of a Nation* (Griffith) 75
Black boys: 'absent father' effect 19; restoring childhood 7–14; school experience paradox 10
Black equality: ineffective approaches and social movements 37–9
Black feminist scholarship 122
Black, H. 43
*The Black Male Handbook* (Powell) 23–4
Black male representations 73–87; concerns 74; contemporary 75; findings and implications 85, *see also The Wire* (Simon and Burns)
Black males: achievement-attitude paradox 111; college admission rates 106; community-based educational spaces 121–34; as damaged 21–3; described by employers 123; dropout rates 106; in educational contexts 124; educational and social disenfranchisement 108; target for public policy 22
*Black Males Left Behind* (Mincy) 7
Black people and poverty 123
Bobo, L.: and Charles, C. 107
Bonilla-Silva, E. 113
Boys & Girls Clubs of America 125
Brewer, B.W.: Murphy, G.M. and Petitpas, A.J. 99
Brown, A.L.: and Brown, K.D. 36; and Donner, J. 1–5, 17–30
Brown, K.D. 29–30; and Brown, A.L. 36; and Kraehe, A. 3, 73–87
Brown, T.N.: *et al* 93
Browne, I.: and Misra, J. 123

capacity-building tools 22
Carter, P. 112
Castellino, D.: Tyson, K. and Darity, W. 111
Census (2000): Metro St. Louis AAmales **61**
Charles, C.: and Bobo, L. 107

# INDEX

Chicago Community Trust 22
Civil Rights Movement 3, 38
cognitive demand 56
College Certificate attainment: Metro St. Louis **65**
College Preparatory Studies Certificate 63; course requirements **64**
Collins, C.: and Williams, D.R. 57
Collins, P.H. 112
*Come On People* (Cosby and Poussaint) 24
community development programs 121–34; importance 125–6
community-based youth organisations 125–7
Conchas, G.Q. 115
control and fear 9–10
Cool Pose 36–7
Cooper, C.: Driskell, J.E. and Moran, A. 98
Cosby, B.: and Poussaint, A. 24–5
Coulter, C.A.: and Smith, M.L. 115
*Countering the Conspiracy to Destroy Black Boys* (Kunjufu) 20
Crenshaw, K.W. 113
crisis of the Black male thesis 20
critical race theory 116
Crowley, Officer J.: arrest of Professor Gates 1
Cullen, C. 42
cultural racism 39
Cummings, S. 58

Darity, W.: Tyson, K. and Castellino, D. 111
Davis, J.E.: Baldridge, B.J. and Hill M.L. 4, 121–34
Denzin, N. 115
Devil's Island: Dreyfus 34; metaphor for AAmales in urban areas 2, 33–46; rare escape from 34
disrespect and apathy 23
*Do the Right Thing* (Lee) 8, 9
Donner, J. 17–30; and Brown, A.L. 1–5
Douglass, F. 43, 74
Dreyfus, A. 34
Driskell, J.E.: Cooper, C. and Moran, A. 98
*Dry Guillotine* (Belbenoit) 33
Du Bois, W.E.B. 35, 110; *Of Work And Wealth* 37, 44
Dupree, D.: Spencer, M.B. and Fegley, S. 54
dysconscious racism 45

Eastside Preparatory Academy 14
Eckholm, E. 8
Edelman, M.: and Bennet, W.L. 17
Editorial Projects in Education 34
education: government spending 28
educational attainment 54
educational opportunities inequality: history and structure 26–8

Edwards, H. 98
Eitzen, D.S. 94
El Puente program Brooklyn 14
Elson, R. 43
employment programs 125
empowerment 25
EmpowerYouth study 121–34; conclusion 133–4; methods and procedures 127–8; methods and study description 126–7; participant interviews 128–33
endangered species: AAmales as 20
Engstrom, C.M.: and Sedlacek, W.E. 98
Entine, J.: *Taboo* 92
Eugenics movement 109

Fader, J.J.: Stern, M.J. and Katz, M.B. 27
Farley, J.E. 37
fear and control 9–10
Fegley, S.: Spencer, M.B. and Dupree, D. 54
Ferguson, A.A. 28, 74, 112
Ferguson, R.F. 55
Fine, M. 125
Flennaugh, T.: and Howard, T.C. 4, 105–17
Football Bowl Subdivision (FBS) 4
Fordham, S. 110
Franklin, J.H.: *Visions of a Better Way* 68

Gates, Prof. H.L. 74–5; arrest by Officer Crowley 1
Geographical Information Systems (GIS) 3, 51–68
Gillborn, D. 29
Glaser, B. 128
Goldring, E.: et al 57
Gordon, C. 60
Gotanda, N. 113
Grant, C.A. 2, 33–46; and Sleeter, C.E. 41
Griffith, D.W.: *The Birth of a Nation* 75
Guinier, L. 57

Haberman, M. 12–13
Haley, A.: *Roots* 34
Hall, S. 76–7
Halstead, M. 39
Harlem Renaissance 42
Harper, H.: *Letters to a Young Brother* 23–4
Harrison, C.K.: Harrison, L. Jr. and Moore, L. 93
Harrison, L. Jr.: et al 3, 91–100; Harrison, C.K. and Moore, L. 93
Harry, B.: and Anderson, M.G. 55
Heiser, J.: and Schwartz, D.L. 59
Henig, J.R.: et al 51, 67
Higginbotham, E.B. 25
high school: dropouts 8; West Philadelphia 13
high school graduation: Metro St. Louis **63**

# INDEX

Hill, M.L.: Baldridge, B.J. and Davis, J.E. 4, 121–34
historical knowledge: AA students 36–7, 41–3
history: and identity formation 41–2; school curriculum problem 42–3
Hogrebe, M.: and Tate, W.F. 3, 51–68
Holt, D. 35
Holt, T.C. 2
hooks, b. 114
Hoover, K. 35
Howard, T.C. 28, 126; and Flennaugh, T. 4, 105–17
Hutchison, E.O. 108

immigrant mantra: fallacy of 44
inequality and globalization 28
infantilization *vs.* criminalization 10
inferiority thesis: textbooks and society 43–4
Intergroup Movement 38

Jackson, R.L. 78
Jacobs, J. 53
Jayaratne, T.E: Sheldon, J.P. and Petty, E.M. 93
Jones, A.: Nasir, N. and McLaughlin, M. 113, 116

Kain, J.F. 58
Katz, M.B.: Stern, M.J. and Fader, J.J. 27
Kelly, R. 116
Kent, G. 42
Kerr, G.A.: and Lally, P.S. 99
King, Martin Luther 36
King, Prof. J. 42
Kluegel, J.R. 40
Kraehe, A.: and Brown, K.D. 3, 73–87
Kunfunju, J.: *Countering the Conspiracy to Destroy Black Boys* 20

Ladson Billings, G. 2, 7–14
Lally, P.S.: and Kerr, G.A. 99
Laslo, D. 60
Lee, S.: *Do the Right Thing* 8, 9
A Legacy of Tradition (ALOT) 22
Legette, W. 20
*Letters to a Young Brother* (Harper) 23–4
Levin, H.: *et al* 28
Liebow, E. 19
Lipman, P. 60
love-hate relationship with Black males 8–9

McKay, C. 42
McKee, A. 77
McLaughlin, M.: Nasir, N. and Jones, A. G. 113, 116
Majors, R.: and Billson; J.M. 36
Marcia, J. 46

Martin, P. 34
Merida, K.: *Being a Black Man* 23
Metro St. Louis 3, 51–68; AAmales 10th grade math MAP Test **66**; AAmales 10th grade science MAP Test **67**; AAmales enrolled in school districts **62**; AAmales high school graduation **63**; biotechnology 58, 60–8; Census (2000) AAmales **61**; College Certificate attainment **65**; kernel density estimation (KDE) 61
Mickelson, R. 111
Middle Passage 34–5
military service 19
Miller, L.S. 57
Milner, H.R. 109, 115
Misra, J.: and Browne, I. 123
Missouri Assessment Program (MAP) 64–7; AAmales 10th grade math **66**; AAmales 10th grade science **67**
Montgomery Bus Boycott 38
Moore, L.: Harrison, L. Jr.; and Harrison, C. K. 93
Moran, A.: Driskell, J.E. and Cooper, C. 98
Moynihan, D.P.: *The Negro Family* 19
multicultural feminist studies 122
Murphy, G.M.: Petitpas, A.J. and Brewer, B. W. 99

Nasir, N.: McLaughlin, M. and Jones, A. 113, 116
The National Collegiate Athletic Association (NCAA) 94
National Educational Longitudinal Survey (1988) 55
*The Negro Family* (Moynihan) 19
neighbourhood and community factors 56
No Child Left Behind Act (2007) 22
*Nobody Knows My Name* (Baldwin) 40
Noddings, N. 8
Noguera, P.A. 28, 94, 111

Obama, B. 9, 20, 42, 107, 121; 'post-racial' era 105; presidential election 1
O'Connor, A. 29
*Of Work and Wealth* (Du Bois) 37
Oglesby, K.T.: *What Black Men Should Do Now* 23
Orfield, M. 52, 59–60, 68
Oyserman, D. and Harrison: K. 35

Parham, T.A.: and White, J.L. 41
Parks, Rosa 36
Payne, C.M. 55
Peterson, D.G. 44
Petitpas, A.J.: Murphy, G.M. and Brewer, B. W. 99
Pettigrew, T. 40

# INDEX

Petty, E.M.: Sheldon, J.P. and Jayaratne, T.E. 93
policy discourse: AAmales 19; crisis of the Black male thesis 20; social inequality 29
Polite, V.: and Davis, J. 8
Popkewitz, T.S. 26
popular visual media 73
post-racial research 105–17; cautions 110–14; colorblind context 113; concerns 112–14; considerations 114; generalization 114; intersectional approaches 122; participants' opinions 128–33; rationale for a measured approach 107–9
Poussaint, A.: and Cosby, B. 24–5
Powell, K.: *The Black Male Handbook* 23
public policy target: AAmales 22

Quarles, B. 43

*Race Ethnicity and Education* 2, 5
racial differences in socioeconomic status 57
racial distrust 37
racial identity development: and athletic identity 93, 95
racial influences in sport 92–3
Reddick, L.D. 78
rigid competitive race relations 37
Rites of Passage programs 25
*Roots* (Haley) 34
Rotich, W.K. 3, 91–100

Sailes, G. 3, 91–100
St. Louis *see* Metro St. Louis
Sanders, M.G.: and Jordan, W.J. 55
school: 'bad boy' tag 12; Black boys' experience paradox 10; racial divide in student treatment 11; as source of problem 12
school curriculum: history study problem 42–3
school opportunity factors 56
Schott Foundation 8, 22
Schwartz, D.L.: and Heiser, J. 59
Scott, D.M. 21
Sedlacek, W.E.: and Engstrom, C.M. 98
Selden, S. 109
self-fulfilling prophesies of defeat 21
Shapiro, T.M. 57
Sheldon, J.P.: Jayaratne, T.E. and Petty, E.M. 93
Simons, J.P.: *et al* 98
Slaughter, J.B. 61
slavery 36
Sleeter, C.E.: and Grant, C.A 41
Smith, M.L.: and Coulter, C.A. 115
Smith, S.J. 35
social inequality: policy discourse framing 29

social policies: historical context 18
social policy approaches 21
social science literature 17
socioeconomic status: racial differences 57
Southgate, B. 35
Spencer, M.B.: Fegley, S. and Dupree, D. 54
sport: AAmales 91–100; athletic identity 93–5; comparison between different races 95–100; NCAA 94; racial influences in 92–3
Stanfield, J. 109
Steele, C.M.: and Aronson, J. 98
Stern, M.J.: Katz, M.B. and Fader, J.J. 27
Stinson, D.W. 113
Stone, C.N. 52; *et al* 58
student and teacher relationships 55

*Taboo* (Entine) 92
Tate, W.F.: and Anderson, C.A. 56; and Hogrebe, M. 3, 51–68
taxation: split-rate method 27
Taylor Gibbs, J. 20
teachers: actions towards Black males 11; attitude towards Black males 11; expectations and support factors 55; and student relationship 55
Tillman, L.C. 109
Tour d' Sol (solar power automobiles) contest 13–14
trade books 23–4; meta-narratives 23
Tushnet, M.V. 38
Tuskegee experiment 108–9
Tyson, K.: Darity, W. and Castellino, D. 111

unemployment rates 8
United States Census (2000) 53
*Up From Slavery* (Washington) 42

*Visions of a Better Way* (Franklin) 68
visual media: Black masculinity and community 73; popular 73

Walters, P.B. 27
Ward, J. 110–11
Washington B.T.: *Up From Slavery* 42
Washington, H.A. 109
Weiner, L. 36
West, C. 106, 117
West Philadelphia: high school 13
*What Black Men Should Do Now* (Oglesby) 23–4
Wheeler, C.H. 58
*When Work Disappears* (Wilson) 76
White, J.L.: and Parham, T.A. 41
Williams, D.R.: and Collins, C. 57
Wilson, W.J. 54, 111; *When Work Disappears* 76

# INDEX

*The Wire* (Simon and Burns) 3, 73–87; Baltimore 76; Bunk 83; Daniels, Lieut. C. 79–82; Little, O. 82; Namond, B. 83–5; representations of Black people 78–87
Woodson, C. 42, 45
Wright, R. 42
Wynter, S. 44

Yosso, T.J. 115

Young, A. 126
young Black male problem 18, 20–1
young Black males: 'post-racial' America 123–4
youth organisations: community-based 125–7

Page numbers in *Italics* represent tables.
Page numbers in **Bold** represent figures.

# SPECIAL ISSUE:
## 'Race', Migration and Education in a Globalised Context

## Irish Educational Studies
Official Journal of the Educational Studies Association of Ireland (ESAI)

**Editors:** Gill Crozier, Kalwant Bhopal and Dympna Devine

Volume 29, Issue 3, 2010

This Special Issue focuses on the relationship between education provision, and practice, migration and globalisation issues. In international discourses on globalisation, migrants have seemingly been positioned, on the one hand, as key contributors to economic development and, on the other, have been constructed as a potential threat to the social stability and harmony of everyday society and the identities of nation states.

Immigration does not take place in a cultural and social void, but becomes mapped to pre-existing systems and structures that exist in the 'host' societies. As a key institution for both the production and reproduction of societal norms, the education system is especially important in mediating both the experiences of immigration, as well as in reflecting the society's response to immigrants.

The articles in this Special Issue focus on Irish and British experiences in the context of migration and education. As such they can be seen as case studies of new and old multiethnic societies. The articles are concerned with the enduring stereotypes in schools and in policy, of pathologising Black and Minority Ethnic children as well as engaging with issues of social class and gender discrimination. The papers featured identify the impact of globalisation in adding to the complexity of racisms, but also forcing to the fore a greater consideration of the nature and impact of Whiteness.

Editorial — FREE to read online

An excavation of the racialised politics of viability underpinning education policy in Ireland
*Karl Kitching*

Reform, racism and the centrality of whiteness: assessment, ability and the 'new eugenics'
*David Gillborn*

Corporate multiculturalism, diversity management, and positive interculturalism in Irish schools and society
*Audrey Bryan*

Immigration and school composition in Ireland
*Delma Byrne, Frances McGinnity, Emer Smyth and Merike Darmody*

Articulating a deficit perspective: a survey of the attitudes of post-primary English language support teachers and coordinators
*Zachary Lyons*

Othering difference: framing identities and representation in black children's schooling in the British context
*Cecile Wright*

Changing the face of the Scottish teaching profession? The experiences of refugee teachers
*Henry Kum, Ian Menter and Geri Smyth*

www.informaworld.com/ies